Impact Evaluation of Infrastructure Interventions

The focus on results in development agencies has led to increased focus on impact evaluation to demonstrate the effectiveness of development programmes. This book illustrates the broad range of methods available for counterfactual analysis of infrastructure programmes such as establishment, rehabilitation and maintenance of roads, water supply and electrical power plants and grids.

Understanding the impact of interventions requires understanding of the context in which the intervention takes place and the channels through which it is expected to occur. For infrastructure interventions it is particularly important to identify the links between the input and the outcomes and impacts because the well-being of people, the ultimate impact, does not change directly as a consequence of the intervention. Therefore impact evaluation of infrastructure programmes typically requires mixing both quantitative and qualitative approaches as illustrated in many of the contributions to this edited volume.

This book was originally published as a special issue of the *Journal of Development Effectiveness*.

Henrik Hansen is Professor of International Economics and Politics at the Institute of Food and Resource Economics, University of Copenhagen, Denmark. He is also Co-Director of the Centre for Social Science Development Research at University of Copenhagen.

Ole Winckler Andersen is Head of the Evaluation Department at Danida, the Ministry of Foreign Affairs of Denmark. He has been a member of management committees for several evaluations including, by appointment of the UN Secretary General, the new evaluation of the UN, Delivering as One.

Howard White is the Executive Director of the International Initiative for Impact Evaluation (3ie). He is also Co-Chair of the Campbell Collaboration International Development Coordinating Group and Managing Editor of the *Journal of Development Studies* and the *Journal of Development Effectiveness*.

Impact Evaluation of Infrastructure Interventions

Edited by
Henrik Hansen, Ole Winckler Andersen and Howard White

Routledge
Taylor & Francis Group

LONDON AND NEW YORK

Publisher's Note
The publisher would like to make readers aware that the chapters in this book may be referred to as articles as they are identical to the articles published in the special issue. The publisher accepts responsibility for any inconsistencies that may have arisen in the course of preparing this volume for print.

Contents

Introduction

Henrik Hansen[a], Ole Winckler Andersen[b] and Howard White[c]

[a]Institute of Food and Resource Economics, University of Copenhagen, Demark; [b]Ministry of Foreign Affairs, Copenhagen, Denmark; [c]International Initiative for Impact Evaluation (3ie), New Delhi, India

The focus on results in development agencies has led to increased focus on impact evaluation to demonstrate the effectiveness of development programmes. A range of methods are available for counterfactual analysis of infrastructure interventions, as illustrated by the variety of papers in this volume. Understanding impact means understanding the context in which an intervention takes place and the channels through which the impact on outcomes is expected to occur. Such analysis typically requires mixing both quantitative and qualitative approaches. The analysis will also anticipate heterogeneity, with conditioning for 'selection bias' being recognised as positive information about for whom and when an intervention works or not.

Introduction

'The operation was a success, but the patient died.' In plain language, all procedures were followed but the hoped for results were not achieved. Maybe evaluations of development assistance cannot really be compared with hospital operations, but it is the case that procedures seem to be being followed. There has been an increasing focus on, and interest in, evaluations: international evaluation quality standards have been developed, and the OECD-DAC's Evaluation Resource Centre (DEReC) includes more than 2000 evaluations of development assistance, and this is an incomplete list.

The large number of evaluations clearly shows that 'the evaluation patient' has not died. But, although there is not a death to report, there is a serious dearth. This dearth is reflected in the fact that, in spite of all these evaluations, there is still a general perception that too little is known about the effects of development assistance and that a better understanding of these effects has to be established. The Evaluation Gap report from 2006 (Centre for Global Development 2006) is one of a number of analyses that has stated this view. Surveys conducted in donor countries have also shown that, while the moral obligation to give aid scores relatively high, the picture is more mixed when it comes to the general public's assessment of the effectiveness of development assistance.

Continued uncertainty about the effects of development assistance make it difficult to create or maintain broad public support for development assistance, especially at a time of widespread cuts in many countries as at the time of writing. Donors have reacted by strengthening their focus on results, as has been demonstrated at several international meetings. The results agenda surfaced in public administration during the 1990s, and has been given momentum in the development field by the widespread adoption of the Millennium Development Goals, which provide a set of outcome-level targets for the development community. More recently the high level meeting in Paris in 2005 endorsed the Paris Declaration, and the meeting in Accra in 2008 endorsed the Accra Agenda for Action. The latter includes as one of three major challenges to accelerate progress on aid effectiveness:

> Achieving development results – and openly accounting for them – must be at the heart of all we do. More than ever, citizens and taxpayers of all countries expect to see the tangible results of development efforts. *We will demonstrate that our actions translate into positive impacts on people's lives.* (Accra Agenda for Action 2008; emphasis added)

The policies and strategies of individual donors have also increasingly focused on results. A comparison of changes over time in Danish development policy demonstrates this trend. The strategy from the year 2000 (*Partnership*) hardly mentions results or evaluations. But the new strategy (*Freedom from Poverty, Freedom to Change*) of 2010 contains a whole section on results. Another example is the explicit results focus of the Millennium Challenge Corporation (MCC), documented in BenYishay and Tunstall (2011), which has manifested itself in the systematic use of rigorous impact evaluation. The same pattern can be found in other donors' policies and strategies, as well as in developing countries, as manifested in the creation of independent evaluation offices in countries such as Argentina, Chile and India.

The uncertainty about the effects of development assistance, combined with donors' focus on results, places new demands on evaluations. In recent years, interest in evaluation methodologies has grown significantly. Specifically, the evaluation community has started new initiatives with focus on impact evaluations, such as the Network of Networks on Impact Evaluation and the International Initiative for Impact Evaluation (3ie). In addition, discussions of impact evaluations and impact evaluation methodologies have been a topic at many evaluation meetings. However, these discussions have usually had a relatively general character and so have not dealt with the specific characteristics and challenges of sectors or thematic areas or with the implications of the specific political and institutional context, within which the impact evaluations are to be conducted. In particular, the political context often puts severe time constraints on evaluations, which require pragmatic solutions to some of the challenges faced in the individual evaluations and a careful selection of evaluation method. In praxis, this will often imply a combination of different evaluation methods.

In order to discuss the challenges evaluations faced within specific sectors or thematic areas, several meetings have been held in very recent years, often with a mixture of participants from academia, evaluation units and consultants, in order to facilitate interaction and learning between researchers, evaluators and staff from donor units responsible for evaluations. One such meeting was held in May 2010, in Copenhagen, which focused on experiences from evaluations of infrastructure interventions. The meeting, which was jointly organised by Danida's Evaluation Department, University of Copenhagen and 3ie, was attended by some 30 participants, who spent three days together discussing both recent research and a number of specific evaluations. This collection presents a selection of papers from that event.

Approaches to impact evaluation for infrastructure

By impact we mean what difference the intervention – that is, the infrastructure construction, rehabilitation or maintenance[1] – has made to people's lives. This definition of impact implies a comparison between the factual and the counterfactual; that is, a comparison between what happened to people in the presence of the intervention compared with how they would have fared without it. We recognise that much of the evaluation community has traditionally used a different definition of the term impact (White 2010). By impact evaluation we mean an ex post analysis of the intervention, although similar concepts may be applied for ex ante analysis; for example, in calculating expected rates of return as is done at the MCC (BenYishay and Tunstall 2011) and Haddad's (2011) application of ex ante computable general equilibrium (CGE) modelling to transport policies in Brazil.

White (2011) distinguishes between large and small n interventions, where n is the number of possible observations at the level of assignment of the intervention. Large n interventions are amenable to statistical analysis in which the counterfactual is constructed using a comparison group with similar characteristics to the treated population. For many, the preferred way of ensuring comparability between the treatment and comparison groups is random assignment of the intervention; that is, a randomised control trial (RCT). Many infrastructure interventions are not suitable for randomisation, either because they are small n (such as port rehabilitation or building a trunk road) or because the technical nature of the intervention prevents randomisation, such as the engineering design determining beneficiary villages for an irrigation scheme. But RCTs should not be ruled out: three of the 14 infrastructure impact evaluations being conducted by the MCC are RCTs (BenYishay and Tunstall 2011), two studies of electrification projects and one of rural water supply. Waddington and Snilstveit's (2009, p. 302) systematic review of water supply and sanitation interventions found 65 rigorous impact evaluations covering 71 interventions, of which 34 were RCTs, although these are not all infrastructure interventions.

But, the majority of infrastructure impact evaluations will either use small n methods, such as CGE models, as recommended by Ravallion (2009) and illustrated by Haddad's (2011) paper in this volume, or, for large n interventions, use quasi-experimental approaches that employ a variety of statistical means to match the comparison and control samples, as in the Rand (2011), Boergaard *et al.* (2011), and Rauniyar *et al.* (2011) papers in this volume. The specific challenges posed in matching, and other aspects of the design of impact evaluations of infrastructure projects, have been discussed in several papers published in previous issues of the *Journal of Development Effectiveness*. In the first issue of the journal, Dominique van de Walle provided a succinct survey of the many issues arising in quantitative evaluations of rural road projects (van de Walle 2009). That paper is already a reference article, often used as a 'handbook of quantitative rural road evaluation'. A later issue in the first volume had several short papers discussing the choice of appropriate evaluation methods by leading experts based on the panel discussion at the 2009 Cairo Conference on Perspectives on Impact Evaluation; see Patricia Rogers (2009), Martin Ravallion (2009) and Dean Karlan (2009).

Against this background we need only briefly summarise the many issues arising in evaluations of infrastructure interventions. We focus on two of the more underexplored topics in this introduction. Specifically, we will briefly discuss the need for a better understanding of the links between the input and the outcomes and impacts, and the importance of understanding the rationale for the specific evaluation when designing the alternative scenario (that is, when choosing the counterfactual).

Simply put, the well-being of people does not change directly as a consequence of a road project. Rather, the impacts of infrastructure interventions are derived from a long chain of intermediate outcomes that interact with other investments, private as well as public, and geographical conditions. As stated in Rogers (2009), an infrastructure project is a 'complicated intervention' exactly because multiple causal strands are needed to produce the impact. The complicated nature of infrastructure interventions calls for formulation of a well-articulated programme theory or, more generally, for theory-based evaluations. Such theory-based impact evaluation of transport infrastructure projects is briefly discussed in Rogers (2009) while more elaborate presentations of the principles can be found in Weiss (2001), Rogers (2007) and White (2009, 2011), with a specific application in Broegaard *et al.* (2011). Following White (2009), a theory-based evaluation should follow six principles – it must: map out the causal chain; understand context; anticipate heterogeneity; do rigorous evaluation of impact using a credible counterfactual; perform rigorous factual analysis; and use mixed methods.

There are a growing number of rigorous impact evaluations of infrastructure projects; for example, the 14 studies being produced by the MCC alone (BenYishay and Tunstall 2011). Many of these studies adhere to the suggestions in van de Walle (2009), such as anticipating heterogeneity, as illustrated by the primary studies in this volume. Rand's (2011) analysis of the employment effects of rural roads in Nicaragua finds that those moving out of unemployment mainly find employment in the agricultural sector (self-employment), whereas those who previously worked in agriculture take the newly created service sector jobs. Boegaard *et al.* (2011) analyse a broader range of impacts of the same rural infrastructure project in Nicaragua, using a mixed-methods design with a strong focus on heterogeneity, which allows them to identify the variation of economic and productive impacts not only between regions but also across different zones within the same region. Rauniyar *et al.* (2011) find that the impact of rural water supply and sanitation in Pakistan on reducing drudgery (self-reported pains from carrying water) is greatest for the lowest socio-economic groups, although other benefits – reduced diarrhoea and increased schooling – are concentrated amongst the better off.

But we would argue that there is a need for increased efforts in mapping out the causal chain, understanding the context, and in using mixed methods; all of these points are elaborated in White's (2011) contribution to this volume and illustrated by the paper of Broegaard *et al.* (2011). To be specific, in several infrastructure evaluations the chosen measures of outcomes and impacts are determined more by data availability than by a hypothesised causal chain. While such data dependency is unavoidable, it is important to put the chosen measures into context. Increased work hours, say – as analysed, for example, in Rand (2011) – may not be important for increased well-being if agricultural land productivity is high in an area with limited market access caused by high transportation costs in the absence of the road. In such a scenario, an evaluation may well show no change in average working hours while well-being in terms of average income or consumption has increased because of increased sales of agricultural products at the market.

As stressed by Woolcock (2009), there is a wide range of possible impact trajectories, a point confirmed by van de Walle's (2009) statement that outcomes and impacts may change over time. One well-known example is the problem of local trade in villages that are connected with larger trade centres. Local trade may increase in the short run because of decreased transportation costs while it decreases later on because of increased competition with the markets in the larger trade centres (consumers rather than goods moving), only to increase again as larger stores set up local departments in the village. Regarding the impact trajectory more generally, benefits may accumulate over time through multiplier and long-run effects or decline after a large initial impact for a variety of reasons. For example, if infrastructure is not maintained then the benefit stream will not be sustained, resulting in low or even negative rates of return. End-of-project impact evaluations cannot directly observe sustainability, so post-endline surveys are a good idea. But even a mid-term or endline evaluation can set out a theory as to how sustainability may be achieved. Carvalho and White (2004) assessed whether the technical, financial and institution pre-conditions are in place for maintaining buildings and other construction by social funds in a number of countries. The rural water supply and sanitation project evaluated by Rauniyar *et al.* (2011) required communities to form maintenance committees. An evaluation of sustainability would assess whether these committees are functioning, and have the necessary technical capacity and finances to perform their tasks.

The second underexplored issue is the importance of understanding the rationale for the specific evaluation when designing the alternative scenario. This point is linked to Rogers' (2009) call for matching impact evaluation design to the purpose of the evaluation. Here, we wish to stress the relation between the purpose of the evaluation and the selection of credible counterfactuals.

A core part of a quantitative impact evaluation is the estimation of the average impact of an intervention on those who receive it; that is, the average treatment of the treated parameter. The potential selection bias in the estimated average impact parameter is probably the best-known problem of all in the impact evaluation literature, and the endogeneity of infrastructure interventions in the form of factors jointly affecting the selection of placement and the outcomes is also well known. However, selection effects are not always unwanted biases: specific sub-groups of the population, with specific characteristics, are targeted on purpose by development agencies – as is very clear from the primary studies in this volume. For example, the study of rural water supply and sanitation in Pakistan documents that selection was on three criteria: dry and brackish areas with no water supply; community willingness to undertake operations and maintenance; and satisfactory feasibility studies including forming community organisations to undertake operations and maintenance (Rauniyar *et al.* 2011).

Hence selection effects should be described as causal mediation effects that are to be included as independent estimates in the final evaluation of an intervention. Clearly, this distinction depends on the context, and in this case the contextual surroundings must include both donor and government motives for the infrastructure intervention as well as the specific purpose of the accompanying impact evaluation.

Consider a situation in which a donor and a government agree on a rural road programme for upgrading of rural roads. The planners agree that an important criterion for placement must be high fertility of the agricultural land in the areas under consideration, as was indeed the case for the Transport Sector Support Program (PAST) in Nicaragua, which is the subject of the papers by Rand (2011) and Broegaard *et al.* (2011) in this volume.

Following the intervention, an evaluation study is conducted. The study has before and after data for both treatment and control groups such that a difference-in-difference (DD) estimator, and even a matched DD estimator, can be used to estimate the impact of the intervention on the selected outcome and impact variables. The average treatment effect is estimated using the standard DD estimator specified in Equation (1) in which y_i is the *change* over time in the outcome variable of interest (such as the value of marketed agricultural produce) and d_i is the treatment indicator variable. The average treatment effect is captured by the regression parameter δ:

$$y_i = \alpha + \delta d_i + u_i \tag{1}$$

As the fertility of the agricultural land is likely to have an effect on the change over time in the outcome variable, it is a factor affecting both selection and outcome so most evaluation studies would condition on a measure of agricultural land fertility and report the DD estimate after controlling for (or matching on) land fertility. Assuming for simplicity a linear effect, we control for land quality by regression, where x_i is the measure of agricultural land fertility used in the selection process. The new impact estimator is given by δ_x in the regression:

$$y_i = \alpha + \delta_x d_i + \beta x_i + v_i \tag{2}$$

The difference between the two estimators of the average impact, the selection bias, is easy to specify as (assuming equation to be the true mode, or data-generation process) we know that:

$$\delta - \delta_x = \beta \frac{\text{cov}(d_i, x_i)}{\text{var}(x_i)} \tag{3}$$

Hence, if land fertility has a positive effect on the change in the outcome variable (so $\beta > 0$) and if the selection on land fertility (the targeting) was successful (so $\text{cov}(d_i, x_i) > 0$), then there will be a positive selection bias in the impact evaluation from Equation (1).[2] So we report the conditional average treatment effect as the estimated impact of the rural road intervention from Equation (2).

But the conditional average treatment estimate is not necessarily the parameter of interest. By conditioning, we are 'taking out' the effect of roads being in high productivity areas. But in projects such as rural road upgrading we have *purposeful selection* (in contrast to uncontrolled self-selection), in the sense that donors and governments are actively targeting specific areas as part of the programme. Hence, when donors and governments are asking for an evaluation of such a project, the selection mechanism should be considered as a possible causal mediation effect and it could well be reported as: 'The road programme had a larger than average effect because of the selection on fertile areas. The selection caused an additional "$\delta - \delta_x$" effect on top of the partial average road effect.'

Obviously, selection effects are not always positive. Another very likely selection mechanism for rural roads would be placement in relatively remote areas. Assuming the programme prefers selection of remote and isolated areas and also that remote and isolated areas have less than average growth prospects, we can simply replace the variable x_i above by the measure of remoteness. Positive selection on remoteness ($\text{cov}(d_i, x_i) > 0$) and a negative partial effect of remoteness ($\beta < 0$) will result in a negative selection effect (bias) and hence a negative causal mediation.

Such a negative mediation is possibly even more important to report in evaluations than a positive effect. In the case considered here, the average partial road impact is the same in both scenarios. But, by selection on, say, agricultural land fertility, the programme would obtain above-average effects; while by selection on, say, remoteness, the programme obtains below-average effects. By specifying such results it is possible for donors and governments to explain to their constituencies why regions with interventions, which has a proven record in terms of positive conditional impacts, do not necessarily grow as much as other areas.

In more complicated settings with non-linearities and interactions, selection effects will have to be estimated by using several control groups. Thus, with purposeful selection, and hence causal mediation in intervention programmes, we should not look for a single relevant counterfactual but rather a set of relevant counterfactuals. In the present collection of papers, this approach is most evident in Boegaard's *et al.* (2011) paper on Nicaragua, which places considerable emphasis on the programme theory and underlying context (geographic isolation, existing economic activities, local governance and ethnic composition). In reporting their findings, the authors explicitly point out that when scaling up the different impact in different settings need be taken into account.

Returning to the message in Rogers (2009), we fully agree that the complicated nature of infrastructure interventions means that impact evaluations should focus on reporting 'contingent messages' describing what works for whom in what situations and over which time frames. By implication we suggest moving away from the 'negative' statistical language of biases towards the more useful notion of mediation mechanisms when the project has purposeful selection.

Acknowledgements

The views expressed here are those of the authors, and not to be taken as representing those of any of the organisations to which the authors are affiliated. Thanks are given to the anonymous referees for each paper, and, in particular, to Professor John Weiss for acting as a reviewer for the collection of papers as a whole. The usual disclaimer applies.

Notes

1. The intervention may also be a policy intervention, such as promoting public–private partnerships.
2. The variance term is, of course, always positive.

References

Accra Agenda for Action, 2008. Available from: http://siteresources.worldbank.org/ACCRAEXT/Resources/4700790-1217425866038/AAA-4-SEPTEMBER-FINAL-16h00.pdf [Accessed 4 December 2010].

BenYishay, A. and Tunstall, R., 2011. Impact evaluation of infrastructure investments: the experience of the Millennium Challenge Corporation. *Journal of development effectiveness*, 3 (1), 103–130.

Broegaard, E., Freeman, T. and Schwensen, C., 2011. Experience from a phased mixed-methods approach to impact evaluation of Danida support to rural transport infrastructure in Nicaragua. *Journal of development effectiveness*, 3 (1), 9–27.

Carvalho, S. and White, H., 2004. Theory-based evaluation: the case of social funds. *American journal of evaluation*, 25 (2), 141–160.

Centre for Global Development, 2006. *When will we ever learn? Improving lives through impact evaluation?* Washington, DC: Centre for Global Development.

Haddad, E., 2011. Assessing the ex ante economic impacts of transportation infrastructure policies in Brazil. *Journal of development effectiveness*, 3 (1), 44–61.

Karlan, D., 2009. Thoughts on randomised trials for evaluation of development: presentation to the Cairo evaluation clinic. *Journal of development effectiveness*, 1 (3), 237–242.

Rand, J., 2011. Evaluating the employment generating impact of rural roads in Nicaragua. *Journal of development effectiveness*, 3 (1), 28–43,

Rauniyar, G., Orbeta, A. and Sugiyarto, G., 2011. Impact of water supply and sanitation assistance on human welfare in rural Pakistan. *Journal of development effectiveness*, 3 (1), 62–102.

Ravallion, M., 2009. Evaluating three stylised interventions. *Journal of development effectiveness*, 1 (3), 227–236.

Rogers, P.J., 2007. Theory-based evaluation: reflection ten years on. In: *Enduring issues in evaluation: the 20th anniversary of the collaboration between NDE and AEA. New directions for evaluation*, 114, 63–67.

Rogers, P.J., 2009. Matching impact evaluation design to the nature of the intervention and the purpose of the evaluation. *Journal of development effectiveness*, 1 (3), 217–226.

van de Walle, D., 2009. Impact evaluation of rural road projects. *Journal of development effectiveness*, 1 (1), 15–36.

Waddington, H. and Snilstveit, B., 2009. Effectiveness and sustainability of water, sanitation, and hygiene interventions in combating diarrhoea. *Journal of development effectiveness*, 1 (3), 295–335.

Weiss, C., 2001. Theory-based evaluation: theories of change for poverty reduction program. *In*: O. Feinstein and R. Piccioto, eds. *Evaluation and poverty reduction*. New Brunswick, NJ: Transaction Publications.

White, H., 2009. Theory-based impact evaluation: principles and practice. *Journal of development effectiveness*, 1 (3), 271–284.

White, H., 2010. A contribution to current debates in impact evaluation. *Evaluation*, 16, 153–164.

White, H., 2011. Achieving high quality impact evaluation design through mixed methods: the case of infrastructure. *Journal of development effectiveness*, 3 (1), 131–144.

Woolcock, M., 2009. Toward a plurality of methods in project evaluation: a contextualised approach to understanding impact trajectories and efficacy. *Journal of development effectiveness*, 1 (1), 1–14.

Experience from a phased mixed-methods approach to impact evaluation of Danida support to rural transport infrastructure in Nicaragua

Eva Broegaard[a], Ted Freeman[b] and Carsten Schwensen[c]

[a]Danidas Evaluation Department, Ministry of Foreign Affairs of Denmark, Asiatisk Plads 2, Copenhagen, DK 1448, Denmark; [b]Goss Gilroy Inc, 150 Metcalfe, Suite 900, Ottawa, ON K2P 1P1, Canada; [c]Orbicon, Lautrupvang 2, DK 2725 Ballerup, Denmark

This study exemplifies and discusses how mixed methods can be used to overcome data shortages in an evaluation of the socio-economic effects of improved transport infrastructure in Nicaragua. Relying on a combination of existing data and a targeted collection of additional qualitative and quantitative information, the approach establishes a counterfactual and analyses the processes of change over a relevant range of impacts, whilst investigating heterogeneity of effects. The approach enabled a small donor agency with scarce evaluation resources to conduct an impact evaluation within data, time and budget constraints, thereby contributing to the foundation for better practice.

1. Introduction

Impact evaluations are perceived to be highly demanding for both data quality and evaluation resources. The notion that 'ideal' conditions are required for assessment of impacts with a credible counterfactual may, however, lead to a premature dismissal of impact evaluations, perceived as unattainable and/or too expensive.

This study documents how a theory-based mixed methods approach can overcome initial barriers of insufficient quantitative data as well as the absence of an adequate baseline in programme information. Based on an evaluation of support to rural transport infrastructure in three regions in Nicaragua, the study illustrates how the application of interweaved mixed methods can generate insights into the impact of an intervention and assist in answering key questions of 'how?' and 'why?' in a policy-relevant manner. The guiding principles for the evaluation design were inspired by current work on impact evaluation of rural roads (Van de Walle 2009), and are closely related to those of White (2009). The evaluation design was developed on the basis of an early analysis of the programme's intervention logic, its implementation, the contexts in which it operates and – of course – data availability.

The establishment of a credible counterfactual enabling a double-difference estimation of quantifiable impacts is a core element of the approach. However, the phased integration of multiple qualitative methods was instrumental in adding towards: (i) an improved understanding of the context and the logic model behind the interventions; (ii) an inclusion of a wider range of effects than would otherwise have been possible; and (iii), most importantly, an evaluation that addresses the heterogeneity of impacts across beneficiary groups and project contexts to a larger degree than would have been possible, had the evaluation only relied on quantitative analysis.

Further details on the use of statistical matching to establish a credible counterfactual and in-depth discussion of selected results can be found in Rand (2010). In the present study, the focus is on the rationale and implications of use of mixed methods, and the specific quantitative methods and results are only addressed as they relate to the specific interplay between qualitative and quantitative methods, and the challenges and opportunities encountered. Selected evaluation results are presented, but mainly to demonstrate the rationale as well as strengths and weaknesses of the methods used. For a full presentation of context and results, the reader is referred to Danida (2010).

The presentation of the mixed methods for the evaluation is guided by a combination of the mixed method typologies presented by White (2008) and Bamberger *et al.* (2006). Adopting a functional perspective, White (2008) identifies three ways of combining quantitative and qualitative methods: (i) *integrating* methodologies whereby qualitative methodologies are used to refine, target or qualify the quantitative collection and/or analysis of data (or vice versa); (ii) confirming/reinforcing, refuting, enriching and explaining the findings of one approach with those of the other (where, for example, quantitative results are verified through the qualitative approach or qualitative methods are used to identify issues or obtain information on variables not covered by quantitative surveys) – for simplicity, this type will overall be referred to as mixed methods for '*analytical enhancement*', with specific indication of the particular (sub)type; and, finally, (iii) White points to *merging* methodologies (and findings) whereby the information provided by both approaches is used to derive one set of policy recommendations.[1]

Bamberger *et al.* (2006) also adopt a functional categorisation of mixed methods, emphasising multiple functions and how different approaches interact. This can, for example, include situations where mixed methods are used to both triangulate results and to extend the comprehensiveness of evaluation findings by broadening the field of analysis. In addition, a range of possible uses of quantitative and qualitative methods at different stages of the evaluation process is outlined. The possible combinations of quantitative and qualitative approaches range from the establishment of the conceptual framework to the collection of data and ensuing analysis. Hence, Bamberger *et al.* (2006) provide an overview of the various forms of mixed methods organised according to the (sometimes multiple and) interdependent functions performed during different stages of an evaluation.

Both typologies are relevant for this study: the sequential typology presented by Bamberger *et al.* (2006) is used to analyse and explain how choice of methodology at one stage affects later stage options and results, whilst the functional typology presented by White (2008) is used to identify implications of the specific mix.

Following this brief introduction, Section 2 will present context and background for the support to rural roads in Nicaragua and its evaluation. Section 3 – the main part of the article – will outline the different steps of the evaluation following the White/Bamberger typology just outlined. Section 4 will present selected results and discuss key implications of the mixed methods approach. Finally, Section 5 concludes.

2. Programme and evaluation background

Danida support to the transport sector in Nicaragua was initiated in the 1980s. Initially, support was provided as project assistance to rehabilitate and reconstruct rural transport infrastructure in the North and South Atlantic Autonomous Regions (RAAN and RAAS). Institutional development activities were added in 1995, and in 1999 the support was organised under the Transport Sector Support Program (or PAST, from its Spanish name). In addition, regional coverage was extended to include the North-Central Nicaraguan area of Las Segovias.

Throughout, the overall objective of PAST was to contribute to poverty reduction through a general improvement of the socio-economic conditions in isolated rural communities. By implication, improvements in transport infrastructure are hypothesised to reduce transport costs, facilitating access to social services and economic and administrative centres. Activities included construction, rehabilitation and maintenance of tertiary roads, bridges, footpaths, and even aquatic transport infrastructure such as wharfs and canals. Construction was undertaken using labour-intensive methods (Mano de Obra Intensivo, in PAST terminology). Benefitting communities and municipalities were to be responsible for respectively routine and periodic maintenance. Programme documentation points to a range of expected economic and social benefits, in line with other work on rural roads and development (Van de Walle and Mu 2007, Van de Walle 2009). In 2006, the programme completion report for Phase One of PAST recommended that an impact evaluation of the support to PAST was carried out (Danida 2010).

Simultaneously, Danida's Evaluation Department (EVAL) increasingly focused on assessing and documenting results. This was in part due to an external review of EVAL in 2003, recommending a stronger focus on documenting outcomes and impacts (Lundgren *et al*. 2003), and in part to supply both internal and external users of EVAL evaluations with information about the impacts of Danida support. Consequently, EVAL decided to undertake a number of impact evaluations. The first two impact evaluations were, however, challenged by, inter alia, a lack of baseline data and an inability to trace baseline households and indicators after the intervention (Danida 2007a, 2009a).

As a result, an exploratory study of data availability and suitability was undertaken prior to initiating the impact evaluation of PAST. The exploratory study identified a variety of existing datasets, but none were assessed to be sufficient to support a rigorous impact evaluation of Danida support (Danida 2007b). Subsequently, an (inconclusive) quantitative analysis of the more general socio-economic effects of improved access was carried out, extending focus to include other transport infrastructure investments than PAST (Danida 2008).

Although the pre-studies indicated challenges for a quantitative impact evaluation covering all PAST interventions, EVAL decided to attempt to assess the impact 'as rigorously as possible', proposing a mixed-methods approach with use of a combination of datasets (Danida 2010). At the time, discussions with the partner ministry were taking place regarding a possible scaling-up of PAST, creating a strong need for policy-relevant information on PAST impacts and the way they were created. The existence of a number of relevant, albeit less than ideal, data sources established by the pre-studies was a concurrent factor. The resulting evaluation was initiated in 2009 and finalised in 2010.

3. Designing an evaluation based on a phased, multifunctional mix of methods

3.1. *Preparing the evaluation: developing the evaluation concept*

The framework for the evaluation as expressed in the Terms of Reference (ToR) was formed by existing qualitative and quantitative information, including the quantitative pre-studies and initial discussions with stakeholders, programme documents and anthropological research.

The central evaluation question in the ToR was, in line with policy needs, whether Danida-supported PAST interventions had contributed positively to improving the socio-economic conditions and thus helped reduce poverty? Although difficulties were expected in the establishment of a credible counterfactual, it was emphasised that evaluation should address the possible variations across contexts and project types. By implication, no form of PAST-supported transport infrastructure or geographical area was excluded from the evaluation. This was motivated by the acknowledgment that impacts were likely to vary across different types of infrastructure and contexts (see also Van de Walle 2009), and the need to ensure that the evaluation could deliver conclusions of relevance to the discussions on a possible scaling up. At the same time, it was expected that prerequisites and possibilities for establishing the counterfactual might also vary, due to differences in data availability across contexts and interventions, resulting in methodological challenges and possibly precluding that all types of infrastructure could be analysed the same way, with the same degree of rigour.[2]

The evaluation set out to include interventions from 1999 to 2004 as well as interventions completed during the second phase from 2004 to 2009. This period was expected to enable both the identification of not just immediate but also medium to longer term impacts and allow an assessment of whether the interventions were maintained (also after the three-year monitoring period, where there would still be contact between PAST and the community in question, creating a possibility of continued informal support), and the implications for sustainability. The PAST implementation model was seen as well established in the evaluation period, based on earlier experience and with a range of technical and organisational guidelines, procedures and designs (Danida 2010). The second phase entailed a stronger focus on transfer of responsibility for management to the municipalities, but with PAST support (and Danida back-stopping as part of a system of checks and balances) to ensure continuity and consistency in the approach.

Economic and social impacts were to be assessed at the household and the community level in all three target regions. Information collected at community and municipal level should include an assessment of whether capacity development and institutional change, as well as other prerequisites for sustainability such as maintenance, were attained. Finally, the evaluation should identify and analyse channels of impact, obstacles to the realisation of impact, and unintended impacts, in line with the focus of theory-based evaluations, in order to provide information of relevance for both practitioners and policy-makers. While not methodologically challenging, this use of both qualitative and quantitative information was an important aspect of 'integrating methodologies' for defining the scope of the evaluation and assessing the basic methodological implications hereof.

3.2. Understanding the object: interventions and contexts

The next step was ensuring the understanding of the intervention logic and contextual factors, in order to establish the analytical design and assess the feasibility of various methods.

First, a model of the PAST intervention logic and expected impacts was established on the basis of programme documents, a desk study of relevant references (for example, Van de Walle and Mu 2007, Van de Walle 2009), and a field trip to the three PAST target regions. The field trip was an opportunity to assess and qualify desk study findings and obtain a better understanding of the PAST model. In particular, information on the selection criteria and process was important for the considerations on how to address the issue of selection bias (see further below).

Overall, expected processes of change were described comprehensively in programme documents, consistent with current literature (Van de Walle and Mu 2007, Van de Walle 2009). The key assumption of PAST was that all-year or seasonal isolation of communities resulted in high transport costs, severely limiting access to social services and commercial centres. Consequently, improved access was expected to lower transaction costs, allowing beneficiaries to increase both market access and utilisation of social services like health and education, leading to increased economic and other opportunities. Possible unintended negative impacts could be seen to include environmental effects from construction and adverse effects of the increased access; for example, illegal logging, leading to deforestation.

The inception report for the evaluation presented the basic programme logic model as shown in Figure 1.

As noted by White (2009) and Van de Walle (2009), contextual factors can influence how the causal chain of an intervention unfolds in practice.[3] Thus, an understanding of key commonalities and differences in context across the three target regions of Las Segovias, RAAN and RAAS was necessary. Knowledge of the PAST context was moreover important for the identification of which impact indicators were to be selected and included in the resurvey, as well as for information for identifying and matching treatment and comparison groups. In this context, the early field trip to all three regions was important.

Overall, the following four key contextual factors were identified as exhibiting both considerable variation across the three regions and possibly influencing results: (1) geographic isolation and transport patterns; (2) economic activities; and (3) community and municipal governance. Variation in these factors coincided with differences in (4) ethnic

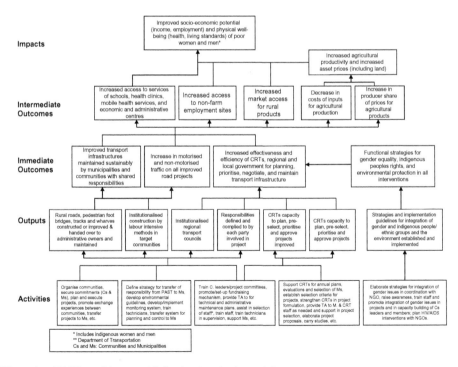

Figure 1. PAST rural transport infrastructure logic model.
Source: Danida (2009b).

composition. This identification was based on analysis of the programme intervention logic and current studies – both on the impact of transport infrastructure in general, and the significance of the contextual factors in the three regions in particular (for example, Hvalkof 2007, Henriksen 2008, Van de Walle 2009, Velleman 2009).

3.2.1. Geographic isolation and transport patterns. Although the three PAST regions – by programme design – were all characterised by limited access, the geographical isolation varied between and within the regions. As noted by Van de Walle (2009), the impact of improved access can be expected to vary with the severity of the initial access problem.

In Las Segovias, the isolation was generally characterised by poor road conditions and seasonal flooding problems. Consequently, PAST projects typically consisted of rehabilitation of access roads and/or construction or improvement of bridges, which improved connections to municipal centres and onto the wider road network. Compared with Las Segovias, PAST communities in RAAN and RAAS were more isolated from both their respective municipal centres. However, the situation within RAAN and RAAS was not uniform. Three geographic zones with distinct transport patterns were identified: the coastal zone (zone i), with communities living near the sea and having access to the municipal centres by boat only; and the central zone (zone ii), where communities lived inland from major navigable rivers, thus experiencing dual problems of both land and water transport to access municipal centres. Additional access problems in relation to the wider transport network (for example, poor primary or secondary road conditions or reliance on water or air transport) was further a constraining factor in these two zones. The last distinct zone is the inland zone (zone iii) where improved access roads would allow the communities to connect to municipal centres and with better access to secondary or primary road network than the first two zones (Hvalkof 2007). The access situation of the latter group of inland zone communities was most similar to that of PAST communities in Las Segovias.

3.2.2. Economic activity, production and the agricultural frontier. As the production patterns vary considerably across regions, the causal chains and the nature of the goods traded (perishable, seasonal, and so forth) were also expected to differ. This could lead to differences in the impact of the improved infrastructure. Ranching and cultivation of basic grains were predominant in almost all Las Segovias communities studied, exhibiting relatively minor differences between agro-climatic zones. In RAAN and RAAS, diversity was more pronounced: the coastal communities and those located on the main rivers (zones i and ii) were typically engaged in commercial fishery for the marketplace, reserving small-scale crop and raising of animals for self-consumption. In zone iii, the predominant production was basic grains for sale and commercial meat and dairy cattle production, in a manner parallel to communities in Las Segovias.

3.2.3. Local governance and maintenance. Since the strategic orientation of PAST focused on transfer of project responsibilities to municipalities and communities, the local government institutions could influence the success, impact, and sustainability of PAST projects. Municipal government engagement in infrastructural matters was moreover expected to depend on a compound of, for example, capacity and interest. Differences were mainly found between Las Segovias on one hand and RAAS and RAAN on the other. For example, while municipalities in all three regions were poor, the fact that municipalities in RAAN and RAAS covers large areas with a scarce and dispersed population created specific challenges, for example, in relation to follow-up and support to maintenance.

3.2.4. Ethnicity. Ethnicity was linked to differences in both impact expectations and measurement. Whilst Las Segovias is ethnically uniform with a Mestizo population,[4] the population of RAAS and RAAN includes six distinct groups of indigenous people and ethnic minorities. Henriksen (2008) outlines how predominantly indigenous communities in RAAN and RAAS normally hold land in common, while Mestizo and other ethnic groups (in RAAN and RAAS as well as in the rest of Nicaragua) have individual landholdings. Consequently, tracking the impact of a road or bridge on land prices and average landholding size might make sense in a Mestizo community, but very little is known where land is communally owned. Within RAAN and RAAS indigenous and minority groups are mostly located in zones i and ii, whilst Mestizo groups are more predominant in zone iii. Ethnicity may thus coincide with productive activities and the level of isolation experienced by a community, and may further influence community use of social services such as health and education.[5]

3.3. Data availability and quality

Following the identification of the programme logic model and the most important contextual factors, an assessment of data needs and availability was undertaken. In this context, the early field trip revealed that high-quality panel data was available to enable a quantitative double-difference analysis, using detailed household-level data from the National Living Standards Survey (*Encuesta Nacional de Hogares sobre Medición de Nivel de Vida* [EMNV]) in combination with data from the national Census (carried out in 2001 and 2005 by the Nicaraguan national statistical bureau).[6] This could serve as a baseline for interventions *after* 2001.[7] A resurvey would provide the data for the post-PAST situation. This was, however, only possible in Las Segovias, since the number of household observations in RAAN and RAAS that could be matched to PAST treatment and comparison communities was insufficient to allow for a solid establishment of a baseline (due to lower population density and the number of beneficiaries). This of course had important implications for the overall design of the evaluation.

3.4. Deciding on the specific design – what should be in the mix?

Since the aim of the evaluation was to assess impacts 'as rigorously as possible', a quantitative double-difference analysis based on existing data formed a natural core of the evaluation design. However, given that sufficient quantitative baseline data from the national livelihood survey and census was only available for Las Segovias, the econometric analysis could not include RAAN and RAAS.

Furthermore, the differences in transport patterns and project types between the three regions meant that the quantitative analysis in practice only covered investments in ground transport infrastructure (such as rehabilitation of access roads or investments in, for example, bridges that created all-year access over land). This reduced the quantitative coverage of other project types undertaken in RAAN and RAAS, such as wharfs and canals, mandating a search for complementary methodologies and data for assessing impacts in different transport settings and contexts.

When it came to assessing whether a specific survey community and household was within the PAST zone of influence or not – that is, whether it could qualify as a control – information on geographical factors and transport options was important. The isolated communities in Las Segovias typically depend on one access road to connect to the road network and the municipal centre. Thus, inter-community contact means exiting the community by one access road, connecting to the wider network and entering another community by another access road. PAST administrative information included definitions, explanations and assessment of projects zone of influence. By overlaying programme administrative information with geographical information and maps on households participating in the surveys and census, it was possible to identify households that qualified for the treatment group.[8] However, more information still was needed in order to identify appropriate comparison communities and households.

3.4.1. Broadening coverage with qualitative methods. The limitations of the econometric assessment to cover only one region and – by implication – certain project types created serious challenges for the evaluation in deciding how to gain information on impacts in other contexts. The geographical focus on Las Segovias meant that a range of concerns on, for example, ethnicity and related issues were in practice excluded from the econometric analysis. However, the evaluation would still need to assess the implications of these issues for heterogeneity of impact in order to be truly policy relevant. By implication, the evaluation would have to investigate the PAST impact in RAAN and RAAS using qualitative methodologies, supplemented by analysis of available quantitative data. Clearly, the assessment of impacts in RAAN and RAAS would have to investigate both 'with' and 'without' as well as 'before' and 'after', across a range of project types and contextual factors. This made it necessary for the evaluation to assess both the level of correspondence between the quantitative and qualitative methods, and the implications for comparing and contrasting of results across the regions. Further, in all three regions the use of qualitative methods allowed the evaluation to include social impacts, for example, in health and education, where quantitative data were insufficient.

3.4.2. A hybrid model: use of mixed methods in preparation and design. The resulting evaluation design was a hybrid between an econometric double-difference assessment in Las Segovias and a pragmatic merge of models based on qualitative methods applied at community level in all three regions. The (modified) typology by Bamberger (World Bank 2006) in Table 1 serves to illustrate how different compositions of methodologies were used to establish the counterfactual 'as credibly as possible'.[9]

In Las Segovias the analytical core was an econometric double-difference analysis, resembling type 1. The collected qualitative and quantitative data informed the decision about which indicators to include, which in turn had implications for the questions in the quantitative resurvey conducted in Las Segovias. The latter was important, given that time and resource constraints did not enable a full replication of the EMNV and the Census. As mentioned, qualitative methods further had to be included to investigate impacts where quantitative data were insufficient; for example, in education and health. This corresponds to an 'enriching' use of mixed methods in the typology by White (2008). Further, the qualitative work was to be conducted after the collection and preliminary analysis of quantitative data, so as to allow analytical enhancement by 'confirming' or 'refuting' the quantitative results, and to 'explore' in greater depth the dynamics behind change (or lack thereof),

Table 1. Four types of impact evaluation with varying strengths of counterfactuals.

Type of evaluation	Before-programme intervention	During-programme intervention	After-programme intervention	Measured comparison (DD)
1. 'Robust' impact evaluation	Treatment group T1, Comparison group C1		Treatment group T2, Comparison group C2	(T2 –T1) compared with (C2 – C1) (double difference)
2. Delayed pre–post test		Treatment group T1A, Comparison group C1A	Treatment group T2, Comparison group C2	T2 –T1A compared with C2 – C1A (still double difference)
3. Pre–post for treatment group, post only for comparison	Treatment group T1		Treatment group T2, Comparison group C2	Single difference T2 – T1, and another single difference T2 – C2
4. Post test only			Treatment group T2, Comparison group C2	Single difference T2 – C2. Lack of baseline data makes controlling for initial differences difficult

Note: DD, double difference.
Source: Adapted from World Bank (2006).

again in line with White (2008). This would also enable the evaluators to assess the level of correspondence between the quantitative and qualitative findings. Whilst substantial differences between the two forms of analysis would necessitate further analyses, a strong concurrence of results across different methodologies, would indicate that the qualitative methods provided reliable information, strengthening confidence in the results achieved from this analysis.

For RAAN and RAAS, the evaluation model included use of existing quantitative and qualitative PAST monitoring data to investigate the pre-PAST post-PAST situations for treatment communities (resembling model 3), and a strong element of qualitative post-intervention comparison of treatment and comparison communities (resembling model 4), with use of recall and existing secondary data to gain as much validated information on the pre-test situation as possible for both treatment and comparison communities. This was done as an attempt to move the qualitative evaluation 'up' the typology ladder, by using a range of data sources and methods to establish the counterfactual as credibly as possible, given data constraints. While this method could not (and was not expected to) deliver the same degree of certainty or specificity of information with regards to the relative significance or strength of impacts as the quantitative double-difference analysis for Las Segovias, it was expected to help identify similarities and differences in impact patterns across contexts.

3.5. Data collection and analysis

3.5.1. Establishing the counterfactual for the double difference analysis: the use of qualitative information. Apart from the use of qualitative information in the preparation as outlined above, qualitative information also played an important role in identifying a suitable comparison group. This was a key concern for the evaluation, since the quantitative data were not sufficient for sampling and matching on all relevant parameters. Careful consideration of possible selection bias and the influence of unobservable parameters was needed. A two-step approach was chosen: first, community-level area based matching was done, considering parameters that could influence project placement and impacts. When a 'long list' of appropriate treatment and comparison communities had been established and household data secured, statistical matching at household level was done (in line with approaches outlined in World Bank 2006).

The point of departure for the sampling was to identify treatment and comparison communities within the same municipality in similar agro-climatic zones, and match them on a range of pre-intervention observables, to use as similar as possible geographical local intact comparison groups (for discussions on the possible advantages hereof when a randomised controlled trial is not feasible, see Cook *et al.* 2008, 2010, Steiner *et al.* 2009). Geographical and administrative information was used to ensure that there was little or no connectivity between treatment and comparison communities, so as to minimise the risk of spillover. In order to minimise the risk of selection biases it was decided that the identification of comparison communities should be based on detailed information about PAST project selection criteria and decision processes. Finally, a pipeline approach was included.

The investigation of the selection process and criteria included study of programme documentation, interviews with municipal and regional technical staff, PAST staff at all levels, independent researchers, and so forth. To counter possible risks of intended and unintended biases, the information provided from PAST staff was validated against other data sources and through the actual visits to communities. Key criteria for selection of PAST communities – and by implication for selection of comparison communities – were:

- *Production.* The communities should be located in areas with a *potential* for high productivity.[10] Thus, comparison communities were selected from areas that had the same agro-climatic and overall production characteristics as PAST communities at the time of selection.
- *Access.* The communities should have had serious access problems in order to qualify for project selection (measured by a PAST access rating system). By implication, comparison communities were only selected if their (historical) access ratings were similar to the treatment communities prior to interventions.
- *Population size.* Population density (for non-aquatic projects) should be, at least, 50 persons per project kilometre. The rationale was to ensure a sufficient population base for the subsequent maintenance. Comparator communities were identified using Census data from 2001 and 2005.
- *'New' projects.* The communities should not previously have been part of other similar interventions undertaken by the Nicaraguan government or other organisations. In addition, comparator communities should not have received support for transport infrastructure improvement during the evaluation period.[11]

Finally, amongst practical pre-conditions were that the interventions had to be feasible for the labour-based methods.

However, this information on the selection process did not fully solve the problem of possible 'hidden' bias. A more detailed assessment was needed; especially, in relation to the pre-selection process and the possible biases related to identifying projects. In particular, issues of self-selection and political favouritism had to be assessed. Detailing the whole process and procedures of the PAST pre-selection is not possible within this article, but it should be noted that the pre-identification of viable projects involved a range of checks and balances and different actors, making it unlikely that any one actor could select 'favourites'.[12] A range of actors could in practice propose projects (although the municipality would be responsible for the formal proposal), and while the community had to agree to the project for it to be carried out, the enthusiasm or capacity of a community was not assessed to be a deciding factor in pre-selection and selection. The use of a range of technical criteria in both pre-selection and selection processes further created a transparency that mitigated the risk of 'non-favourites' being disqualified on criteria not consistent with the formal procedure.

The risk of bias towards more resourceful communities (wealthier or better organised) had to be addressed as well. The first step of the matching included the criteria of productive potential, but requirements for actually carrying out the projects were also relevant: According to PAST procedures, communities had to ensure a counterpart funding of 5 per cent of project costs, in cash or in kind, for the project to be carried out, possibly creating a bias against poorer communities. However, while some communities found it more difficult to comply with this than others, the programme allowed a flexible time frame and approach for fulfilling requirements. Thus, it was in practice not a matter of whether a community could put together its counterpart funding, but rather how much time would be needed.[13]

Finally, there was seen to be a risk that the information on expected change in access and cost used in the selection process could have led to a prioritisation of the communities with the most difficult access situation. This could then possibly link to other differences in the pre-intervention conditions (in line with PASTs own intervention logic on access as a bottleneck for development and discussions in current studies; Van de Walle and Mu 2007, Van de Walle 2009). The matching on pre-intervention access went some way to control for this, but since the ranking was based on a rough one to five scale, more specific matching and testing was needed. Quantitative data were not available to compare access conditions and change. However a range of other parameters on pre-intervention characteristics was used for the next step of statistical matching (Danida 2010, Rand 2010).

To further ensure an appropriate composition of the comparison group, the selected comparison communities included 'pipeline projects' that were part of the 2010 municipal project proposals to PAST. This provided a clear indication that these communities could have qualified for PAST projects.[14]

Finally, the sampling had to consider the contextual factors mentioned earlier. Consequently, treatment and comparison communities were spread over the range of municipalities in Las Segovias to avoid bias. As explained above, ethnic and intervention type concerns were not relevant in this region, and the issue of agro-climatic zones and production patterns was covered in other steps of the sampling.

The pool of suitable comparison communities was then matched to survey and census information, so as to find the households to be included in the resurvey. Once the data had been collected, statistical matching was then carried out (further detailed in Rand 2010). After data cleaning, the sample covered EMNV-based data from 16 treatment and 21 comparison communities, covering 14 municipalities, and census-based data from 36 treatment and 37 comparison communities, covering 17 municipalities (out of the 20 municipalities in Las Segovias where PAST projects had been concluded in the relevant timeframe).

3.5.2. The qualitative fieldwork. As noted above, a qualitative investigation at community level was to be carried out in all three regions. In line with the ToR, it should meet the following requirements:

- It should include treatment and comparison communities in all three regions, so as to address economic and social conditions related to infrastructure and the impact hereof.
- It should include different geographic, economic, and ethnic zones as well as different types of projects.
- At the same time, it should select comparator communities that support the implied assumption that conditions in the comparison and treatment communities were equivalent in the pre-project period.
- It should assess impact areas not covered by the quantitative datasets, in particular health and education, as well as address possible unintended/unexpected impacts.
- It should be phased to enable the qualitative analysis to support and, to some degree, explain the results of the quantitative analysis in Las Segovias.
- It should be carried out with uniform application of a common set of tools, so as to facilitate that results could be contrasted and compared.

3.5.3. Selection of treatment and comparison communities for qualitative fieldwork. Information from PAST offices was important for the selection and matching of treatment and comparison communities, but care was taken to validate this through other data sources and informants as well as during the actual field visits, in line with the process of establishing the list of comparator communities for the quantitative analysis. A total of 39 communities were selected for evaluation using qualitative Participatory Rural Appraisal (PRA) methods in the three regions; 26 were treatment communities, whilst 13 were comparison communities.[15] The criteria used in this selection process were similar to the ones applied for selection of communities for the quantitative analysis, in order to identify similar communities. However, in the case of RAAN and RAAS, additional criteria had to be applied to be able to address the contextual factors identified as important. As a consequence, the selection had to include treatment and comparison communities:

- from different municipalities (16 of 18 municipalities in RAAN and RAAS covered);
- from different productive and agro-climatic zones in each region (zones i, ii and iii covered);
- with different ethnic compositions (Mestizo, indigenous and ethnic groups covered); and
- with different levels of isolation and transport modes and related PAST supported infrastructure (zones i, ii and iii as well all project types included).

The additional information was found in programme documents and municipal information, and was validated through existing secondary information and the fieldwork. Since formal requirements and 'protocol' are less stringent for qualitative methods, it follows that consistency depends on the skill of the investigators in applying the tools in a uniform manner, while still being responsive to the particularities. To facilitate this, work was conducted based on a single set of operational guidelines and with a common reporting format, to help identify patterns across the (considerable) material. In every community, the three field teams used a common set of participatory evaluation techniques including a graphic depiction of community changes before and after PAST project(s) (community in transition mapping). In addition, separate workshops with male and female community members, transect walks and mappings of community services available 'before' and 'after' were included. Tools were field tested and revised prior to application, and the early field trips as well as the quantitative re-survey provided information for this process.

In addition to the community fieldwork, interviews and other material was collected at municipal level. This did not, however, include any comparison communities, since PAST had some presence in all municipalities in the three regions.

The analysis for Las Segovias was conducted separately, to make the most of the possibility of confronting the qualitative and quantitative information in a systematic way. It was found that for the impact areas covered by both the quantitative and qualitative investigation, results were highly similar; for example, for reported levels of change in prices and other areas where results were comparable. This indicated that the qualitative analysis captured relevant impacts in concurrence with the quantitative analysis and enhanced the analytical confidence in the qualitative results (including recall data). Further, this facilitated the comparison of qualitative results across the three regions.

4. Achievements and limitations of the use of qualitative methods in the mixed approach

This section contains a short description of key results, and how the interplay between quantitative and qualitative analysis was important in achieving them.

4.1. Results and conclusions based on the mixed-methods approach in Las Segovias

The quantitative double-difference covering Las Segovias found a range of statistically significant impacts, including the following:

- reductions in the time required by community members to access services outside the community (walking time/kilometre) (assessed at 1 per cent significance level);
- increases in the level of paid employment among heads of households (assessed at 1 per cent significance level);
- increase in number of bedrooms in the house (assessed at 5 per cent significance level);
- increased access to publicly provided electrical supply (assessed at 10 per cent significance level); and
- greater inflows of development projects to the participating communities (assessed at 10 per cent significance level).

In addition, a number of findings pointed to areas where the impact indicators had changed markedly more for treatment communities than for comparison communities, but without the double-difference being significant; for example, where assessment was based on relatively few observations. Some of these include:

- changes in crop composition;
- raising value of land for agricultural use;
- changes in the size of landholdings devoted to agriculture; and
- index of ownership of durable goods.

The qualitative analysis both confirmed the results with regards to the significant impacts and further helped deepen the understanding of the dynamics at play. For instance, it is hardly surprising that construction of an all-weather access road to a community significantly reduces the travel time for the population living in the community and for visitors for economic transactions or social purposes. But it is still an important finding that signifies that improved access had actually been established, enabling improved contact to the outside world and change in development processes. Supplementary quantitative data showed increased traffic levels and establishment of scheduled transport services in PAST communities. The qualitative analysis further helped explore the specific way in which this had affected the communities; for example, in relation to employment.

The quantitative analysis, for example, indicated that the percentage of main household providers with employment had increased significantly in the treatment communities, without similar increases in the comparison communities. It further showed that almost all household providers that had not previously been employed gained 'entrance' in the agricultural sector, but that the construction sector had also increased its overall share of employment (outside rural road construction and maintenance, which could be directly PAST related). No change in sector composition was found for comparison communities.

Furthermore, the qualitative investigation strongly supported and helped explain these findings. With regards to the increased share of employment in the construction sector, it was found that municipalities had adopted the labour-based method for projects funded with non-PAST resources (a result of the institutional analysis), and that community members with experience in labour-based methods were finding employment in local municipal centres. Thus, it is likely that not just the improved access but also the training and experience from PAST played a role in employment generation.[16]

With regards to the agricultural sector, the quantitative findings were also strongly supported by the results of the qualitative fieldwork. For all treatment communities it was emphasised that the change in access had led to changes in relative prices on agricultural inputs and outputs, and strengthened the incentives for agricultural production. This had reportedly led to the increases in amount of land used for agricultural production and in the demand for farmhands. In particular, members of PAST-supported communities pointed to more frequent, timelier and less expensive contacts with markets and buyers for community agricultural products. They also pointed to change in production patterns and improved prices for their products resulting from lessened damage and/or the ability to transport higher value perishable products (such as fresh milk or damageable crops as tomatoes, lettuce, and so forth). The comparison communities did not report similar gains. Again, these results were in strong concurrence with the quantitative results, helped interpret possibly relevant but non-significant quantitative findings and added to the understanding of the programme dynamics.

4.2. Results and conclusions based on the qualitative analysis across regions

As mentioned above, qualitative methods were also used for enriching purposes, by addressing indicators not sufficiently covered by the quantitative material. This was highly relevant for the issues of health and education. Treatment communities in all three regions reported the improved access to health services, especially in emergency cases, as an important social impact. It was also found that access contributed to a positive impact on frequency of visits of health personnel, inspections, and so forth. Similar changes were not reported in the comparison communities. Positive impacts were similarly identified in education: less problems with attendance of teachers; more material; new or rehabilitated schools; and more children attending secondary schools outside the community, since they could now reliably get to school and back within the same day.

It was considered whether the increase in visits from health and education personnel was related to changes in political priorities related to a change of government, rather than access. However, comparison communities did not report any change in attendance, and this was seen as an indication that improved access at least contributed to the reported change, although not necessarily being solely responsible.

In other areas, heterogeneity of impacts was found. When comparing the findings on employment and economic activity in Las Segovias with the results from RAAN and RAAS, clear differences were identified. While the treatment communities did point to some economic impacts, the relative level and importance of these impacts were generally much less pronounced in RAAN and RAAS. An interesting modification was that in the communities where the situation was most similar to Las Segovias (for example, in type of access problems and production patterns), similar types and levels of impacts were found. In the coastal areas, where the economic activities were more focused on fisheries and less on agriculture, and where the interventions included more aquatic infrastructure projects targeting a different type of access problems, the benefits was found to be less pronounced. Thus, the mixed methods approach helped identify the variation of economic and productive impacts not only *between* regions but also across different zones *within* the same region.

This allowed the evaluation to conclude that important heterogeneity of (economic) effects could be encountered, if scaling up, and to point to some of the factors influencing the type and level of impact to be expected. In comparison, social impacts in health and education were found to be more homogeneous.

Even if the assessment of heterogeneity based on mixed methods is less specific than it would have been, had it been possible to use quantitative data for all three regions, this contribution from qualitative analysis has important implications for policy and practice. These would have been missed, if this 'less-than-perfect' approach had not been pursued.

This illustrates how mixed methods can be used for *analytical enhancement*, facilitating the creation of a foundation for an important *merging* of results from both quantitative and qualitative analysis to develop recommendations of relevance for policy and practice, following White (2008).

4.3. *Organisational capacity, maintenance and sustainability*

The final result area to be outlined is the issue of organisational capacity, maintenance and sustainability. While some aspects were assessed for both treatment and comparison communities (for example, inflow of development projects and cooperation with outside actors), the important issues of maintenance and sustainability did naturally focus on PAST communities and municipalities.

At community level, the evaluation found maintenance committees had been established and had demonstrated an ability to continue organising, funding and executing routine maintenance of the original works, also after project completion and end of PAST monitoring presence. This was seen as linked to the training and practical involvement of the communities, increasing local capacity both for the technical aspects of construction and maintenance, and for the organisation and interaction with the municipalities and other actors.[17]

At municipal level, the evaluation found that the PAST-trained staff remained with the municipalities, which contributed to the continued dialogue with the project committees and resulted in generally satisfactory levels of maintenance. The assessment at municipal level did not, however, include comparison municipalities. To help validation and triangulation, the assessment from actors expected to have a better overview and basis for comparison was collected. In this context, it is notable that the national fund for road maintenance (FOMAV) reported that PAST municipalities submitted project proposals of a markedly higher quality than non-PAST municipalities (Danida 2010).

Based on the combination of assessment of technical–physical maintenance status of projects, continued existence and functioning of maintenance committees and the continued presence of trained staff in the municipalities, the evaluation concluded that important prerequisites for the sustainability of the infrastructure investments were in place. This bodes well for the continuation of the stream of benefits stemming from the improved access.

5. Conclusion

The evaluation of the impacts of PAST support to rural transport infrastructure has demonstrated how mixed methods can be relevant in all phases of evaluation work, and how it can fruitfully be applied in relation to *integration, analytical enhancement* and *merging of results* for policy recommendations, to use the typology of White (2008).

Without the early consideration of both quantitative and qualitative data, including early field exposure, the evaluation would have run high risk of missing opportunities of accessing and combining existing datasets. Both quantitative and qualitative data helped shape the overall evaluation approach, and mixed methods were used in an *integrative* manner in the more specific design; for example, when qualitative information helped focus and streamline the quantitative investigation, and where quantitative (and qualitative) information helped identify parameters to be considered to ensure adequate coverage of contexts for the qualitative analysis.

Further, the iterative process of contrasting and comparing qualitative and quantitative results for *analytical enhancement* helped the evaluation to gain a deeper understanding of quantitative results, in line with the second of the three dimensions of combining qualitative and quantitative methods presented in White (2008). The evaluator assessment of concurrence between qualitative and quantitative results strengthened the confidence in the results of the qualitative analysis. This again enhanced the contrasting and comparison of qualitative results between and within regions, whereby the evaluation could address issues that were insufficiently covered by the quantitative datasets. In particular, the mixed methods helped identify heterogeneity of impacts, something that was considered highly relevant in a situation where scaling up was considered. The inclusion of qualitative methods also allowed the evaluation to assess the prerequisites for sustainability and continuation of the stream of benefits in more detail and nuance. This combination of qualitative and quantitative methods thereby facilitated the *merger* of results for identification of lessons learned and policy recommendations that had more resonance and relevance, than would otherwise have been possible.

Thus, it is evident that the qualitative methods in important ways added to the quality of the evaluation, in particular its usefulness and relevance for policy and practice. The 'success' of the qualitative methods, however, is heavily dependent on the evaluation core of a more 'robust' econometric double-difference analysis, which identified a range of significant impacts. Without this core, both as a source of specific knowledge on impacts and as backdrop for assessment of qualitative tools and calibration of the expectations, the results from the qualitative analysis would have been much less informative and the qualitative information on, for example, sustainability of investment of less relevance to policy-makers.

So is it worthwhile to attempt to carry out mixed methods evaluations, even if data constraints only allow for a partial core of 'robust' double-difference analysis? From a donor agency perspective, the answer is yes: knowledge on impact is scarce, as is information on how programme intervention logics function in practice. This means that even less-than-perfect information is worth pursuing, and that investing in data availability studies and exploration of 'pragmatic' alternatives to more rigorous – but for donors often less applicable – approaches (such as randomised controlled trials) can be worthwhile. At the same time, however, it is important to be sensitive to the fact that such approaches, including the present example, *are* less than perfect. In particular, data constraints in controlling for biases, matching, and so forth, are not to be taken lightly. While the second step of matching at household level did allow the evaluation to do important controls, it would have benefitted from the availability of more specific measurements on, for example, pre-intervention access. Similarly, while a qualitative assessment of heterogeneity against a core of quantitative analysis is markedly better than no assessment of heterogeneity, the limitations of the results and conclusions should be kept in mind.

A related challenge for the *use* of the results of a mixed-method evaluation, as presented in this study, concerns the different types and levels of analysis and conclusions. This entails a risk that evaluation users miss some of the implications of the differences and nuances between conclusions based on different types of analysis. While this makes the communication of the evaluation and its results challenging, it should not discourage from attempting to undertake a 'less than perfect' impact evaluation. The knowledge gained may still be sufficiently well founded and policy relevant to represent a step forward for the individual donor. It might even form a small addition to the body of knowledge about the impacts of, for example infrastructure programmes. Consequently, the PAST case indicates a 'niche' for small agencies that want to undertake 'as rigorous as possible' impact evaluations, and – in the process – contribute to the discussion of evaluation approaches and enhanced knowledge for policy and practice.

Notes

1. It should be noted that the use of mixed methods does not necessarily imply the notion that qualitative and quantitative data can be used interchangeably. Clearly, quantitative and qualitative data have different characteristics that influence their use. However, such differences do not mean that data and conclusions stemming from different methodologies cannot be fruitfully used in combination: while significant findings from a quantitative analysis would not be rendered non-significant when facing differing qualitative results, their interpretation might well be challenged or informed hereby. Thus, it could be argued that in this context, 'challenging' (rather than 'refuting') might be relevant term for this specific use of mixed methods. See examples on how quantitative analysis may be informed by qualitative findings and vice versa in White (2008), and a brief discussion on characteristics and differences of qualitative and quantitative data in Bamberger *et al.* (2006).
2. See for instance van de Walle (2009), who notes that small rural roads projects expected to have local impact are often more conducive to the construction of a credible counterfactual than more ample interventions.
3. Likewise, project placement may not be (and was indeed not) random and can be linked to context as well. The issue of links between context, selection process and expected impacts is further addressed below.
4. With the exception of few communities outside the PAST focus.

5. Velleman (2009), in a recent assessment of factors affecting access to healthcare in RAAS, argues that, while geographic and transport barriers are important, the single most important factor limiting access for Miskito community members to healthcare was discriminatory treatment by health workers (Creole nurses and Mestizo doctors). Without either accepting or rejecting this claim it seems clear that, for example, linguistic problems in accessing healthcare could be a major factor for some ethnic groups.

6. This option of combining datasets was not fully explored by the earlier pre-study (Danida 2008).

7. This meant that the timeframe for the quantitative analysis was reduced in comparison with the original expectations. It was assessed that the resulting eight-year period was still sufficient to cover medium to longer-term impacts, although possibly not to the same degree. It further meant that the assessment of longer term sustainability in the qualitative analysis had to include 'old' projects.

8. Defining the zone of influence with a sufficient degree of certainty would have been substantially more difficult, for example, for an improved central wharf, used by a dispersed group of communities. See also Van de Walle (2009) for considerations on beneficiaries and zone of influence.

9. This typology (and indeed the 'real world approach' to impact evaluation that it represents) might be contested, since it can be seen to advocate an eclectic use of methods and data sources to gain 'good enough' information on impact, thus possibly seen by some to not focus sufficiently on establishing the counterfactual with a high degree of statistical certainty, and therefore not being sufficiently 'robust'. Without entering into a substantial discussion on criteria for methodological rigour it is, however, noted that the labelling of category 1 as a 'robust' impact evaluation often would typically imply a foundation in quantitative data allowing for econometrical analysis or similar.

10. Projects could also be justified by lack of access to social services. While this was particular relevant for justifications in RAAN and RAAS, it meant that care had to be taken when matching based on these criteria, also in Las Segovias, and considering existence of and access to social services.

11. This was due to the objective of the evaluation, which was to assess the possible impact of the PAST interventions, rather than comparing the PAST interventions with other interventions. While this would also have been a very relevant question, which could allow for an assessment of cost-effectiveness, this was seen as being a rather more ambitious task than intended for the present evaluation. While other actors were involved in transport infrastructure, especially in recent years, the approaches were typically quite different from PAST, according to information available.

12. Actual collusion amongst actors is perceived to be unlikely – and unlikely not to have been discovered over time, had it been the case.

13. As an example of the level of programme 'patience', it can be mentioned that programme information showed that a project was 'waiting' almost 10 years, before all guarantees (in this particular case including environmental mitigation measures) were in place and the project was carried out.

14. A 'regression discontinuity'-oriented aspect was considered, by including communities that were fully eligible on all other criteria than physical–technical requirements for Mano de Obra Intensivo (for example, the slope of a hill), and where other agencies had not implemented projects, as possible comparison communities. However, in practice no such projects were found, where sufficient information was available to assess that to what degree other criteria were fulfilled.

15. The uneven distribution between comparison and treatment communities is due to the inclusion of more treatment than comparison groups in RAAN and RAAS. This was due to an assessment of the need to investigate a range of projects and project context in depth. By implication and due to resource constraints, the number of comparison communities was limited. While not ideal, care was taken to include make sure a sufficient range of community contexts were included.

16. The evaluation is clear in stating that it cannot differentiate between the strength of influence of the improved access in itself, and the influence of other elements of the PAST model. While consistent with the focus on the specific impact of PAST support, this is clearly an important factor when considering the implications of the evaluations results.

17. Interestingly, the quantitative analysis showed a significantly higher inflow of other development projects to PAST communities than to comparison communities, and the evaluation points to that the improved access for non-government organisations and other development actors and increased capability of the communities may in combination have brought this change about (Danida 2010).

References

Bamberger, M., Rugh, J. and Mabry, L., 2006. *Real world evaluation: working under budget, time, data and political constraints.* Thousand Oaks, CA: Sage.

Cook, T.D., Sahdish, W.R. and Wong, V.C., 2008. Three conditions under which experiment and observational studies produce comparable causal estimate: new findings from within-study comparisons. *Journal of policy analysis and management,* 27 (4), 724–750.

Cook, T.D., Scriven, M., Coryn, C.L.S. and Evergreen, S.D.H., 2010. Contemporary thinking about causation in evaluation: a dialogue with Tom Cook and Michael Scriven. *Americal journal of evaluation,* 31 (1), 105–117.

Danida, 2007a. *Impact evaluation of Hima Iringa Region Tanzania.* Prepared by Orbicon and Goss Gilroy. Copenhagen: Danish Ministry of Foreign Affairs, Denmark.

Danida, 2007b. *Evaluating the impact of rural roads in Nicaragua.* Prepared by Nina Blöndal, Endeleza International Development Consulting. Copenhagen: Ministry of Foreign Affairs, Denmark, Evaluation Study 2007/3.

Danida, 2008. *General study of the impact of rural roads in Nicaragua.* Prepared by COWI A/S. Lyngby: Ministry of Foreign Affairs, Denmark.

Danida, 2009a. *Impact evaluation of aquaculture interventions in Bangladesh.* Prepared by Orbicon and Lamans. Copenhagen: Danish Ministry of Foreign Affairs, Denmark.

Danida, 2009b. *Impact evaluation of Danida support to rural transport infrastructure in Nicaragua. Inception report.* Prepared jointly by Orbicon A/S and Goss Gilroy. Copenhagen: Danish Ministry of Foreign Affairs, Denmark.

Danida, 2010. *Impact evaluation of Danida support to rural transport infrastructure in Nicaragua.* Prepared jointly by Orbicon A/S and Goss Gilroy. Copenhagen: Danish Ministry of Foreign Affairs, Denmark.

Henriksen, K., 2008. Ethnic self-regulation and democratic instability on Nicaragua's Atlantic Coast: the case of Ratisuna. *European review of Latin American and Caribbean studies,* 85, 23–40.

Hvalkof, S., 2007. *Technical mission to the transport sector programme support in Nicaragua.* Report submitted to Danida. Copenhagen: Danish Ministry of Foreign Affairs, Denmark.

Lundgren, H.E., North, W.H. and Rist, R.C., 2003. *A review of evaluation in Danida.* Copenhagen: Danish Ministry of Foreign Affairs, Denmark.

Rand, J., 2010. Evaluating the employment generating impact of rural roads in Nicaragua. *Journal of development effectiveness,* 3 (1), 28–43.

Steiner, P.M., Wroblewski, A. and Cook, T.D., 2009. Randomized experiments and quasi-experimental design in educational research. *In*: R.K.E. and J.B. Cousins, eds. *The SAGE international handbook of educational evaluation.* Los Angeles: SAGE Publications, 75–97.

Van de Walle, D., 2009. Impact evaluation of rural roads projects. *Journal of development effectiveness,* 1 (1), 147–168.

Van de Walle, D. and Mu, R., 2007. *Rural roads and poor area development in Vietnam.* Washington, DC: World Bank, Policy Research Working Paper 4340.

Velleman, Y., 2009. *Access to health care services in Nicaraguas South Atlantic region – a report.* Gosport: Hoveraid.

White, H., 2008. Of probits and participation: the use of mixed methods in quantitative impact evaluation. *Nonie Working Paper 7,* January.

White, H., 2009. Theory-based impact evaluation: principles and practice. *3ie Working paper 3.*

World Bank, 2006. *Conducting quality impact evaluations under budget, time and data constraints.* Prepared by Michael Bamberger. Washington, DC: Independent Evaluation Group, The World Bank Group.

Evaluating the employment-generating impact of rural roads in Nicaragua

John Rand

Institute of Food and Resource Economics, University of Copenhagen, Rolighedsvej 25, DK-1958, Frederiksberg, Denmark;

This paper analyses the employment-generating impact of a tertiary road project in Nicaragua, applying a matched double-difference approach to control for initial conditions and time variant factors that simultaneously influence the placement of roads and subsequent employment growth rates. Results are promising. The author's estimates indicate an increase in hours worked per week attributable to the intervention of around 9.5–12.3 hours. Moreover, he observes tendencies of a graduation process taking place in the labour market: individuals moving out of unemployment predominately achieve employment in the agricultural sector (self-employment), whereas newly created service sector jobs primarily are taken by workers previously working in agriculture. Finally, the analysis suggests that the employment-generating effect comes through a combination of reduced travel time and better access to markets and larger, more integrated road networks.

1. Introduction

Improvement of existing roads and development of new roads has long been a central part of the donor toolbox with the aim to reduce poverty in the developing world. However, the poverty-reducing effect of these interventions are often not well documented, although there has been a substantial amount of work to evaluate the impact of infrastructure improvements on different socio-economic indicators.[1] Most of these evaluations have been qualitative in nature, maybe due to the large data requirements and methodological difficulties faced when carrying out solid quantitative assessments of infrastructure investments.

The central empirical obstacle to estimating road impacts has been reverse causation. Non-theoretical reduced form models focusing on ex-post impact evaluation has been instrumental in addressing this exact problem, and in this paper we restrict our discussion to the use of this methodological approach.[2] The causality problem basically boils down to the fact that roads are not randomly placed, as roads are constructed in certain locations based on the attributes of those locations. Examples of endogenous road placement are numerous. If roads are built in places experiencing higher growth, there will be problems in disentangling the road's impact on incomes. Moreover, if locations with higher agricultural potential are selected for road improvements, then a bias can be expected when assessing road impacts on agricultural production. Van de Walle (2009, p. 19) therefore highlights that 'understanding the potential sources of endogeneity is critical to collecting the right data and choosing the right methodology for estimating unbiased impacts' of roads. She also notes that a credible ex-post evaluation methodology needs to correct for the potential sources of selection bias through a careful construction of a counterfactual. Furthermore, given that roads may have dispersed effects, pre-intervention data for both treated and control communities must be available. Evaluation methods that use a single cross-section are not a well-suited instrument as control communities might have been contaminated by the road investment project. Finally, evaluation of secondary/tertiary/feeder roads using ex-post impact evaluation methods seem especially strong if pre-intervention data exist for both treated and control communities.

In this paper, we analyse the potential impact of the Danida-supported Transport Sector Support Program (PAST) in Las Segovias, Nicaragua. A combination of the Nicaraguan household census (CENSO) from 2005 and a follow-up sub-sample survey of randomly selected households in 2009 constitute the pre-intervention and post-intervention data. In each survey the data contain information on the same 345 households (146 treatment and 199 comparison households), making the use of a matched double-difference approach particularly appropriate.

Several authors (Van de Walle and Mu 2007, Ravallion and Chen 2005, Lokshin and Yemtsov 2005) have successfully used this conventional double-difference approach in combination with different matching procedures to control for initial conditions and any time variant factors that simultaneously influence the placement of roads and subsequent growth rates.[3] Lokshin and Yemtsov (2005), who study the impacts of road rehabilitation in Georgia, find that impacts vary between poor and non-poor households and that opportunities for off-farm and female wage employment were significantly increased in project versus control villages. However, off-farm employment improved solely for non-poor households and female wage employment increased for poor women only.

Khandker *et al.* (2009) use a fixed-effects regression method, with regression controls for initial conditions. They find that road investments in Bangladesh reduced poverty significantly by raising agricultural production, wages and output prices and lowering input and transport costs. Their results also suggest that schooling outcomes for both boys and girls improved as a result of the road improvements. Impacts were found to be proportionately higher for the poor relative to the non-poor.[4]

Gibson and Rozelle (2003) take another approach by using an instrumental variable that determines road placement but does not determine outcomes conditional on placement. More specifically, using data from Papua New Guinea, Gibson and Rozelle (2003) argue that the year a district was linked to the national highway system was not a function of a region's wealth or productivity potential and this therefore provides a good instrument for subsequent access to rural roads. Their results appear to support the argument that poor areas have the least access to infrastructure and so people in those areas may benefit the most from new investments. Thus, infrastructure spending, whether on new assets or maintenance of existing facilities, can provide a form of targeted interventions that favour the poor.

The Nicaragua CENSO survey instrument is particularly detailed with regards to employment. In this paper we therefore focus on the potential impact of roads on employment generation. Using four different employment definitions, we find that the PAST programme had substantial employment gains, especially in regions with lower poverty rates, on average. Moreover, individuals moving out of unemployment predominately achieve employment in the agricultural sector (self-employment), whereas newly created service sector jobs primarily are taken by workers previously working in agriculture. As such we observe a kind of graduation process in the labour market. Furthermore, the PAST tertiary road project does not increase job migration. Jobs are generated locally (within the municipality) and more jobs are considered non-seasonal in character. Finally, the analysis suggested that the employment-generating effect came through a combination of reduced travel time (creating a relative increase in labour supply) and better access to markets and larger more integrated road networks (increasing labour demand).

As such, the results differ from papers finding that roads predominantly raise labour opportunities outside the agricultural sector (see, for example, Gashassin *et al.* 2010), whereas the result that most new jobs (due to the road placement) are generated locally is in accordance with the finding by Fafchamps and Schilpi (2008) that road improvements slow down migration substantially.

The remainder of this paper is organised as follows. Section 2 outlines the PAST Phase II in some detail, and Section 3 describes the data. Section 4 presents results while conclusions follow in Section 5.

2. The Transport Sector Support Program

The Transport Sector Support Program (PAST, from its Spanish name Programa de Apoya Al Sector Transporte) was designed as a follow-up to phase I of PAST (1999–2004). Besides continuing work in other regions (RAAN and RAAS, especially), an added component to support improvement of tertiary infrastructure was introduced in the Las Segovias region. This component included both a construction and a maintenance plan. In this paper, the focus is solely on evaluating the employment-generating impacts of this tertiary road project in areas with significant new construction plans, although the data allow for several issues to be analysed (for details, see Orbicon and Lamans 2010). Phase II of PAST covered the period from 2005 to 2009 and had the immediate objective to improve access in Las Segovias (and RAAN and RAAS) by connecting rural areas with difficult access to social services and economic and administrative centres.[5]

The overall development objective of phase II of PAST was to contribute to poverty reduction through the improvement of socio-economic conditions of the population in the isolated rural areas of Las Segovias (and the provinces RAAN and RAAS). This included addressing both the social and economic well-being of the poorest elements in the target regions. As stated in Orbicon and Lamans (2010), the four immediate objectives of phase II of PAST were as follows:

- To improve access in Las Segovias by connecting rural areas with difficult access to social services and economic and administrative centres.
- To ensure sustainable maintenance of the improved transport infrastructure, sharing responsibilities at municipal and community levels.
- To strengthen the capacities of Regional Transport Councils (CRTs) as well as local and regional government for planning, defining priorities, negotiating and maintaining the transport infrastructure, so as to progressively assume PAST activities.
- To establish and implement strategies on the cross-cutting issues of gender equality, environmental protection and the rights and needs of indigenous people and ethnic groups, taking into consideration the priority themes, including gender and environment.

In this paper we limit our analysis and reasoning to the effects of improved access without discussing the political/governance aspects of the intervention.

The projects covered during the second phase of PAST were primarily rural roads that could be built and maintained by the communities themselves using labour-intensive methods. A key strategic priority of phase II of PAST was a commitment to transfer responsibility for planning, management, procurement, and supervision (largely undertaken during phase I of PAST by regional transport support teams) to regional, municipal and community partners. This was done in order to motivate local partners to undertake project and programme functions in a sustainable way.

As highlighted in van de Walle (2009), roads are seldom randomly placed. This is also the case of phase II of PAST. First, road project proposals (submitted by municipalities) needed to be *pre-approved* for submission to the annual meeting of the CRT, where it was decided whether a project should be approved for funding or not. The submission criteria can be summarised as follows:

(1) *Execution*: the project must be capable of execution within two years, which normally means that road projects should not exceed 15 km.
(2) *Labour-intensive methods*: it must be possible to construct the project using labour-intensive methods, so sufficient manpower needed to be available in the community.
(3) *Road system*: the project should provide a year-round connection to the secondary and primary transport system and access to an urban centre or market.
(4) *Contamination*: the project should not be the object of investments by other organisations.
(5) *Endogenous road placement*: project proposals must be accompanied by documentation showing that the implementation area is particularly well suited for support from a social or economic point of view (for example, especially showing areas high agricultural potential would be favoured).

Points 1–3 do not pose a serious problem to our analysis as we only focus on Las Segovias. Abundant labour is readily available and most tertiary roads needed do not have to exceed 15 km in order to reach secondary and primary road systems, which under normal circumstances are accessible year-round.[6] Moreover, we do not expect to experience infrastructure contamination problems as road investments are centrally planned and well documented, and we did not find other ongoing road projects in either treatment or control communities during the period under consideration. However, through the use of household survey (EMNV [Encuesta Nacional de Hogares sobre Medición de Nivel de Vida]) data and municipality interviews, we found a few systematic differences between treatment and comparison communities when studying changes in the allocation of other government projects in Las Segovias. Out of 22 government projects analysed, we found that treatment communities were more likely to receive funds for health campaigns and installation of latrines than comparison communities. But importantly, we found no systematic differences between treatment and control areas in government-funded employment programmes (see Orbicon and Lamans 2010 for details).

Finally, point 5 above (endogenous road placement) is of special concern to our analysis. It is well known that a conventional double-difference approach will bias estimates if outcome changes are a function of initial conditions that also influenced assignment of the communities between treatment and comparison groups. To help address this issue we control for initial heterogeneity using nearest-neighbour matching methodology. Retrieving unbiased estimates thereby assumes that we are able to control for all factors that jointly influence project placement and outcomes, leaving no selection bias due to latent heterogeneity. Moreover, we note that our comparison communities are located in the same municipalities that received treatment, which helps us ensure that it is not municipality (social and economic) characteristics driving the effects. Finally, it is also reassuring that a significant number of the selected comparison communities are part of the 2010 municipal project proposals to PAST, which is why these communities can be considered 'pipeline projects'. This is a particular strength, since it provides a clear indication that these communities would actually qualify for the project.

After pre-approval, the CRT and the Executive Committee (CED) prioritise projects based on the following four criteria: cost per kilometre of road, cost per beneficiary (per capita) of the project, expected net change in access measured on a scale of one to five, and ability of the community to provide 5 per cent of the capital costs of construction.[7]

As such, an important characteristic of the PAST model of support to rural transport infrastructure is the clear and objective criteria for setting priorities and approving projects. However, it is also clear that the process highlights the importance of controlling for differences in the administrative capacity of local communities. This feature of the project made the selection of potential comparison communities a relatively demanding task, a procedure described in the following section.

3. Data description and summary statistics

A combination of the Nicaraguan household census (CENSO) from 2005 (described in detail in INIDE 2008) and a follow-up sub-sample survey in 2009 (described in Orbicon and Lamans 2010) is the main data source relied upon in this paper. In each survey the data contain information on the same households in Las Segovias in the districts of Estelí, Madriz and Nueva Segovia, which is where part of the Danida-funded Transport Sector Support Program (PAST) was implemented. From the 2005 CENSO the survey team in 2009 identified 17 relevant municipalities, including 36 treatment communities found in the PAST project database (2005–2008 projects).

Moreover, as mentioned in the previous section a particular challenge was the identification of a sufficiently large number of suitable comparison communities for the re-survey in Las Segovias. The survey team therefore visited all project communities within Las Segovias, where round-table discussions were held with technical staff from the municipalities and PAST staff. Following the PAST pre-selection project criteria described in detail in the previous section, the survey team was able to identify 37 relevant control communities. In each CENSO community, eight households were randomly selected for the re-survey. In the household-level analysis below we use statistical matching to ensure the quality of the match, and since the sample is designed with matching in mind, the data collected from comparison communities are less likely to be outside the region of common support, since we already matched at the community level prior to collecting the post-intervention data.

After completing the 2009 re-survey, the survey team made strong efforts to check the consistency of the data, ensuring that it was in fact the same households being interviewed in both 2005 and 2009. Moreover, a data cleaning process was undertaken excluding all inconsistent answers and missing observations. This data cleaning process focusing on the employment module left 345 CENSO households with consistent information in both survey years (690 observations). These observations covered 146 treatment households and 199 control households within 15 municipalities (municipio), 48 regions (comarca) and 61 communities (comunidad), with 29 treatment and 32 control communities, respectively.[8] Table 1 presents an overview of the data available for analysis. More details on the re-survey in Las Segovias are found in Orbicon and Lamans (2010).

Table 1. Data overview.

	A: Communities		B: Households	
	Control	Treatment	Control	Treatment
2005	61	0	345	0
2009	32	29	199	146
Total observations	122	690		

The focus in this paper is on the employment-generating effects of the PAST project. Better access to roads may improve job opportunities, by allowing them to look for jobs beyond their immediate settlement areas and take advantage of seasonal work in neighbouring rural areas or cities. In addition to the direct employment-generating effects, we also look at the location (within the community or outside the community) and characteristics (wage worker or self-employment and employment in agriculture/manufacturing/services) of the jobs.

We work with four different employment definitions, defined at the level of the household head:[9]

(1) Indicator variable taking the value one if the individual worked (for wages) during the past week, and zero otherwise.
(2) Hours worked during the past week.
(3) Indicator variable taking the value one if the individual worked (for wages) during the past week (based on consistency in the reporting in definitions 1 and 2), and zero otherwise.
(4) Indicator variable taking the value one if the individual worked (for wages) *full-time* during the past week (where a full-time working week is defined as 48 hours), and zero otherwise.

Although we distinguish between permanent and seasonal job creation, results presented may be affected by survey timing. In 2009 data were collected in the months of June, July and August, whereas the reference months in the CENSO 2005 data were May and June. Results may therefore to some extent be affected by seasonality differences between baseline and the follow-up survey.

Table 2 summarises these main outcome variables by treatment category and survey year. Looking at employment definition 1, we see that only 67.8 per cent of the treatment group had some sort of employment in 2005, as compared with 76.4 per cent in the control group. However, some individuals reported no employment if they were not full-time employed. Correcting for this (employment measure 3) shows closer baseline correspondence between treatment (82.2 per cent) and comparison (80.9 per cent) communities. Finally, around one-half of individuals living in treatment communities had full-time employment in 2005, as compared with 52.8 per cent in comparison areas. Independent of the employment measure used we observe increases in employment between 2005 and 2009 in the treatment communities, whereas the employment situation in comparison areas in the same period worsened on average.

Table 2 also provides information on the following three employment variables: location of main employment (within community = 1, outside community = 0), seasonal or

Table 2. Employment outcome indicators – summary statistics by treatment category and survey year.

	2005		2009	
	Treatment	Control	Treatment	Control
Employed (yes = 1, no = 0)	0.678	0.764	0.842	0.739
	(0.469)	(0.426)	(0.366)	(0.440)
Hours worked	35.000	36.603	38.945	33.704
	(19.215)	(20.135)	(19.497)	(20.177)
Employed, corrected (yes = 1,	0.822	0.809	0.856	0.799
no = 0)	(0.384)	(0.394)	(0.352)	(0.402)
Employed full-time (yes = 1,	0.493	0.528	0.548	0.447
no = 0)	(0.502)	(0.500)	(0.499)	(0.498)
Location of main job	0.970	0.961	0.967	0.966
(within municipality = 1,	(0.172)	(0.195)	(0.178)	(0.182)
outside municipality = 0)				
Seasonal or permanent	0.737	0.612	0.691	0.680
employment	(0.442)	(0.489)	(0.464)	(0.468)
(seasonal = 1, permanent = 0)				
Self-employed or employee	0.737	0.809	0.821	0.850
(self-employed = 1, wage	(0.442)	(0.394)	(0.385)	(0.358)
worker = 0)				
Total observations	146 [99]	199 [152]	146 [123]	199 [147]

Note: Standard deviations in parentheses and numbers of employed household heads in square brackets.

permanent employment (seasonal = 1, permanent = 0), and self-employed or employee (self-employed = 1, wage worker = 0). The table shows that most jobs (both before and after treatment) are located within the same municipality. Around 70 per cent of the jobs are seasonal, but we do observe a slight increase in the number of permanent jobs in treatment areas between 2005 and 2009, combined with an on average decrease in permanent employment in comparison areas in the same period. Finally, most employed individuals are self-employed (in agriculture) and we see an increase in the share of self-employed between 2005 and 2009 in both treatment and control communities.

Table 3 documents the observable household, community and municipality characteristics included as control variables in the analysis. Numbers are reported separately for 2005 and 2009. Due to the nature of the application process, where unobserved municipality characteristics (ability to organise and develop) may influence project selection, we control for potential location-specific effects through inclusion of a set of municipality indicator variables. The table shows that the municipality distribution across survey years is the same given that the households have been followed over time and migrated households have not been traced. Moreover, we include municipality pre-treatment changes in poverty based on calculations in Gomez et al. (2008) to evaluate whether pre-treatment poverty dynamics make a difference.

Table 3 also shows that micro-regional differences between treatment and control communities exist. The total population of treatment communities is on average larger than the observed 2005 CENSO numbers for comparison areas. Moreover, five variables defined in the CENSO at the regional level (micro regions as defined in the CENSO) are also included.[10] These numbers are also only recorded in 2005. First, around 35 per cent of households in a micro-region live in 'overcrowded' conditions (Indicator 1). This means

Table 3. Control variables – summary statistics by treatment category and survey year.

		2005		2009	
		Treatment	Control	Treatment	Control
HH characteristics	HH gender (male = 1, female = 0)	0.842	0.839	0.856	0.809
	HH age	45.370	45.176	50.658	50.975
	HH education 1[a]	0.452	0.382	0.466	0.462
	HH education 2[a]	0.507	0.548	0.493	0.467
	HH education 3[a]	0.041	0.070	0.041	0.070
	HH married (yes = 1, no = 0)	0.822	0.814	0.822	0.774
	HH literate (literate = 1, read only = 2, illiterate = 3)	1.890	1.789	1.801	1.804
	HH members	5.555	5.121	5.493	5.357
Community and micro-regional characteristics	Size of community (number of people in the comarca)	442	347	..	..
	Indicator 1: Overcrowding	34.789	34.999		
	Indicator 2: Inadequate housing	36.744	43.473	..	..
	Indicator 3: Underserved - public utilities	9.458	8.287	..	..
	Indicator 4: Low education	26.523	30.314	..	..
	Indicator 5: Economic dependence	49.657	48.719	..	..
Municipality characteristics	Changes in poverty levels (1998–2005)	−5.947	−5.168	..	..
	Location 1 (Japala)	0.034	0.060	0.034	0.060
	Location 2 (El Jicaro)	0.027	0.050	0.027	0.050
	Location 3 (Quilali)	0.055	0.101	0.055	0.101
	Location 4 (Wiwilli)	0.014	0.050	0.014	0.050
	Location 5 (Somoto)	0.062	0.095	0.062	0.095
	Location 6 (Telpaneca)	0.041	0.025	0.041	0.025
	Location 7 (San Juan de Rio Coco)	0.068	0.030	0.068	0.030
	Location 8 (Palacaguina)	0.055	0.050	0.055	0.050
	Location 9 (Yalaguina)	0.041	0.030	0.041	0.030
	Location 10 (San Lucas)	0.137	0.015	0.137	0.015
	Location 11 (San Jose de Cusmapa)	0.082	0.095	0.082	0.095
	Location 12 (Pueblo Nuevo)	0.096	0.101	0.096	0.101
	Location 13 (Esteli)	0.007	0.060	0.007	0.060
	Location 14 (La Trinidad)	0.144	0.070	0.144	0.070
	Location 15 (Condega)	0.137	0.166	0.137	0.166
Total observations		146	199	146	199

[a]Household head (HH) education 1, never attended school; HH education 2, attended and passed primary school; HH education 3, attended secondary school and above.

Table 4. Balancing of pre-treatment initial characteristics.

		Coefficient	Standard error
HH characteristics	HH gender (male = 1, female = 0)	0.001	(0.114)
	HH age	−0.003	(0.002)
	HH education 2	−0.250	(0.170)
	HH education 3	−0.244	(0.156)
	HH married (yes = 1, no = 0)	0.001	(0.110)
	HH literate (literate = 1, read only = 2, illiterate = 3)	−0.095	(0.089)
	HH members	0.027**	(0.012)
Community and micro-regional characteristics	Community size (log)	0.190***	(0.070)
	Indicator 1: Overcrowding	−0.017**	(0.007)
	Indicator 2: Inadequate housing	−0.004*	(0.002)
	Indicator 3: Underserved - public utilities	0.010	(0.006)
	Indicator 4: Low education	−0.019***	(0.004)
	Indicator 5: Economic dependence	0.009**	(0.004)
Municipality characteristics	Changes in poverty levels (1998–2005)	−0.007	(0.020)
Location dummies included		Yes	
Pseudo R-squared		0.21	
Total observations		345	

Notes: Probit estimates, marginal effects. Standard errors (reported in parentheses) are heteroskedasticity robust. Base: Household head (HH) education 1 and Condega.
*, **, ***Significance at a 10 per cent, 5 per cent and 1 per cent level, respectively.

that around one-third of households do not have premises suitable for housing all members of their household. Second, treatment and control groups differ in terms of 'inadequate housing' (Indicator 2 captures the share of households in a micro-region below a certain threshold quality of the construction materials of walls, ceilings and floors of the house), with 37 per cent of households in a micro-region having an inadequate dwelling in treatment areas, as compared with 44 per cent in control communities.

Third, 9 per cent of treatment households do not have adequate water supply and systems of sewage disposal (Indicator 3), as compared with 8 per cent in control areas. Fourth, between 27 and 31 per cent of households in a micro-region have at least one child, 7–14 years of age, who does not attend school (Indicator 4). Fifth, the 'economic dependence' variable (Indicator 5) captures baseline micro-regional employment rates, which is shown to be 49 and 50 per cent on average in control and treatment communities, respectively.

Finally, we include a series of household-specific characteristics in the control set.[11] Among these household characteristics, only size (number of members) are significant in the probit estimation carried out using 2005 information (results are reported in Table 4). As suggested above, we find a number of significant covariates of programme participation among the micro-regional indicators. Figure 1 also shows that the propensity score distribution differs somewhat between treatment and control households. However, there is a reasonable overlap in the densities of the estimated propensity scores for treated and non-participating households. Consequently, restricting the analysis to the common support should not significantly reduce the sample under consideration (20 observations dropped, when restricting the analysis to the common support).

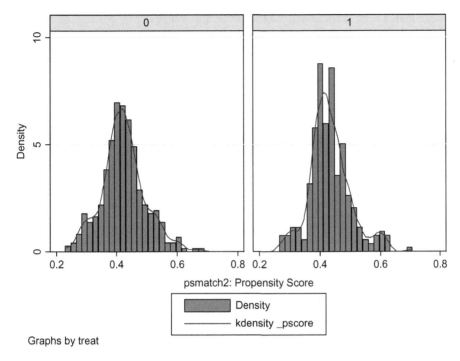

Figure 1. Distribution of estimated propensity scores.
Note: 0 = non-participants and 1 = treatment households.

4. Results

Table 5 provides the matched double-difference results following three different approaches all applying the bias-corrected matching estimator suggested by Abadie and Imbens (2002). First, using a *levels* specification, we allow individual observations to be used more than once by allowing for four matches. Second, in addition to the *levels* of our matching variables, we include *differences* in household characteristics as control variables.

Third, as highlighted above, employment information is only available for the head of households. Since some of these main providers of the family are above the retirement age, we check the robustness of the results obtained when limiting the age group to 15–65. This reduces the sample to 273 observations (117 treatment and 156 comparison households).[12]

First, using only the *levels* of the independent variables and allowing for four matches leads to point estimates which are somewhat different from the unmatched estimates reported in Appendix 1. Moreover, coefficient estimates are well determined on three out of our four employment variables. Second, including *differences* in household characteristics in the control set and using a bias-adjusted approach leads to a significantly lower point estimate on employment definitions 1 and 2, whereas the average treatment effects on the treated (ATT) on hours worked and full-time employment remains well-determined using a weighted matched double-difference approach. Third, reducing the sample to household heads between the age of 15 and 65 inflates coefficient estimates, and ATTs are well determined for all employment definitions used, definition 1 being the exception. Overall, we conclude that there is a positive and well-determined impact of PAST on 'hours worked per week' (ATT of between 9.5 and 12.3 hours per week) and on generating more full-time jobs.

Table 5. Employment effect: matched double-difference estimates.

		ATT	Standard error
Levels only, $n =4$ and weight adjusted	Employment definition 1 (yes = 1, no = 0)	0.097	(0.080)
	Hours worked	10.952***	(3.252)
	Employment definition 2 (yes = 1, no = 0)	0.138**	(0.066)
	Full-time employed (yes = 1, no = 0)	0.198**	(0.088)
Levels and differences, $n =4$ and weight adjusted	Employment definition 1 (yes = 1, no = 0)	0.029	(0.069)
	Hours worked	9.516***	(2.925)
	Employment definition 2 (yes = 1, no = 0)	0.088	(0.059)
	Full-time employed (yes = 1, no = 0)	0.200***	(0.077)
Levels and differences, $n =4$ and weight adjusted (only HH heads between the age of 15 and 65 considered)	Employment definition 1 (yes = 1, no = 0)	0.117	(0.075)
	Hours worked	12.278***	(3.003)
	Employment definition 2 (yes = 1, no = 0)	0.147**	(0.058)
	Full-time employed (yes = 1, no = 0)	0.252***	(0.085)

Notes: Average treatment effect of the treated (ATT), standard errors in parentheses. Nearest-neighbour matching ($n = 4$). Full sample based on 345 observations (146 treatment and 199 control units). Twenty observations off common support. Estimations carried out in Stata using the commands psmatch2 (see Leuven and Sianesi 2006) and nnmatch (Abadie et al. 2004).
*, **, ***Significance at a 10 per cent, 5 per cent and 1 per cent level, respectively.

To disentangle the reason for this observed positive employment impact, we looked closer into these employment effects. In terms of sector and location we found that most households work within agriculture, and most of the new jobs are also created within this sector. This also explains the increase in treatment communities in the share of self-employed (reported in Table 2). However, while around 90 per cent of the household heads worked in agriculture in 2005, this share has declined to 85 per cent in 2009. Data also show that nearly all new jobs were created within the same municipality and nearly all of the household heads moving out of unemployment are now working in agriculture. This indicates that entry into the job market goes through the agricultural sector and that those obtaining employment in other sectors come from previous work in agriculture. Orbicon and Lamans (2010) also document significant reductions in average travel time, so relatively more time can be spent working.

Moreover, as noted above, the job creation was mainly realised within the same municipality (97 per cent worked within their municipality both before and after the intervention). This observation was strongly supported by findings from the qualitative fieldwork done by Orbicon and Lamans (2010). In all treatment communities, reference was made to the positive impact from PAST interventions on local agricultural production and employment. This suggests that the improved access led to changes in relative prices on agricultural inputs and outputs and provided more incentives for increasing agricultural production. The 'Job-migration' effect of the PAST intervention therefore seems to be limited.

Table 6.   Impact differences by community size.

| | Community size below/above median | | | |
| | Below | | Above | |
	ATT	Standard error	ATT	Standard error
Employment definition 1 (yes = 1, no = 0)	0.239**	0.111	0.135	(0.116)
Hours worked	0.704	5.142	14.891***	(4.284)
Employment definition 2 (yes = 1, no = 0)	−0.017	0.094	0.219***	(0.085)
Full-time employed (yes = 1, no = 0)	0.108	0.125	0.082	(0.109)

Notes: Average treatment effect of the treated (ATT), standard errors in parentheses. Nearest-neighbour matching ($n = 4$). Levels specification including household, micro-regional characteristics and pre-2005 municipality poverty changes. Weight adjusted. Estimations carried out in Stata using the nnmatch command.
*, **, ***Significance at a 10 per cent, 5 per cent and 1 per cent level, respectively.

Another reason for the significant increase in hours worked can be found through impact differences by 'access to markets'. Looking at data for treatment communities on distance to markets and on distance to larger road networks, we found a strong positive association between these distance measures and community size; households in larger communities report shorter distance to both markets and larger road networks.[13] In Table 6, we therefore differentiate the impact of the PAST road intervention by looking at differences in ATTs below and above the median community size, in order to (indirectly) evaluate whether PAST impacts differ by distance to markets and road networks.

First, using employment measure 1 we find a higher (and well-determined) effect in below-median-sized communities, indicating that individuals that worked (for wages) during the past week have increased more in relatively 'remote' areas. However, looking at hours worked and the corrected employment indicator (employment definition 2) suggests that the aggregate impacts are largely driven by effects obtained in larger communities with better connected road networks and easier access to markets. As such, the results support the conclusion that the increase in hours worked goes through both overall reductions in travel time and that households have improved their immediate access to markets and better developed road networks (and so increased labour demand).

In Table 7 we take a closer look at the potential impact differences between low and high poverty micro-regions. The 2005 CENSO reports micro-regional poverty rates, where the poverty measure documented in the CENSO is calculated based on the information obtained from the five micro-regional indicators reported above. Table 7 report matched (nearest neighbour with four matches, weight adjusted) double-difference estimates comparable with the level specification in Table 5. The first column shows the results comparing below median poverty micro-regions only, whereas the second column reports the ATTs from comparing above median poverty micro-regions. Interestingly, we find that most of the average PAST impact found in the aggregate using employment definitions 1 and 2 and hours worked is driven by large treatment effects in 'low poverty' micro-regions. This could suggest that the PAST rural roads project has had larger employment-generating effects in lower poverty micro-regions than in areas with above median poverty rates. However, coefficient estimates on full-time employment suggests that more permanent jobs are generated in 'wealthier' communities.

Table 7. Impact differences in low and high poverty micro-regions.

| | Micro-regional poverty rates below/above median | | | |
| | Below | | Above | |
	ATT	Standard error	ATT	Standard error
Employment definition 1 (yes = 1, no = 0)	0.289**	(0.116)	0.120	(0.097)
Hours worked	13.078**	(6.160)	8.987**	(3.841)
Employment definition 2 (yes = 1, no = 0)	0.167	(0.102)	0.018	(0.077)
Full-time employed (yes = 1, no = 0)	0.133	(0.127)	0.226**	(0.105)

Notes: Average treatment effect of the treated (ATT), standard errors in parentheses. Nearest neighbour matching ($n = 4$). Levels specification including household, community size and pre-2005 municipality poverty changes. Weight adjusted. Estimations carried out in Stata using the nnmatch command.
*, **, ***Significance at a 10 per cent. 5 per cent and 1 per cent level, respectively.

5. Conclusion

There seems to be a general consensus about infrastructure improvements reducing poverty through the creation of new job opportunities. However, recent literature has suggested that especially areas with surroundings appropriate for non-farming activities benefit from improved road systems (see, for example, Lokshin and Yemtsov 2005). Other studies (see, for example, Khandker *et al.* 2009) have found road investments to reduce poverty for especially poor farming households by raising agricultural production and output prices.

In this paper we analysed the employment-generating impact of a tertiary road project in Nicaragua implemented between 2005 and 2009 in the area of Las Segovias. Applying a matched double-difference approach to control for initial conditions and any time-variant factors that simultaneously influence the placement of roads and subsequent employment growth rates, we obtain an increase in hours worked per week attributable to the road intervention of around 9.5–12.3 hours. Using detailed information on individual employment status and job characteristics, we also found that individuals moving out of unemployment often start up as self-employed in the agricultural sector. Moreover, employment dynamics arc also found for individuals initially self-employed in agriculture, as we are more likely to observe a diversification out of agriculture into off-farm service-based activities in treatment areas. We therefore conclude that there seems to be an employment graduation process taking place in the labour market. Moreover, the PAST road project does not increase work migration. Jobs are usually generated within the municipality and are to larger extent permanent (non-seasonal) in character. Finally, the analysis suggested that the employment-generating effect came through a combination of reduced travel time (creating a relative increase in labour supply) and better access to markets and larger more integrated road networks (increasing labour demand).

The qualitative fieldwork documented in Orbicon and Lamans (2010) strongly supports the quantitative findings found above. According to the interviews, the improved access to roads led to huge changes in relative prices on agricultural inputs and outputs providing more incentives for increasing agricultural production in treatment communities, which reportedly led to increases in land size (and land prices) for agricultural production and in the demand for farm labourers. Moreover, it was also reported that the experience and knowledge gained from the Danida PAST interventions, through the adoption a labour-intensive methodology upgraded the skill level in treatment communities through society learning effects. However, this statement was not possible to verify using the quantitative data collected.

The PAST project therefore seems to have been highly successful in improving employment possibilities in local communities through a combination of improved conditions in agriculture for formerly unemployed labourers and enhanced off-farm employment possibilities for incumbent workers. However, this conclusion is based on evidence from Las Segovias only. Whether the employment-generating impact of PAST (largely driven by a combination of increases in both labour supply and demand conditions) can be widely applicable to the more secluded provinces of RAAN and RAAS is questionable, giving doubt to the external validity of the results reported.

Acknowledgements

The author appreciates the comments by the Editor and the referee, and suggestions received from participants at the International Workshop on Evaluating Infrastructure held in Copenhagen, 25–27 May 2010, and by the Editor. The standard caveats apply.

Notes

1. NCG (2008) provides an overview and synthesis of 27 road sector evaluations and study reports carried out between 1997 and 2007. However, no assessment on the quality of the evaluations is made explicitly.
2. One can divide road evaluation studies into two broad categories: non-theoretical reduced form models, and structural methods using either partial or general equilibrium setups. The former is surveyed in Van de Walle (2009), whereas the later is well summarised in Jensen (2009).
3. The combined matching and DD approach may still yield biased estimates if there are unobservable characteristics that affect both placement and outcome changes.
4. Van de Walle (2009) mentions that controlling for initial conditions in a linear regression is similar to doing so non-parametrically with matching generally not yielding the same results. The methods make a number of different assumptions, including on functional form and the use of the full sample versus trimmed or re-weighted samples. Van de Walle and Mu (2007) compare the two approaches and find striking differences in the impact estimates despite controlling for the same conditions.
5. It should be noted that phase two of PAST was ongoing at the time of the evaluation, still including support to rural transport infrastructure, but with an enhanced focus on reaching most of the municipalities in the target regions.
6. Extreme weather conditions (for example, Hurricane Felix in 2007 and Hurricane Mitch in 1998) are of course exceptions, which limits general infrastructure access.
7. The 5 per cent cost was usually gathered through a subscription charge on producers in the community while the cost of routine maintenance was financed through tolls or a combination of subscription and toll charges.
8. We follow the location classifications described in the CENSO, which means that we have information for three districts (Departamento), 15 municipalities (Municipio), 48 regions (Comarca), 61 communities (Comunidad). The treatment indicator variable is defined at the community level.
9. We would have preferred employment status numbers for all household members, but unfortunately this information was not available. However, CENSO 2005 information indicates that household heads often are the main providers of the family. Furthermore, the sensitivity analysis below limit the analysis to individuals aged 15–65 in order to avoid retirement age problems in the employment numbers.
10. We follow the definition of micro-regions used in the CENSO (INIDE 2008). The 'Extreme Municipality Poverty Map' reported in the CENSO comes from the 'Eighth National Census of Population and Housing' in 2005 and it is based on the methodology of Unsatisfied Basic Needs (NBI). The NBI method is based on the identification of a minimum level of satisfaction of basic needs using the five indicators included in this study: overcrowding, inadequate housing, inadequate services (water and sanitation), low education, and economic dependence.

11. Average household age differences between 2005 and 2009 are 5.3 and 5.8 for treatment and control groups, respectively. These two numbers contrast with the time span covered between the two surveys (four years). This difference may, to some extent, be accounted for by differences in implementation month of the surveys and by different people heading the household? The only remaining explanation is entry mistakes of age in one of the surveys.

12. Appendix 1 gives the unmatched estimates of mean impacts on the four selected employment measures using the entire sample. The estimated double difference indicates a significant employment increase attributable to the PAST intervention of 19 percentage points, using employment measure 1. Using hours worked per week (employment measure 2) does not change the overall conclusion. Here we get a significant double difference estimate of 6.8 hours per week. Finally, we also find a well-determined impact of PAST on the creation of full-time jobs.

13. It should be noted that information on 'distance to markets' and 'distance to larger road networks' is available only for treatment communities.

References

Abadie, A. and Imbens, G., 2002. *Simple and bias-corrected matching estimators for average treatment effects*. NBER Technical Working Paper T0283. Cambridge, MA: National Bureau of Economic Research.

Abadie, A., Drukker, D., Herr, J. and Imbens, G., 2004. Implementing matching estimators for average treatment effects in Stata. *Stata journal*, 4, 290–311.

Fafchamps, M. and Schilpi, F., 2008. *Determinants of choice of migration destination*. World Bank Policy Research Working Paper 4728. Washington, DC: World Bank.

Gaschassin, M., Najman, B. and Raballand, G., 2010. *The impact of roads on poverty reduction: a case study of Cameroon*. World Bank Policy Research Working Paper 5209. Washington, DC: World Bank.

Gibson, J. and Rozelle, S., 2003. Poverty and access to roads in Papua New Guinea. *Economic development and cultural change*, 52, 159–185.

Gomez, L., Martinez, B., Modrego, F. and Ravnborg, H.M., 2008. *Mapeo de Cambios en Municipios de Nicaragua: Consumo de los Hogares, Pobreza y Equidad 1998–2005*. Documento de Trabajo No. 12, Programa Dinamicas Territoriales RuralesRimisp – Centro Latinoamericano para el Desarrollo Rural.

INIDE, 2008. *CENSO 2005: Documentation'. Instituto Nacional de Información de Desarrollo*. Managua: Instituto Nacional de Información de Desarrollo.

Jensen, H.T., 2009. General equilibrium impact evaluation of road sector investment projects in Ghana. Paper presented at the Twelfth GTAP Conference, 10–12 June 2009, Santiago, and the ECOMOD 2009 Conference, 24–26 June 2009, Ottawa.

Khandker, S., Bakht, Z. and Koolwal, G., 2009. The poverty impact of rural roads: evidence from Bangladesh. *Economic development and cultural change*, 57 (4), 685–722.

Leuven, E. and Sianesi. B., 2006. *PSMATCH2: Stata module to perform full Mahalanobis and propensity score matching, common support graphing, and covariate imbalance testing*. Statistical Software Components S432001. Boston, MA: Boston College Department of Economics.

Lokshin, M. and Yemtsov, R., 2005. Has rural infrastructure rehabilitation in Georgia helped the poor? *World Bank economic review*, 19 (2), 311–333.

NCG, 2008. *Synthesis report: overview and synthesis of road sector evaluations*. Nordic Consulting Group, Denmark, mimeo.

Orbicon and Lamans, 2010. *Impact evaluation of Danida support to rural transport infrastructure in Nicaragua*. Report prepared for Danida. Available from: http://www.um.dk/en/menu/DevelopmentPolicy/Evaluations/Publications/ReportsByYear/2010/ [Accessed 26 January 2011].

Ravallion, M. and Chen, S., 2005. Hidden impact? Household saving in response to a poor-area development project. *Journal of public economics*, 89, 2183–2204.

Van de Walle, D., 2009. Impact evaluation of rural road projects. *Journal of development effectiveness*, 1 (1), 15–36.

Van de Walle, D. and Mu, R., 2007. Fungibility and the flypaper effect of project aid: micro-evidence for Vietnam. *Journal of development economics*, 84 (2), 667–684.

Appendix 1. Employment effect: simple double difference estimates

	Definition 1: employed			Definition 2: hours		
	Before	After	Difference	Before	After	Difference
Treatment communities	0.678	0.842	0.164	35.000	38.945	3.945
	(0.039)	(0.030)	(0.049)	(1.590)	(1.614)	(2.266)
Control communities	0.764	0.739	−0.025	36.603	33.704	−2.899
	(0.030)	(0.031)	(0.043)	(1.427)	(1.430)	(2.021)
Difference	−0.086	0.104	0.190***	−1.603	5.242	6.845**
	(0.048)	(0.045)	(0.069)	(2.152)	(2.168)	(3.170)

	Definition 3: employed, corrected			Definition 4: fulltime		
	Before	After	Difference	Before	After	Difference
Treatment communities	0.822	0.856	0.034	0.493	0.548	0.055
	(0.032)	(0.029)	(0.043)	(0.042)	(0.041)	(0.059)
Control communities	0.809	0.799	−0.010	0.528	0.447	−0.080
	(0.028)	(0.028)	(0.040)	(0.035)	(0.035)	(0.050)
Difference	0.013	0.057	0.044	−0.034	0.101	0.135*
	(0.042)	(0.042)	(0.062)	(0.055)	(0.054)	(0.076)

Notes: Difference-in-difference estimates. Standard errors reported in parentheses.
*, **, ***Significance at a 10%, 5% and 1% level, respectively.

Assessing the ex ante economic impacts of transportation infrastructure policies in Brazil

Eduardo Amaral Haddad[a,b], Fernando Salgueiro Perobelli[c], Edson Paulo Domingues[d] and Mauricio Aguiar[e]

[a]Fipe and Department of Economics, University of Sao Paulo, Av Prof. Luciano Gualberto 908, FEA 1, Cidade Universitaria, Sao Paulo 05458-001, Brazil; [b]Regional Economics Applications Laboratory, UIUC, USA; [c]Department of Economics, Federal University of Juiz de Fora, Juiz de Fora, Brazil; [d]Department of Economics, Federal University of Minas Gerais, Belo Horizonte, Brazil; [e]Tectran Técnicos em Transporte Ltda., Belo Horizonte, Brazil

This paper uses a fully operational inter-regional computable general equilibrium (CGE) model implemented for the Brazilian economy, based on previous work by Haddad and Hewings, in order to assess the likely economic effects of road transportation policy changes in Brazil. Among the features embedded in this framework, modelling of external scale economies and transportation costs provides an innovative way of dealing explicitly with theoretical issues related to integrated regional systems. The model is calibrated for 109 regions. The explicit modelling of transportation costs built into the inter-regional CGE model, based on origin–destination flows, which takes into account the spatial structure of the Brazilian economy, creates the capability of integrating the inter-regional CGE model with a geo-coded transportation network model enhancing the potential of the framework in understanding the role of infrastructure on regional development. The transportation model used is the so-called Highway Development and Management, developed by the World Bank, implemented using the software TransCAD. Further extensions of the current model specification for integrating other features of transport planning in a continental industrialising country like Brazil are discussed, with the goal of building a bridge between conventional transport planning practices and the innovative use of CGE models. In order to illustrate the analytical power of the integrated system, the authors present a set of simulations, which evaluate the ex ante economic impacts of physical/qualitative changes in the Brazilian road network (for example, a highway improvement), in accordance with recent policy developments in Brazil. Rather than providing a critical evaluation of this debate, they intend to emphasise the likely structural impacts of such policies. They expect that the results will reinforce the need to better specifying spatial interactions in inter-regional CGE models.

1. Introduction

One of the main obstacles to economic development in Brazil is the so-called *Custo Brasil*, the extra costs of doing business in the country. Enterprises are faced with a heavy burden that competing firms in other countries do not confront, hampering competitiveness. It includes different components that represent distortions in the relation between the public and the private sectors, reflecting inadequate legislation and deficient provision of public goods. Ongoing debate centres on the contribution of different sectors to the *Custo Brasil*: labour costs; transportation infrastructure; the tax system; and the regulatory system.

A study by the World Bank (1996) in the mid-1990s provided a comprehensive examination of the diverse components of the *Custo Brasil* and an exploration of their implications for total firm costs. Regarding land transport costs, which are often viewed as a significant component of the *Custo Brasil*, the available evidence collected for the report suggested that the costs of providing rail and trucking services were high in Brazil. Nevertheless, because of overcapacity and significant competition in trucking, these costs are not passed on to shippers; transport rates per ton-kilometre are low by international standards. The principal problem with land transportation, from the point of view of shippers, is not the unit costs of different modes of transportation, but rather excessive reliance on trucking. Railroad and barge transport over long distances are far cheaper than trucking, particularly for bulk commodities. Inefficiencies and low productivity in the railroad sector have meant that the percentage of total cargo carried by trucks in Brazil is approximately twice as large as the share in Australia and the United States.

More than 10 years after the aforementioned World Bank study, the situation in the transportation sector did not change. Brazilian transport infrastructure is deteriorating fast from lack of investment and maintenance, showing an increased number of critical points, or bottlenecks, in most of the corridors. Decay in the transportation system curtails economic growth, hampering competitiveness both in the internal and external markets. Deterioration of Brazil's transportation network in the past years contributed to high operational costs, obstructing the competitive integration of the country.

The federal government has signalled its intention in reviving long-term planning in transportation in the country. The design of an ambitious *Plano Nacional de Logística e Transportes* (National Plan of Logistics and Transportation) has been initiated, involving different stakeholders. It aims at supporting decision-makers in attaining economic objectives through policy initiatives related to both public and private infrastructure and organisation of the transportation sector.[1]

At the state level, few initiatives have taken place in the realm of transport planning. States such as Bahia, Rio Grande do Sul, Minas Gerais and Pará have all developed thorough diagnosis of the sector, including forward-looking exercises with a long-term view on the available possibilities for policy intervention within the respective state borders.[2]

As a recent report by the World Road Association (2003, p. 7) points out, there is a growing need for economic and socio-economic models for helping improving road management. This paper provides an attempt to meet this requirement. We use a fully operational inter-regional computable general equilibrium (CGE) model implemented for the Brazilian economy, based on previous work by Haddad and Hewings (2005), in order to assess the likely economic effects of recent road transportation policy changes in Brazil. Among the features embedded in this framework, modelling of external scale economies and transportation costs provides an innovative way of dealing explicitly with theoretical issues related to integrated regional systems. The explicit modelling of transportation costs built into the inter-regional CGE model, based on origin–destination flows, which takes into account the spatial structure of the Brazilian economy, creates the capability of integrating the inter-regional CGE model with a geo-coded transportation network model enhancing the potential of the framework in understanding the role of infrastructure on regional development. The transportation model used is the so-called Highway

Development and Management Model, developed by the World Bank, implemented using the software TransCAD.

It is important to notice that the existing, commonly-used policy tools to address issues related to the economic impacts of transportation infrastructure policies do not come any-where close to capturing some of the most important channels through which exogenous and transportation policy shocks are transmitted to the various dimensions of regional eco-nomic structures. Models are issue-specific; trying to 'force' a model to answer questions that it is not designed to address hampers our ability to address relevant policy questions (see Agénor *et al.* 2007). Thus, this paper provides quantitative and qualitative insights (general equilibrium effects) into trade-offs commonly faced by policy-makers when deal-ing with infrastructure projects in a spatial context. It shows that, given different policy options, decision-makers face non-trivial choices, as different projects perform differently in different dimensions, usually presenting outcomes with different hierarchies related to multi-dimensional policy goals.

The remainder of the paper is organised as follows. After the discussion of relevant modelling issues – focusing on the treatment of transportation costs in CGE models – in the next section, Section 3 will present an overview of the CGE model to be used in the simulations, focusing on its general features. After that, the simulation experiments are designed and implemented, and the main results are discussed in Section 4. Final remarks follow in an attempt to evaluate our findings and put them into perspective, considering their extensions and limitations.

2. Modelling issues

The development of regional and inter-regional CGE modelling has experienced, in the past 15 years, an upsurge in interest. Different models have been built for different regions of the world. Research groups, located especially in Australia, Brazil, Canada, Germany, Scotland, and the United States, as well as individual researchers, contributed to these developments through the specification and implementation of a variety of alternative mod-els. Recent theoretical developments in the new economic geography bring new challenges to regional scientists, in general, and inter-regional CGE modellers, in particular.[3]

Among the potential uses of inter-regional CGE models, we can mention the analysis of transport planning policies with ranging effects on regional and national economies. National and/or state-wide transport planning is a widely institutionalised process in sev-eral countries. The use of model-based analytical procedures is in the state of practice, including the application of conventional input–output methods for forecasting freight movements. Nevertheless, the feedback impact of transport actions on the regional and/or national economies is not fully accounted for in these procedures. In recent years, the development of improved techniques was the focus of several efforts joining the trans-port and economics research fields in the USA (for example, Friez *et al.* 1998) and the European Union (for example, Bröcker 2002), without forgetting efforts of Asian countries (for example, Miyagi 2001) and Brazil (for example, Pietrantonio 1999).

Investments in highways and other forms of improvements in the transportation sys-tem represent an important way of achieving regional and national economic growth. Expansion and improvements of transportation facilities can be used as a means to reduce firms' transaction costs and to expand the economic opportunities in a region/country, as it potentially helps to increase income and improve the standard of living of the resident population.

However, investments in transportation, in addition to its impact on systemic productivity, have potential differential impacts across economic spaces. Spatially localised interventions may increase regional competitiveness. External scale economies and accessibility effects would produce the expansion or contraction of the local firms' market areas and generate opportunities to access broader input markets. One of the fundamental elements to be taken into account is the spatial interaction among regions: changes in a given location may result in changes in other regions through the various types of relations (complementary and competitive) associated with the regional agents in the relevant economic spaces.

In this context, the modelling procedure developed in this paper represents an attempt to address some of these issues in the context of a unified approach, which enables the proper treatment of the role of transportation infrastructure in the allocation of resources in a given economy. The explicit modelling of transportation costs, in an inter-regional CGE model integrated into a geo-coded transportation network infrastructure model, will allow us to assess, under a macro spatial perspective, the economic effects of specific transportation projects and programmes.

2.1. Treatment of transportation costs

It has been noticed elsewhere (Haddad 2004) that current CGE models are not without their limitations to represent spatial phenomena. Isard's vision of integrated modelling, which anticipated the proposals reported in Isard and Anselin (1982), provided a road map for the development of more sophisticated analysis of spatial economic systems (Hewings 1986, Hewings *et al.* 2003). Given their many virtues, however, if adequately coped, inter-regional CGE models are the main candidates for the core subsystem in a fully integrated system.

The embedding of spatial trade flows into economic modelling, especially those related to inter-regional trade linkages, usually should go along with the specification of transportation services. Given existing inter-regional CGE models, one can identify at least three approaches for introducing the representation of transportation, all of them considering the fact that transportation is a resource-demanding activity.[4] This basic assumption is essential if one intends to properly model an inter-regional CGE framework, invalidating the model's results if not considered (see Isard *et al.* 1998).

3. The inter-regional CGE model

Our departure point is the B-MARIA model, developed by Haddad (1999). The B-MARIA model – and its extensions – has been widely used for assessing regional impacts of economic policies in Brazil. Since the publication of the reference text, various studies have been undertaken using, as the basic analytical tool, variations of the original model.[5] Moreover, critical reviews of the model can be found in the *Journal of Regional Science* (Polenske 2002), *Economic Systems Research* (Siriwardana 2001) and in *Papers in Regional Science* (Azzoni 2001).

The theoretical structure of the B-MARIA model is well documented.[6] In this paper, we develop a version of the B-MARIA model specified to deal with transportation policies in the state of Minas Gerais. We use a similar approach to Haddad (2004), and Haddad and Hewings (2005) to integrate the inter-regional CGE model with a geo-coded transportation network infrastructure model. However, instead of using a simpler transportation network

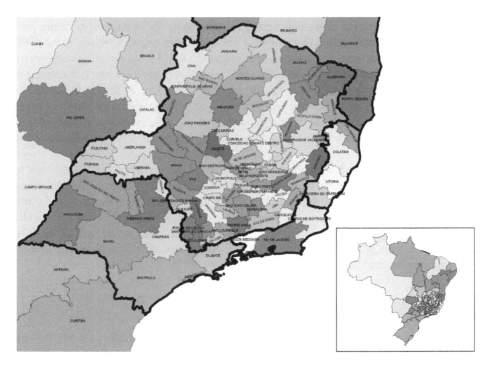

Figure 1. Regional setting in the B-MARIA-MG model.
Source: Elaborated by the authors.

model based on only one attribute of the links to deal with accessibility (that is, maximum speed), we use a more sophisticated model, the Highway Development and Management (HDM-4), developed at the World Bank.[7]

The model recognises the economies of 109 Brazilian regions, 75 within the state of Minas Gerais (Figure 1). Results are based on a bottom-up approach – that is, national results are obtained from the aggregation of regional results. The model identifies eight production/investment sectors in each region producing eight commodities,[8] one representative household in each region, regional governments and one Federal government, and a single foreign area that trades with each domestic region, through a network of ports of exit and ports of entry. Three local primary factors are used in the production process, according to regional endowments (land, capital and labour). The model is calibrated for 2002; a rather complete dataset is available for that year, which is the year of the last publication of the full national input–output tables that served as the basis for the estimation of the inter-regional input-output database (FIPE 2007), facilitating the choice of the base year.

The B-MARIA-MG framework includes explicitly some important elements from an inter-regional system, needed to better understand macro spatial phenomena; namely, inter-regional flows of goods and services, transportation costs based on origin-destination pairs, inter-regional movement of primary factors, regionalisation of the transactions of the public sector, and regional labour market segmentation. We list below the additional structural modifications implemented in the basic model, related both to specification issues and to changes in the database.

First, we have introduced the possibility of (external) non-constant returns in the production process, following Haddad (2004). This extension is essential to adequately

48

represent one of the functioning mechanisms of a spatial economy. The modelling procedure adopted in B-MARIA-MG uses constant elasticity of substitution (CES) nests to specify the production technology. Given the property of standard CES functions, non-constant returns are ruled out. However, one can modify assumptions on the parameters values in order to introduce non-constant returns to scale. Changes in the production functions of the manufacturing sector[9] in each one of the 109 regions were implemented in order to incorporate non-constant returns to scale, a fundamental assumption for the analysis of integrated inter-regional systems. We kept the hierarchy of the nested CES structure of production, which is very convenient for the purpose of calibration (Bröcker 1998), but we modified the hypotheses on parameters' values, leading to a more general form. This modelling trick allows for the introduction of parametric external scale economies (rationalised as agglomeration economies), by exploring local properties of the CES function.

The second main modification, which addresses some of the modelling issues discussed in the previous section, refers to the introduction of links between the inter-regional CGE core and a geo-coded transportation network model, allowing for a more adequate characterisation of the spatial structure of the economy, in which the role of the transportation infrastructure and the friction of distance is explicitly considered.

3.1. Modelling of transportation costs

The set of equations that specify purchasers' prices in the B-MARIA model imposes zero pure profits in the *distribution* of commodities to different users. Prices paid for commodity *i* supplied from region *s* and consumed in region *q* by each user equate to the sum of its basic value and the costs of the relevant taxes and margin-commodities.

The role of margin-commodities is to facilitate flows of commodities from points of production or points of entry to either domestic users or ports of exit. Margin-commodities, or, simply, margins, include transportation and trade services, which take account of transfer costs in a broad sense.[10] Margins on commodities used by industry, investors, and households are assumed to be produced at the point of consumption. Margins on exports are assumed to be produced at the point of production.

In B-MARIA, transportation services (and trade services) are produced by a regional resource-demanding optimising transportation (trade) sector. A fully specified production possibility frontier has to be introduced for the transportation sector, which produces goods consumed directly by users and consumed to facilitate trade; that is, transportation services are used to ship commodities from the point of production to the point of consumption. The explicit modelling of transportation costs, based on origin–destination flows, which takes into account the spatial structure of the Brazilian economy, creates the capability of integrating the inter-regional CGE model with a geo-coded transportation network model, enhancing the potential of the framework in understanding the role of infrastructure on regional development.

3.2. Structural database

The CGE core database requires detailed sectoral and regional information about the Brazilian economy. National data (such as input–output tables, foreign trade, taxes, margins and tariffs) are available from the Brazilian Statistics Bureau (IBGE). At the regional level, a full set of accounts was developed by FIPE (2007). These two sets of information were put together in a balanced inter-regional social accounting matrix. Previous work in this task has been successfully implemented in inter-regional CGE models for Brazil (for example, Haddad 1999, Domingues 2002, Perobelli 2004, Porsse 2005).

3.3. Behavioural parameters

Experience with the B-MARIA framework has suggested that inter-regional substitution is the key mechanism that drives model's spatial results. In general, inter-regional linkages play an important role in the functioning of inter-regional CGE models. These linkages are driven by trade relations (commodity flows), and by factor mobility (capital and labour migration). In the first case, of direct interest to our exercise, inter-regional trade flows should be incorporated into the model. Thus, inter-regional input–output databases are required to calibrate the model, and regional trade elasticities play a crucial role in the adjustment process.

One data-related problem that modellers frequently face is the lack of such trade elasticities at the regional level. An extra effort was undertaken to estimate model-consistent regional trade elasticities for Brazil (see Haddad and Hewings 2005).

Other key behavioural parameters were properly estimated; these include econometric estimates for scale economies (Haddad 2004); econometric estimates for export demand elasticities (Perobelli 2004); as well as the econometric estimates for regional trade elasticities. Another key set of parameters, related to international trade elasticities, was borrowed from a recent study developed at IPEA (Instituto de Pesquisa Econômica Aplicada) (Tourinho et al. 2002), for manufacturing goods, and from model-consistent estimates in the EFES (Economic Forecasting Equilibrium System) model (Haddad and Domingues 2001) for agricultural and services goods.

3.4. Closures

In order to capture the effects of improvements in the transportation network, the simulations were carried out under two standard closures, referring to the short run and the long run. A distinction between the short-run and long-run closures relates to the treatment of capital stocks encountered in the standard microeconomic approach to policy adjustments. In the short-run closure, capital stocks are held fixed; while, in the long-run, policy changes are allowed to affect capital stocks. In addition to the assumption of inter-industry and inter-regional immobility of capital, the short-run closure would include fixed regional population and labour supply, fixed regional wage differentials, and fixed national real wage. Regional employment is driven by the assumptions on wage rates, which indirectly determine regional unemployment rates. On the demand side, investment expenditures are fixed exogenously – firms cannot re-evaluate their investment decisions in the short run. Household consumption follows household disposable income, and real government consumption, at both regional and federal levels, is fixed (alternatively, the government deficit can be set exogenously, allowing government expenditures to change). Finally, preferences and technology variables are exogenous.

A long-run (steady-state) equilibrium closure is used in which capital is mobile across regions and industries. Capital and investment are generally assumed to grow at the same rate. The main differences from the short-run are encountered in the labour market and the capital formation settings. In the first case, aggregate employment is determined by population growth, labour force participation rates, and the natural rate of unemployment. The distribution of the labour force across regions and sectors is fully determined endogenously. Labour is attracted to more competitive industries in more favoured geographical areas, keeping regional wage differentials constant. While in the same way, capital is oriented towards more attractive industries. This movement keeps rates of return at their initial levels.

4. Transportation infrastructure projects

In this section, we illustrate the analytical capability of the unified framework in the evaluation of specific transportation projects contemplated in the *Plano Estadual de Logística e Transportes* (PELT Minas). The case study under consideration refers to two projects of improvement of federal highways – BR-262 and BR-381 – in the State of Minas Gerais (Figure 2). The following analysis suggests a strategy of application of the framework developed here for the ex ante impact assessment of a project in a systemic context, in its operational phase. The impacts of the investment phase are not considered in these illustrative exercises. The goal is to explore the characteristics of the integrated model in the simulation phase and not to proceed with a systematic evaluation of the project, which is outside the scope of this paper. In what follows, we will assess the impacts on national variables, and on a broader set of socio-economic state variables.

The characteristics of the projects are detailed in a document prepared by FIPE (2007) for the Secretaria de Transportes e Obras Públicas. The guidelines that have been used to justify the choice of these specific tracks of the BR-262 and BR-381 highways to be improved are based upon the grounds of the strategic location of this network links in the national transportation system, which constitute two of the main corridors related to the more dynamic regions of the country. Moreover, it is hoped that such improvements will foster regional development in the State of Minas Gerais, one of the leading economies of the country.

With a total length of 441 km, between Betim and Uberaba, the BR-262 project consists of the duplication of the existing road link between Betim and Nova Serrana, and the construction of climbing and passing lanes between Nova Serrana and Araxá. Total costs of the project are estimated in BRL 554 million.[11]

The BR-381 project considers the duplication of the track between Belo Horizonte and Governador Valadares, in a total length of 304 km. Total costs of the implementation are estimated in BRL 1395 million.

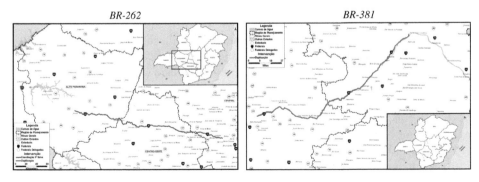

Figure 2. Location of road improvement projects.

Source: Elaborated by the authors based on the Secretaria de Transportes e Obras Públicas, Minas Gerais.

The distinction between the two projects lies on the role they play in the integration of Brazilian regions. While the BR-262 project constitutes a major improvement on the east–west integration of the country, linking the coast of the Southeast to the more agricultural areas of the Midwest, the BR-381 has a strategic role in the integration of the Northeast with the Southeast and South of the country. These distinct axes of integration play different roles in the inter-regional Brazilian system, as spatial competition occurs in a lower degree in the case of the BR-262 than in the case of the BR-381 link. In the latter case, denser economic spaces are directly involved in the spatial process, while in the former case, more specialised spaces have more prominent roles.

4.1. Functioning mechanism

The simulation exercise considers the implementation of two projects related to road improvements in the State of Minas Gerais. According to the model structure, this may represent a margin-saving change; that is, the use of transportation services per unit of output is reduced, implying a direct reduction in the output of the transportation sector. The reduction in transport cost decreases the price of composite commodities, with positive implications for real regional income: in this cost-competitiveness approach, firms become more competitive – as production costs go down (inputs are less costly); investors foresee potential higher returns – as the cost of producing capital also declines; and households increase their real income, envisaging higher consumption possibilities. Higher income generates higher domestic demand, while increases in the competitiveness of national products stimulate external demand. This creates room for increasing firms' output – directed for both domestic and international markets – which requires more inputs and primary factors. Increasing demand puts pressure on the factor markets for price increases, with a concomitant expectation that the prices of domestic goods would increase.

Second-order prices changes go in both directions – decrease and increase. The net effect is determined by the relative strength of the countervailing forces. Figure 3 summarises the transmission mechanisms associated with major first-order and second-order effects in the adjustment process underlying the model's aggregate results.

4.2. Results

The B-MARIA-MG model was used to estimate the short-run and long-run impacts of both projects, during their operational phases. The main results are discussed below.[12]

4.2.1. National impacts. Table 1 presents simulation results for national aggregates. Two distinct pictures emerge, embedding the specific structural differences between the two projects. In the case of the BR-262 project, more standard outcomes associated with commonsense expectation on infrastructure project arise.

Gains in efficiency (real Gross Domestic Product [GDP] growth) are positive in both the short run and the long run, while welfare gains (equivalent variation) are revealed only in the long run. Noteworthy is that, in the long run, the effects on GDP are magnified.

Changes in terms of trade tend to benefit Brazilian exports only in the short run, as the results point to increasing competitiveness of Brazilian products. This conclusion is reinforced by the performance of the international trade sector: exports volumes increase, leading GDP growth in the short run. When compared with other GDP components, international trade is the only component that presents a positive performance in the short run.

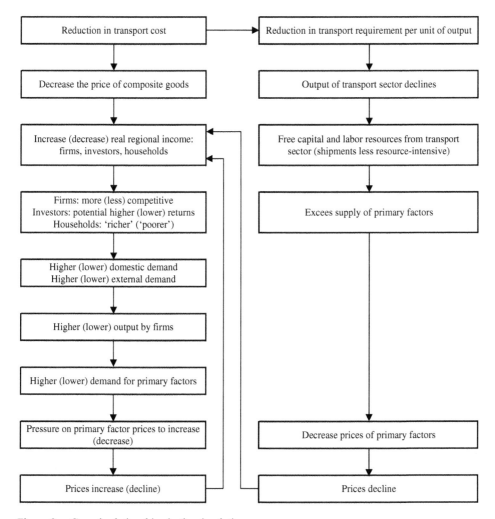

Figure 3.   Causal relationships in the simulation.
Source: Elaborated by the authors.

In the long run, however, this situation is reversed. While stronger penetration of imported products is verified, due to the reversal of the terms of trade result, domestic absorption becomes the component in chief, leading GDP growth. The rationale behind this result is as follows. In the short run, components of domestic absorption are less prone to change; while in the long run, primary factors (both labour and capital) are more flexible. Pressures on primary factor prices to increase are, thus, less sensitive, allowing stronger fall in domestic costs of production. However, in this specific simulation, prices of exports tend to increase in relation to domestic prices, hampering the international trade balance.[13] This fact is intrinsically related to the location of the project, which situates in a position linking agricultural markets (in the west and central parts of the country) to important domestic centres of consumption, in the east. As this east–west link is not substantially associated with export corridors of the agricultural production, the positive impacts are heavily associated with benefits to domestic markets. Moreover, the very distinct nature of the respective

Table 1.   National results: selected variables (percentage change).

	BR-262		BR-381	
	Short run	Long run	Short run	Long run
Aggregates				
Real GDP	0.00022	0.00105	0.00018	(0.00293)
Equivalent variation – total (change in $1,000,000)	(12.3)	58.6	(48.3)	6.4
Economy-wide terms of trade	(0.00180)	0.00040	(0.00674)	0.00299
GDP price index, expenditure side	(0.00240)	(0.01598)	(0.00818)	0.00242
GDP components				
Real household consumption	(0.00047)	0.00139	(0.00132)	(0.00344)
Real aggregate investment		0.00001		(0.00002)
Real aggregate regional government demand	(0.00217)	0.00129	(0.01301)	(0.00156)
Real aggregate federal government demand	(0.00047)	0.00139	(0.00132)	(0.00344)
International export volume	0.00385	(0.00017)	0.01456	(0.00683)
International import volume	(0.00239)	0.00019	(0.00823)	(0.00397)

Source: Elaborated by the authors.

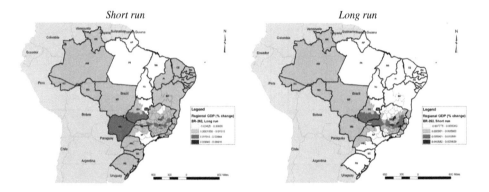

Short run   *Long run*

Figure 4.   Spatial results: real GDP (percentage change): BR-262 project.
Source: Elaborated by the authors.

economic structures of the linked spaces imposes very weak spatial competition among regions in the area of influence of the BR-262.

In this sense, the spatial effects on GDP (Figure 4) reveal, both in the short run and in the long run, positive impacts in regions directly influenced by the BR-262. Noteworthy is that these positive impacts spread over space in the long run. Moreover, re-location effects tend to be directed to the agriculture-producing regions in the West as well as to the areas directly linked to the project itself within the borders of Minas Gerais.

Regarding the BR-381 project, macroeconomic short-run results are qualitatively equivalent to those presented by the BR-262 project: GDP growth led by the international sector and improvement in the terms of trade, as well as increasing overall competitiveness.

However, a seemingly surprising (to commonsense) result occurs: real GDP in the long run is projected to decrease, after the duplication project starts to operate. It should be

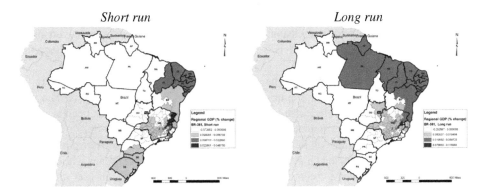

Figure 5.   Spatial results: real GDP (percentage change): BR-381 project.
Source: Elaborated by the authors.

emphasised that BR-381 has a relevant role in the integration of the country – it is part of one of the major routes linking the Northeast to the South of the country.

Figure 5 helps us clarify this issue. It presents both short-run and long-run results on GDP, from a spatial perspective. Looking more closely at such results for the long run, an 'accounting' explanation for the negative real GDP result emerges. Regional contributions for national GDP show that regions with positive performance (74 of them) represent a total impact of 0.00388, while regions with negative performance (35) represent a total impact of –0.00682. Thus, the negative impact, in absolute terms, is 75 per cent greater than the positive one. The map indicates that negative impacts are concentrated in the whole South region, all regions in the states of São Paulo and Rio de Janeiro. Fifty-eight per cent of the total negative impact comes from the São Paulo regions, and 12 per cent from Rio de Janeiro. In the regions that present a positive performance, major contributions come from the Northeast, especially Salvador, Aracaju, and Fortaleza, representing 68 per cent of the total positive impact on GDP growth.

Short-run results represent a counterfactual situation characterised by less flexible mechanisms of inter-regional transmission, as the possibility of inter-regional factor mobility is precluded. In the case of the South (including São Paulo), there seems to be stronger competitive interdependence with Minas Gerais and the eastern economies of the Northeast, mainly the more industrialised ones. The results for real GDP, in percentage terms, make this feature more evident, as economic growth of Minas Gerais and the Northeast is verified at the expense of growth in those economies south of Minas Gerais, even though the western economies of the Northeast, Tocantins and Mato Grosso present negative performance.

In the long run, the behavioural parameters have an even more prominent role in the functioning of the model. Re-location effects of capital and labour operate defining a new geography of winners and losers. The state of Minas Gerais and the Northeast place themselves as the main attractors of economic activity, competing directly with the centre-South of the country. The net result is the re-location of activities towards those areas, providing two distinct spatial regimes of potential winners and losers.

In summary, in the case of the BR-381 spatial competition clearly plays a prominent role. Given the favourable scenario for relative costs of production in the Northeast, in a context of systemic low quality of transport infrastructure, the Northeast increases its spatial market area while the richer Southeast suffers from the network (congestion) effects. Lower growth with decreasing regional inequality is the main long-run macro result (see localised spillover models – Baldwin and others 2003 – for a theoretical view).

Before moving to the analysis of the specific impacts in the State of Minas Gerais, it is important to emphasise the systemic nature of the problems under analysis. The issue of coordination of spatial policies should be given its proper role. As has been seen, isolated projects may promote undesirable outcomes if not considered within a context of a well-specified programme of investments. The integrated nature of transport systems may induce policy-makers to achieve mistakes when designing programmes without sound knowledge of this property. Accordingly, it would be important to consider differences between modes of transportation (that is, highways, railways and waterways) and different flows of goods. These requirements imply the need not only for a network model of multi-modal transport – as the one used in this paper – but also a more detailed specification of products in the CGE model – still to be developed.

4.2.2. Regional impacts. As both projects locate in the State of Minas Gerais, it is important to assess the specific state impacts. Policy-makers in Minas Gerais may have special interests in such projects, given their strategic role in the state transport network.

Common patterns appear related to aggregate effects of both projects with Minas Gerais (Table 2). In general, positive outcomes are stronger in the BR-262 project than in the BR-381 project. However, they go in the same direction for most of the indicators. Overall, gains in efficiency (real GDP growth) are positive, with bigger impacts occurring in the long run. Real tax revenue also follows the same pattern. Competitiveness indicators suggest improvements in the terms of trade with other countries, and a reduction in the *Custo Minas* – measured in terms of the state GDP deflator. Noteworthy is that in the long run the effects on terms of trade are magnified, what does not happen to *Custo Minas* in the BR-381 project. In the long run, a less favourable situation emerges, as Minas Gerais overall competitiveness seems to be hampered by production costs increases associated with increases in consumer good prices, also affecting welfare in terms of the equivalent variation. This effect is connected with direct spatial competition with similar economies in the Northeast.

Table 2.   State results: selected indicators (percentage change).

	BR-262		BR-381	
	Short run	Long run	Short run	Long run
Real GDP	0.00765	0.01554	0.00532	0.00686
Equivalent variation – total (change in $ 1,000,000)	15.4	30.1	7.7	(7.5)
Real tax revenue	0.00269	0.01381	0.00297	0.00425
Terms of trade	(0.00024)	(0.00216)	(0.00001)	(0.00274)
Custo Minas	(0.00379)	(0.02270)	(0.00870)	(0.00629)
Regional concentration	(0.00757)	(0.01528)	(0.00478)	(0.00640)
Poverty	(0.28963)	(1.12426)	(0.16286)	(0.28925)

Source: Elaborated by the authors.

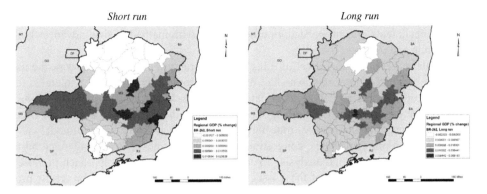

Figure 6.   Spatial state results: real GDP (percentage change): BR-262 project.
Source: Elaborated by the authors.

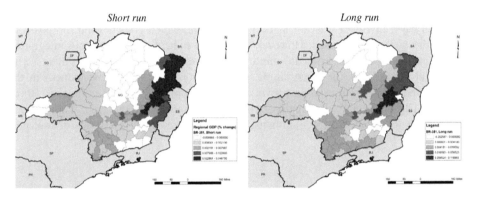

Figure 7.   Spatial state results: real GDP (percentage change): BR-381 project.
Source: Elaborated by the authors.

In terms of regional concentration, our indicator considers the relative growth of poorer regions of the State – North and Jequitinhonha/Mucuri. This outcome reveals that both projects are pro-concentration, but it happens to a lesser degree in the BR-381 project. Finally, both projects are also pro-poor, projecting reductions in the headcount poverty index for the State of Minas Gerais, both in the short (weaker) and long run (stronger). In this case, however, the BR-262 project performs better.

Figures 6 and 7 depict the spatial GDP effects of both projects, focusing on the regions of Minas Gerais. Overall, the stronger effects on the areas of influence of the projects are clearly perceived. Moreover, these effects tend to spread over time, as suggested by the smaller number of regions presenting negative performance in the long run.

5.   Final remarks

Appropriate tools are needed to assess the ex ante economic impacts of transportation infrastructure policies. This paper has attempted to tackle this issue. It has been suggested that inter-regional CGE models can potentially be used for the analysis of transport planning policies. We have illustrated a way in which this potential use can be implemented.

However, this tool is not yet a recurrent part of the transport planning process. To do so, further amendments are still needed, in order to cope with methodological advances both in economic and transport modelling.

Despite representing the effect of transport infrastructure in a consistent way, the use of current versions of inter-regional CGE models has some drawbacks when intended for replacing conventional models used in national or state-wide transport planning. Future versions of inter-regional CGE models should envisage the incorporation of some usual features of conventional models of transport planning, such as a broader multimodal view, quality and non-price attributes, congestion effects, and a finer spatial disaggregation to allow for finer intra-regional analysis. To some extent, the integrated approach proposed here directly addresses some of these issues. More importantly, however, the results provided are encouraging in the sense that the broader issues dealt in this paper, while difficult, are not insurmountable.

The policy conclusions that can be derived from the results of this study indicate the potential effects (both national and regional) road investments may play in the Brazilian economy. A detailed analysis of the shortage of infrastructure (that is, roads, railways and waterways) in Brazil was not made in the article, which goes beyond the possibilities of the methodology used. However, the results indicate that economic integration of regional markets in Brazil can amplify the benefits of transport investments with differential spatial impacts. Accordingly, given the systemic interconnectedness in the economy and in the transportation network, more appropriate transport policies in Brazil would envisage national coordination, which very often is not the case. Coordination may play an important role in optimising the multi-dimensional outcomes of transport policies.

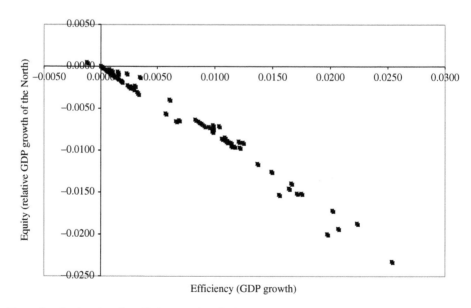

Figure 8.   Regional equity-efficiency trade-off of transportation infrastructure investments in Minas Gerais, Brazil.

Source: Elaborated by the authors.

This paper makes it clear that the choice of the 'best' infrastructure projects depends on the policy goals to be achieved. Different trade-offs may appear when considering different investment alternatives. Time trade-offs (short run versus long run), political trade-offs (regional versus national effects), and policy outcomes trade-offs were present in the two illustrative cases drawn from the PELT Minas case.

To make this point stronger, a closer look at the complete portfolio of multimodal infrastructure projects within the PELT Minas reveals further evidence about the nature of the relationship between the provision of transport infrastructure and regional equity. Indeed, transport infrastructure is strongly region-dependent. The spatial structure of the provision of transport infrastructure matters in this question, playing a fundamental role in determining its effects on the economic system.[14]

Fifty-three projects (simulations) were analysed with a view to the efficiency-equity trade-off associated with investments in transportation infrastructure. Among the 53 projects, three are investments in waterways, five in railways, three in pipelines, and 42 in roads.[15] Figure 8 summarises the results for the effects on efficiency (measured in terms of real gross regional product growth) and regional disparity (measured in terms of the relative growth of the poor regions in the north of the state and the state as a whole; a negative value indicates that the poor region is growing at a slower pace). The results reflect a long-run environment. There is a clear trade-off between efficiency and regional equity. Projects that produce higher impacts on GDP growth also contribute more to regional concentration. Such trade-offs are commonly faced by policy-makers.

Acknowledgements

Financial support by CNP_q, Fapesp and Rede CLIMA is acknowledged.

Notes

1. See www.centran.eb.br (*Programa Nacional de Logística e Transportes*).
2. In the Minas Gerais case, the *Plano Estadual de Logística e Transportes* (PELT Minas) was based in the use of state-of-the-art methodological approaches to deal explicitly with the interface between transport and economy, from diagnostics to evaluation of transport projects. A similar approach was followed in Pará.
3. See, for instance, Fujita *et al.* (1999) and Fujita and Thisse (2002).
4. First, it is possible to specify transportation technology by adopting the iceberg transportation cost hypothesis, based on Samuelson (1952). Second, one can assume transport services to be produced by a special optimising transport sector. Finally, a third approach to introduce transportation in CGE models consists of the development of a satellite module, for the transportation system.
5. Among them, five doctoral dissertations: Domingues (2002), Perobelli (2004), Porsse (2005), Ferraz (2010), and Santos (2010).
6. See Haddad (1999), and Haddad and Hewings (2005).
7. See http://www.worldbank.org/transport/roads/tools.htm
8. Agriculture, mining, manufacturing, construction, transportation, trade, public administration, and other services.
9. Only the manufacturing activities were contemplated with this change.
10. Hereafter, transportation services and margins will be used interchangeably.
11. Values as of December 2006.
12. Simulations results were computed using GEMPACK (Harrison *et al.* 1994).
13. Marginal trade balance is assumed to be in equilibrium in the long run.
14. See Almeida *et al.* (2010).
15. Two of them were analysed in more detail in the article.

References

Agénor, P.R., Izquierdo, A. and Jensen, H.T., 2007. *Adjustment policies, poverty, and unemployment: the IMMPA framework*. 1st ed. Oxford: Wiley-Blackwell.

Almeida, E.S., Haddad, E.A. and Hewings, G.J.D., 2010. The transport–regional equity issue revisited. *Regional studies*, 44 (10), 1387–1400.

Azzoni, C.R., 2001. Book review: regional inequality and structural changes – lessons from the Brazilian experience. *Papers in regional science*, 83 (2).

Baldwin, R., Forslid, R., Martin, P., Ottaviano, G. and Robert-Nicoud, R., 2007. *Economic geography and public policy*. Princeton: Princeton University Press.

Bröcker, J., 1998. Operational computable general equilibrium modeling. *Annals of regional science*, 32 (3), 367–387.

Bröcker, J., 2002. Spatial effects of European transport policy: a CGE approach. *In*: G.J.D. Hewings, M. Sonis and D. Boyce, eds. *Trade, networks and hierarchies*. Berlin: Springer-Verlag, 11–28.

Domingues, E.P., 2002. *Dimensão Regional e Setorial da Integração Brasileira na Área de Livre Comércio das Américas*. PhD dissertation. São Paulo, FEA/USP.

Ferraz, L.P.C., 2010. *Essays on the general equilibrium effects of barriers to trade on economic growth, foreign trade and the location of economic activity in Brazil*. PhD dissertation. Rio de Janeiro: EPGE/FGV.

FIPE, 2007. *Estudo com Vistas a Subsidiar o Programa Estadual de Logística de Transporte do Estado de Minas Gerais*. Belo Horizonte: Governo do Estado de Minas Gerais.

Friez, T.L., Suo, Z.-G. and Westin, L., 1998. Integration of freight network and computable general equilibrium models. *In*: L. Lundqvist, L.G. Mattsson and T.J. Kim, eds. *Network infrastructure and the urban environment – advances in spatial systems modeling*. Berlin: Springer-Verlag.

Fujita, M. and Thisse, J-F., 2002. *Economics of agglomeration*. 1st ed. Cambridge: Cambridge University Press.

Fujita, M., Krugman, P. and Venables, A.J., 1999. *The spatial economy: cities, regions and international trade*. 1st ed. Cambridge: MIT Press.

Haddad, E.A., 1999. Interregional computable general equilibrium models. *In*: M. Sonis and G.J.D. Hewings, eds. *Tool kits in regional science: theory, models and estimation*. Berlin: Springer-Verlag, 119–154.

Haddad, E.A., 2004. Interregional computable general equilibrium models. *In*: G.J.D. Hewings and M. Sonis, eds. *Reassessment of regional science theories*. Berlin: Springer-Verlag.

Haddad, E.A. and Domingues, E.P., 2001. EFES – Um Modelo Aplicado de Equilíbrio Geral para a Economia Brasileira: Projeções Setoriais para 1999–2004. *Estudos econômicos*, 31 (1), 89–125.

Haddad, E.A. and Hewings, G.J.D., 2005. Market imperfections in a spatial economy: some experimental results. *The quarterly review of economics and finance*, 45 (2–3), 476–496.

Harrison, W.J., Pearson, K.R. and Powell, A.A., 1994. *Multiregional and intertemporal AGE modelling via GEMPACK*. IMPACT Project. Clayton: Monash University, Preliminary Working Paper no. IP-66, September.

Hewings, G.J.D., 1986. Problems of integration in the modelling of regional systems. *In*: P.W.J. Batey and M. Madden, eds. *Integrated analysis of regional systems*. Pion: London Papers in Regional Science.

Hewings, G.J.D., Nazara, S. and Dridi, C., 2003. *Channels of synthesis forty years on: integrated analysis of spatial economic systems*. Regional Economic Applications Laboratory, University of Illinois at Urbana-Champaign, Discussion Paper REAL 03-T-27, Urbana, IL.

Isard, W. and Anselin, L., 1982. Integration of multiregional models for policy analysis. *Environment and planning A*, 14 (3), 359–376.

Isard, W., Azis, I.J., Drennan, M.P., Miller, R.E., Saltzman, S. and Thorbecke, E., 1998. *Methods of interregional and regional analysis*. 1st ed. Aldershot: Ashgate.

Miyagi, T., 2001, *Economic appraisal for multiregional impacts by a large scale expressway project: a spatial computable general equilibrium approach*. Tinbergen Institute, The Netherlands, Discussion Paper 2001-066/3, Amsterdam.

Perobelli, F.S., 2004. *Análise das Interações Econômicas entre os Estados Brasileiros*. PhD dissertation. São Paulo, FEA/USP.

Pietrantonio, H., 1999. *Land use and transport integrated models – basic relations and solution approaches*. Laboratory of Methodological Studies in Traffic and Transportation (LEMT/PTR-EPUSP), University of São Paulo, Work Report No.04/99, San Paulo, Brazil.

Polenske, K.R., 2002. Book review: regional inequality and structural changes – lessons from the Brazilian experience. *Journal of regional science*, 42 (2), 411–452.

Porsse, A. A., 2005. Competição Tributária Regional, Externalidades Fiscais e Federalismo no Brasil: Uma Abordagem de Equilíbrio Geral Computável. PhD dissertation. Department of Economics, Federal University of Rio Grande do Sul.

Samuelson, P., 1952. Spatial price equilibrium and linear programming. *American economic review*, 42, 283–303.

Santos, G., 2010. *Política energética e desigualdades regionais na economia brasileira*. PhD dissertation. São Paulo, FEA/USP.

Siriwardana, M., 2001. Book review: regional inequality and structural changes – lessons from the Brazilian experience. *Economic systems research*, 13 (1), 129–130.

Tourinho, O.A.F., Kume, H. and Pedroso, A.C.S., 2002. *Elasticidades de Armington para o Brasil: 1986–2001*. Rio de Janeiro: IPEA, Texto para Discussão 901.

World Bank, 1996. *Brazil: the Custo Brasil since 1990–1992*. Latin America and the Caribbean Region, World Bank Report No. 15663-BR, December. Washington, DC: The World Bank.

World Road Association, 2003. *The role of economic and socio-economic models in road management*. Paris: PIARC Technical Committee on Road Management.

Impact of water supply and sanitation assistance on human welfare in rural Pakistan

Ganesh Rauniyar[a], Aniceto Orbeta, Jr[b] and Guntur Sugiyarto[c]

[a] *Independent Evaluation Department, Asian Development Bank, Manila, Philippines;*
[b] *Philippine Institute of Development Studies, Manila, Philippines;* [c] *Economics Research Department, Asian Development Bank, Manila, Philippines*

The paper examines impact of two water supply and sanitation projects in rural Pakistan in improving access to water supply and sanitation and on health, education, and labour supply based on a household survey of 1300 project and 1300 comparison households. The impact was estimated using treatment effects based on a control-function approach. Overall findings show that the projects improved households' access to water supply, reduced drudgery associated with fetching water and improved attendance of high-school-age girls in schools. However, the projects had no significant impact on the incidence and intensity of diarrhoea and on increasing labour force participation and hours available for work.

Introduction

The impact of water supply and sanitation (WSS) interventions has gone a long way from being output-oriented to delivering a wide-range of development impact. The United Nations Millennium Project Task Force report on Water and Sanitation argues that better WSS will contribute to reduced income-poverty, improved health and nutrition outcomes, higher educational attainment, and greater gender equity. However, until recently, the majority of the research in this area focused on health impact, particularly on the incidence of diarrhoea among children under five years of age (IEG 2008). For instance, the IEG review of 100 WSS impact studies revealed that over 30 per cent of them used child diarrhoea as the outcome indicator.

Given the possible impact of a WSS project, it has been argued that a good impact evaluation should be theory based, tracing the causal chain from inputs to outcomes (Carvalho and White 2004, White and Massey 2007). This paper examines the impact of the Asian Development Bank's (ADB) assistance to Pakistan's rural WSS on intermediary outcome such as improving access to water supply, and the final impact on health, education, and labour supply.[1] In the absence of valid baseline data, this ex-post study adopted a quasi-experimental method and used a synthetic comparison group developed by directly matching villages to be surveyed based on a parsimonious set of characteristics, which were derived from Census data combined with local knowledge. The main findings show that the projects had a large impact on the intermediate outcome of improving access to water supply but a more limited and tentative impact on final outcomes, such as on health, education, and labour supply. No significant impact was observed as a result of ADB's assistance for sanitation and hygiene education. The findings of this study are consistent with other similar studies, including IEG (2008), and also provide quantitative estimates of outcomes and impacts resulting from rural WSS interventions.

Evidence from the literature

A review of literature on the impacts of WSS interventions suggested three sets of impacts – health, education, and labour supply (as a proxy for income). Most authors have adopted a number of health indicators as outcome variables: diarrhoea, child mortality, drudgery from fetching water (IEG 2008), and diarrhoea and drudgery (Zwane and Kremer 2007). Mosley and Chen (1984) developed an integrated framework and argued that the 'black box' of socio-economic determinants of health outcomes can be broken down into environmental/personal preventive conditions and therapeutic measures, which are also the primary elements in the bio-medical literature. This perspective led to the identification of personal, household, and community determinants of morbidity and mortality that underlie their current modelling, including the studies on the role of WSS interventions on health outcomes. The studies on the impact of water connection on health outcomes show mixed results (IEG 2008). Some studies have reported that WSS interventions lower morbidity and mortality incidence, but others show indifferent results.

Using propensity score matching at the household and community levels, Jalan and Ravallion (2003) estimated the impact of piped water on diarrhoea among children younger than five years of age in rural India, and found that the prevalence and duration of diarrhoea among the children were significantly lower for families with piped water than for identical households without piped water. They also found that the impact was not significant for poor families (40th quintile and under), particularly when mothers were poorly educated. Similarly, piped water supply connection both inside and outside the house had no significant impact on diarrhoea incidence. However, it significantly reduced the duration of illness, particularly in non-poor households (above the 40th quintile). Moreover, these results were obtained only when matching was done at the household level. The statistical significance did not hold when matching was done at the village level.

Using a case–control method, Wang et al. (1989) found that the incidence of acute watery diarrhoea in the rural China was 38.2 per cent lower in project than the control regions. On the other hand, in a study of two urban areas of Brazil, the incidence of diarrhoea from improved water supply was significantly lower but the intervention did not influence duration of diarrhoea (Gross et al. 1989). The study also reported that the prevalence of diarrhoea declined by 45 per cent in households with piped water, and that income level did not influence incidence and intensity of diarrhoea. A meta-analysis by Fewtrell and Colford (2004) concluded that water supply interventions in developing countries had no health benefits, while Semenza et al. (1998) reported diarrhoea incidence remained unaffected if there was contamination in the piped water. The latter also showed that piped water connection performed poorly compared with chlorinated water at point of use even in the absence of piped water to house.

Conceptually, the provision of WSS may save time from fetching water, and for school-age children this can increase school attendance. Other reported benefits from WSS interventions include increasing convenience for puberty-age girls (Burrows et al. 2004) and more time for income-generating activities, thereby contributing to a better education of children (Hutton *et al.* 2006, IEG 2008). However, the evidence from impact evaluation of WSS interventions on education is scant. Khandekar (1996) found interesting gender-differentiated impacts of provision of tube-well drinking water. The intervention did not affect school enrolment and the dropout rates of boys. The dropout rate of girls, however, declined. Furthermore, availability of water supply in school did not affect schooling attainment of both sexes but lowered the failure and dropout rates of boys. Finally, having a separate toilet in schools did not affect the schooling attainment rate of boys but increased that of the girls. The dropout rates of both boys and girls were also not affected. A less rigorous analyses employing a simple comparison shows that a proximity with water supply increased school attendance in Tanzania (Burrows *et al.* 2004), while a provision of water supply and toilet facilities in the school increased school attendance and reduced dropout rate in India (Kumar and Snel 2000).

The IEG (2008) study identified a weak link between the provision of improved water supply and time savings in fetching water. Drawing from Cairncross and Valdmanis (2006) and Dutta (2005) from 14 different studies, Hutton *et al.* (2006) noted that the time saved ranged from six minutes per day for men in Nepal to seven hours in rural Nigeria during the dry season. Similarly, Blackden and Wodon (2006) reported varied estimates of time saving in several sub-Saharan African countries. Ilahi and Grimand (2000) analysed the time allocation of women in rural Pakistan using the 1991 Pakistan Integrated Household Survey, and they found a significant negative and quadratic relationship (that is, market work time falls with a distance but at decreasing rate) between time for market work and distance to a water source. In addition, they also found that proximity to a water source was negatively (and linearly[2]) related to total market and non-market work burden, which they argued to be a measure of the women's leisure time. An interesting implication they put forward was that investing in a more accessible water source is similar to buying leisure for women in rural Pakistan. The authors refrained from claiming impact on household income because they did not study market time for men, which could potentially correlate with market time for women. In addition, more work and working hours may not always mean uniformly higher income in a developing country context. Banerjee and Duflo (2007), for instance, pointed out that the poor people do a lot of jobs or entrepreneurial activities that fill up because of a lack of specialisation and economics of scale that does not necessarily mean more income for them.

The literature on the impact of WSS interventions on household welfare reveals some gaps, mostly from the use of diarrhoea as the most common outcome indicator. This may be due to its relative ease in measuring and its short response time. On the contrary, no study has looked at the impact on drudgery of fetching water reflected by pain from muscle strain, blisters, and back ache. In terms of labour supply, most studies limit their impact estimations on time saved from fetching water and on the reduction in sick days, and very few explicitly estimate the impact on labour supply. On the impact on education, again very few studies provide direct estimates since most of them prefer to assume that the impacts are reflected indirectly in time saved in fetching water and reduction in sick days. This study intended to fill these gaps by directly measuring the impacts of WSS intervention on those household welfare indicators and disaggregating them by socio-economic group.

Description of the projects

The ADB approved a $42.97 million loan for the Punjab Rural Water Supply and Sanitation Project (PRWSSP) in 1995 (ADB 1994) and the project was closed in June 2003. The project completion report (PCR) in 2003 concluded that it was overall *partly successful* and *highly relevant*, but *less effective, less efficient*, and *less likely to be sustainable*. On the Pakistani government's request, the ADB approved another $50 million loan to implement a follow on Punjab Community Water Supply and Sanitation Project (PCWSSP) in 2002 (ADB 2002), which was officially closed in December 2007. The PCR of PCWSSP in 2009 rated the overall project as *highly successful*, based on *highly relevant, effective, efficient*, and *most likely sustainable* ratings.

The PRWSSP provided support for construction or rehabilitation of the water supply and drainage system, a hygiene education programme, and institutional strengthening, covering seven districts of Punjab on a pilot basis; while in the PCWSSP the coverage was expanded to 30 of the 35 districts in Punjab with an additional support for the Social Uplift and Poverty Eradication (SUPER) programme. The community participation, hygiene education and SUPER received strong emphasis but attracted only a very small portion of the total project resources.[3] The construction and/or rehabilitation of the water supply and drainage system in the PCWSSP included gravity and pump-based schemes, as well as rainwater harvesting schemes. The PCWSSP had reportedly more intensive community participation in the design, implementation and management, compared with the PRWSSP.

Both projects followed similar selection criteria broadly comprising three steps: (i) listing of communities in brackish and dry land (barani) areas with no water supply and applying for inclusion in the project; (ii) assessing the communities' willingness to operate and maintain the projects upon completion; and (iii) conducting feasibility and sustainability studies, including forming community organisations[4] responsible for operation and maintenance.

Community Liaison Workers were engaged during the process, and in the PCWSSP the step also included a collection of joint deposit of two months operation and maintenance cost with the Punjab Public Health Engineering Department. Therefore, there was no explicit targeting of poor communities even though the projects' rationale stated that 'the project will help the Government to reduce poverty' and that the overall goal was 'to reduce poverty' (ADB 1994, para. 16).[5] This would have been due to the fact that a majority of households in rural Punjab was poor anyway.

Methodology

A conceptual framework for evaluating the impact of the project was developed based on the review of literature on WSS impacts and relevant project documents, and discussions with key stakeholders. The logic model envisages WSS impacts in three key areas – health, education, and labour supply. The intermediate outcomes from project interventions include better access to water and sanitation services and improved water handling and sanitation practices. The provision of improved water supply, sanitation, and training and educational materials on improved water and sanitation practices comprised the key project outputs, while the exogenous variables included personal (that is, age, sex, and education), household (that is, age, sex, educational attainment of household head, expenditure on consumption items, and proxy wealth indicators including housing conditions), and community (that is, presence of education, health, water and sanitation facilities, and other village development indicators) factors that generated project outputs.

One of the key challenges in conducting the study was to find a valid counterfactual or a comparison group against which the treatment group was to be compared, given that the project did not have valid baseline data. Hence, the evaluation adopted a one-time survey using ex-post treatment–comparison groups by applying a single-difference method.[6] To implement the treatment–comparison group design, a matching comparison village was selected and enumerated for each treatment or project village. The treatment and comparison villages were directly matched based on their characteristics before the project started; that is, by using four Census-based indicators: village population size, absence of potable water source at the time the project was introduced, similarity of geographic area of the village, and literacy rate. The lack of village-level data was the main reason for using this matching method[7] since the 1998 district Census reports were the only available data source in Pakistan for this purpose. The importance of using the characteristics of the village prior to the intervention, as opposed to the current conditions, as the basis for matching is emphasised in Pattanayak et al. (2007).[8] Jalan and Ravallion (2001)[9] have also argued in favour of the superiority of a matched sample compared with an unmatched sample in the estimation of the impact of interventions. In each treatment and comparison village, an equal number of household samples were randomly selected. This randomisation was expected to normalise the distribution of outcomes at the village level. Therefore, the matching was essentially done at the village level rather than at the household level, which is usually done in the propensity score matching studies.[10]

Impact estimation was first done using differences in means between project and comparison villages, and their difference was tested for their significance using t-tests.[11] The single-difference method of the projects' impact was measured in two ways. This involved computing simple weighted difference in outcomes between the treatment and comparison villages given by the equation:[12]

$$\Delta\bar{y} = \sum_{j=1}^{T} \omega_j(\bar{y}_j^1 - \bar{y}_j^0) = \sum_{j=1}^{T} \omega_i \Delta\bar{y}_j \qquad (1)$$

where $\bar{y}_j^k$ is the mean values of outcome y for household type k in village j, $k = 1$ (treatment), 0 (comparison); $\Delta\bar{y}_j$ is the difference in mean outcome y for matched treatment and comparison village j; T is the number of treatment villages, which is equal to the number of comparison villages; and ω is the sampling weights if the sampling scheme is not self-weighting. However, since the sampling design was proportional to the number of schemes for the seven provinces randomly selected, the sample is self-weighting and implies $\omega = 1$.

The method in Equation (1) assumed that other variables affecting the outcomes of interest were identical for both the treatment and comparison households as in the case of a randomised experiment. If the characteristics were not identical, the difference in means would not correctly estimate the impact, instead it would have included the effects of other characteristics. Hence, the second way of estimating the impact applied was by using a regression method in the form given by:

$$y_i = \beta_o + \beta_1 t_i + \beta\mathbf{X}_i + \varepsilon_i \qquad (2)$$

where y is the outcome of interest, t is the treatment variable ($t = 1$ if treated, 0 otherwise), $\mathbf{X}$ is the vector of independent variables, β is the vector of coefficients, and ε is the error term.

In Equation (2), β_1 was an estimate of impact like $\overline{\Delta y}$ in Equation (1). The advantage of this regression-based approach over the simple difference in means (and proportions) was that the former could control the effects of other observable variables that could independently affect the project's outcomes. These variables were represented by vector $\mathbf{X}$ in

Equation (2). Note that if these other variables were not included in the equation, β_1 was then expected to be identical to $\overline{\Delta y}$ in Equation (1). Thus, the simple difference in means effectively assumed that the treatment and comparison households were identical on average, except for the project intervention. The specification in Equation (2) was assumed for continuous dependent variables. However, some of the outcomes such as diarrhoea incidence or school attendance were binary or dichotomous variables. Therefore, non-linear models such as probit or logit were needed and hence the Equation (2) was re-specified as follows:

$$y_i = F(\beta_o + \beta_1 t + \boldsymbol{\beta} \mathbf{X}_i + \varepsilon_i) \tag{3}$$

where $F(\ldots)$ is normal in the case of probit and logistic in the case of logit.

To estimate the impact, the study employed the average treatment effects estimation using a control function approach (Wooldridge 2002). This method uses independent variables X as elements of the control function in addition to treatment variable and it controls for selection bias. The functional form of the control function depended on whether the outcome of interest was modelled linearly or non-linearly. For a linear model, the elements of control function were the independent variables and the interaction between the treatment variables and the demeaned[13] values of the independent variables. Wooldridge (2002, p. 613) argues that demeaning the variables ensures that the coefficient of t in the equation above would be the average treatment effect. For a non-linear model, such as probit or logit, the propensity score,[14] the product of the treatment variable and the demeaned values of the estimated propensity score, were the elements of the control function.[15] Woodridge (2002, p. 637) specifically recommends the use propensity score approach because the assumptions needed to arrive at Equation (4) will not be tenable for non-linear models. The estimation equation for linear models was:

$$y_i = \beta_o + \beta_1 t_i + \boldsymbol{\beta}_2 \mathbf{X} + \boldsymbol{\beta}_3 t_i (\mathbf{X} - \overline{\mathbf{X}}) + \varepsilon_i \tag{4}$$

where y is the outcome of interest, t is the treatment variable ($t = 1$ if treated, 0 otherwise), $\mathbf{X}$ is the vector of independent variables, β_i is the coefficients, and ε_i is the error term.

On the other hand, Equation (5) represented the non-linear model:

$$y_i = F[\beta_o + \beta_1 t_i + \boldsymbol{\beta}_2 P(t_i|\mathbf{X}) + \beta_3 t_i (P(t|\mathbf{X}) - \overline{P(t|\mathbf{X})}) + \varepsilon_i] \tag{5}$$

where

$$P(t|\mathbf{X}) = \text{propensity score}$$

In the linear model, the estimate of the average treatment effect (the average effect of a binary or dichotomous explanatory variable) was given directly by β_1, while for non-linear models it was given by the difference in expected value of y given X for the treatment and comparison groups; that is, the marginal effects of the treatment variable.[16]

The basic treatment variable was the presence or absence of the project. Given the project outcomes, one could have considered piped water connection to beneficiary households as the primary intervention. However, not all households in project villages had piped water. Therefore, the project presence was used as the treatment variable yielding what is known in the literature as the *intension to treat* effect.[17] Other independent variables used in the model were those commonly used in the literature (for example, Mosley and

Chen 1984, Jalan and Ravallion 2003), including household, community and individual characteristics. Household characteristics included the household head's age, sex, education, occupation, sector of work, household expenditures, housing characteristics, and assets. Community characteristics included location dummies, school and health facilities, other development indicators (for example, transport facilities), demographic characteristics (population, number of households), and main sources of livelihood. Individual characteristics included age, sex and education.

Sampling design and data

At the survey design stage, the only available information on the projects was the location, type, and number of beneficiaries by subprojects. Given the limited resources, only seven of 30 districts where the project operated were considered in the sampling. They were selected randomly using two important criteria of project phase (PRWSSP or PCWSSP) and types of water supply (barani or brackish). To capture the main features of the project, sampling of the subprojects was done utilising the project's features, such as nature of intervention (that is, a new construction or a rehabilitation) and type of intervention (that is, water supply only or water supply and sanitation).[18] Figure 1 shows a schematic diagram of the sampling scheme.

The distribution of subprojects and household samples is given in Table 1. The community survey covered 115 treatments and an identical number of comparison villages, and each sample subproject covered a village. Fifty sample subprojects were under PRWSSP and another 65 subprojects under PCWSSP. The household survey enumerated a total of 2602 households consisting of 1301 treatments and 1301 comparison households.

Two types of survey questionnaires were developed for the household and village, respectively. The questionnaires covered measures of project impacts on health, education, and labour supply, as well as on specific project intermediate outcomes, outputs, and inputs. The questionnaires also covered other non project intervening factors known to affect the outcomes of interest both at the household and community levels. The household questionnaire had 10 sections: (i) household identifiers; (ii) personal characteristics of individual household members; (iii) water borne-related and other morbidity information; (iv) education; (v) employment and livelihood; (vi) water sources; (vii) sanitation facilities and

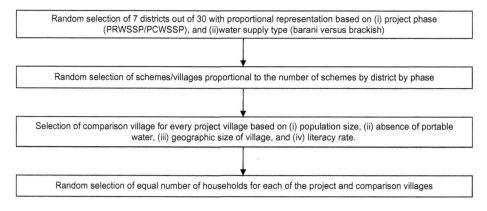

Figure 1.   Sampling scheme.

Table 1. Sampling distribution of subprojects and households.

District	Total number of subprojects			Number of sample subprojects			Number of sample households			Comparison households	Grand total
	PRWSSP	PCWSSP	Total	PRWSSP	PCWSSP	Total	PRWSSP	PCWSSP	Total		
Rawalpindi	47	34	81	12	6	18	118	67	185	185	370
Chakwal	47	43	90	12	9	21	173	123	296	296	592
Bahwalpur	54	34	88	13	8	21	124	79	203	203	406
RY Khan	54	38	92	13	8	21	102	56	158	158	316
Sargodha		53	53	0	9	9	0	95	95	95	190
Fasialabad		40	40	0	7	7	0	76	76	76	152
DG Khan		82	82	0	18	18	0	288	288	288	576
Total	**202**	**324**	**526**	**50**	**65**	**115**	**517**	**784**	**1301**	**1301**	**2602**

Source: PCWSSP and PRWSSP project databases and information provided by the Public Health Engineering Department, Government of Punjab, Lahore, 2008.

Table 2. Distribution of sample subprojects by typology.

Item	PRWSSP			PCWSSP			Total		
	WS	WSS	Total	WS	WSS	Total	WS	WSS	Total
Rehabilitated									
Average months since handover				32.7	31.8	32.6	32.7	31.8	32.6
Frequency				19.0	4.0	23.0	19.0	4.0	23.0
Proportion to total				16.5	3.5	20.0	16.5	3.5	20.0
New									
Average months since handover	98.9	84.7	86.7	36.5	33.8	35.2	51.5	68.6	63.2
Frequency	7.0	43.0	50.0	22.0	20.0	42.0	29.0	63.0	92.0
Proportion to total	6.1	37.4	43.5	19.1	17.4	36.5	25.2	54.8	80.0
Total									
Average months since handover	98.9	84.7	86.7	34.7	33.5	34.3	44.1	66.4	57.1
Frequency	7.0	43.0	50.0	41.0	24.0	65.0	48.0	67.0	115.0
Proportion to total	6.1	37.4	43.5	35.7	20.9	56.5	41.7	58.3	100.0

Note: PCWSSP = Punjab Community Water Supply and Sanitation (Sector) Project, PRWSSP = Punjab Rural Water Supply and Sanitation (Sector) Project, WS = water supply, WSS = water supply and sanitation.
Source: Independent Evaluation Department, 2008. *Rigorous Impact Evaluation Survey of Water Supply and Sanitation in Punjab (Pakistan)*. Manila.

practices; (viii) health education, community participation and institutions; (ix) housing characteristics; and (x) household assets and expenditures.

The village questionnaire, on the other hand, had five sections: (i) physical characteristics; (ii) demographic characteristics; (iii) basic services and institutions such as education, health, water, waste disposal, and transportation; (iv) other non-ADB-supported water and sanitation projects; and (v) electricity services availability. The household and community questionnaires were linked via geographic codes. The survey itself was conducted by a local research firm from August to September 2008. Table 2 shows the distribution of the sample by subproject typologies.

Results

Intermediary outcomes

Table 3 shows that the project had significant positive impact on improving access to water supply in project villages compared with the counterfactual communities for all types of water use such as for drinking, hand washing, cooking, toilet, other domestic uses, and livestock. However, no significant impact was observed with respect to sanitation facilities. The result is not surprising because almost 90 per cent of project resources were dedicated to improving access to water supply. On the other hand, very few households treated their drinking water and the difference in the project and non project areas was statistically insignificant (that is, 3.5 per cent in project area compared with 2.6 per cent in comparison area). With respect to per-capita monthly expenditure on water, households in project areas spent significantly less on water in general (PRs22.58 vs. PRs31.32) and on drinking water (PRs20.40 vs. PRs25.83). This finding should be interpreted with the caution that relatively fewer households paid for their water in the comparison areas.

Table 3.   Intermediate outcomes from rural water supply and sanitation interventions.

Variables	Project		Non-Project		Difference	T	Sig. level
	Mean	Frequency	Mean	Frequency			
Water on premises (proportion):							
Drinking	0.952	1,301	0.843	1,301	0.108	9.254	0.000
Handwashing	0.964	1,301	0.862	1,301	0.102	9.392	0.000
Cooking	0.958	1,301	0.851	1,301	0.108	9.504	0.000
Toilet facility	0.971	1,289	0.873	1,275	0.098	9.464	0.000
Other domestic uses	0.972	1,300	0.869	1,301	0.102	9.802	0.000
Livestock	0.932	941	0.865	896	0.067	4.799	0.000
Sanitation (proportion)							
Toilet facility in house	0.819	1,301	0.812	1,301	0.007	0.454	0.650
Use cleaning agent in handwashing	0.998	1,301	1.000	1,301	(0.002)	(1.415)	0.157
Covered sewerage	0.272	1,301	0.283	1,301	(0.011)	(0.613)	0.540
Water treatment and expenditure							
Households that treat drinking water (proportion)	0.035	1,301	0.026	1,301	0.008	1.257	0.209
Per capita monthly expenditure on drinking water[a] (rupees)	20.395	1,037	25.832	251	(5.438)	(3.609)	0.000
Per capita monthly expenditures on water[ab] (rupees)	22.580	840	31.320	228	(8.740)	(4.655)	0.000

Note: ( ) = negative, Sig. = significance, T = student's t-statistic.
[a]Excludes those who reported zero expenditure.
[b]Substantial number of households did not provide breakdown on expenditures.
Source: Socio-economic survey, 2008.

The project was expected to change the primary sources of water. Of the six different uses of water (drinking, hand washing, cooking, toilet, other domestic uses, and livestock), drinking water has been used here to illustrate the impact on alternative sources of water because it is a good representation of other uses. The results suggest a very distinct difference in the sources of drinking water. In project areas, about 71 per cent of households had access to piped water compared with only 10 per cent in non-project areas (the difference is highly significant as reflected by the value of $p < 0.001$). Tube well/borehole (39 per cent) and hand pump (31 per cent) were the two most important sources of drinking water in the non-project areas. Similarly, accessibility to water supply was also much better in project areas. This can be seen in both time spent and distance travelled to fetch water for various purposes, including for drinking. The project households spent 90 minutes less time per week and travelled 5 km less distance than their comparison counterparts ($p < 0.001$).[19]

Health impact

Significant health and sanitation benefits were expected from the WSS projects (ADB 1994, para. 83). In particular, it was stated that 'the availability of clean water will create better and healthy conditions for the people' (ADB 2002, para. 68). In addition, the projects were expected to relieve women from the stress and discomfort of hauling water

(ADB 1994, para. 65). The health impacts covered in the study were: the incidence and severity of water-borne diseases (for example, diarrhoea),[20] and drudgery.

As mentioned earlier, the significance of the project impact was first determined by examining the simple differences in means and/or proportions of indicators of interest between project and non project areas using t-tests. The results show that the difference in health outcomes of project and non-project areas was mild at most. Only drudgery, measured by the proportion of households with members complaining about pain from fetching water, was statistically significant ($p < 0.001$). The proportion was 5 per cent lower in project areas compared with non-project villages. Although diarrhoea incidence among children younger than five years of age, and diarrhoea severity for all household members and for children younger than five years of age were lower in project areas, the estimates were not statistically different from those in the non-project areas.

Table 4 compares the health indicators in project and non-project areas, showing that there was no significant difference between the diarrhoea incidence and the number of sick days due to diarrhoea. The incidence of diarrhoea in the last month as a reference point was estimated to be 1.8 per cent for all ages and about 6 per cent for children younger than five years of age. These estimates are lower compared to the estimates reported in other publications. In particular, the Pakistan Social and Living Standards Measurement Survey 2006–2007[21] estimates were 11 per cent for all of Pakistan, 10 per cent for urban Punjab and 11 per cent for rural Punjab.[22]

The validity of a simple comparison of means as the basis for establishing causal effects is critically dependent on the similarity of the project and non-project households in all characteristics, except for the presence of the treatment in project areas, such as those achieved in randomised experiments. Since the evaluation design was an ex-post single-difference method (with and without project), there is no guarantee that this in fact was obtained. The comparisons of personal, household and community characteristics (Appendices 1 and 2) suggested that although households in the project and non-project areas were similar in many characteristics, they also differed in other characteristics. These differences were expected to affect the health outcomes and other impacts of the project.

To establish the causality under these circumstances, regression estimates with a control for other important variables were used. Based on human capital and health production function models, the incidence and number of sick days due to diarrhoea were known to be determined by personal, household, and community characteristics.[23] The primary variable

Table 4. Health outcomes in project and non-project areas.

Variables		Project		Non-project		Difference	T	Sig. level
		Mean	Frequency	Mean	Frequency			
Diarrhea incidence,	All	0.018	7,682	0.018	7,520	0.001	0.37	0.710
	5 and under	0.058	886	0.061	756	(0.003)	(0.28)	0.779
Diarrhea sick days,	All	3.128	141	3.341	132	(0.213)	(0.57)	0.569
	5 and under	2.255	51	2.543	46	(0.289)	(0.44)	0.662
Pain[a] from fetching water		0.032	1,295	0.084	1,301	(0.051)	(5.62)	0.000

Note: ( ) = negative, Sig. = significance, T = student's t-statistics.
[a]Muscle strain, blisters or backache.
Source: Socio-economic survey, 2008.

of interest was the treatment variable – presence or absence of the project intervention. The personal characteristics included age, sex and education, while the household characteristics include the characteristics of parents/household head such as age, sex, education, occupation, sector of work and the housing characteristics or wealth indicators. The community characteristics, on the other hand, included presence of health facilities and other development indicators including demographic characteristics.

Since diarrhoea incidence and the likelihood of experiencing pain from fetching water were binary variables, these variables were estimated using probit models. The number of sick days, on the other hand, was treated as count data and hence estimated using Poisson regression. In estimating treatment effects using probit models (or any non-linear model), the propensity score method is recommended.[24] Estimation results showed that none of the personal characteristics were significantly different in project and non-project areas, but there were several significant differences in the household characteristics. The education of the household head was found to be significantly lower in project areas and the household size was larger in project areas. A higher proportion of household heads in project areas were working in agricultural and service professions. The average number of rooms was higher and there were also more households with finished floors in project than in non-project areas. Finally, a lower proportion of households had structured roof in project areas compared with comparison areas.

In terms of community characteristics, there were more villages with a primary school, a middle school, and a high school but fewer had a tertiary school in project areas compared with non-project areas. There were more villages with medical facilities in project areas compared with non-project areas. More villages in project areas had bus services while non-project areas had more villages with motorcycle or tricycles (*rikshaws*). Project villages had a smaller population size. Households in project villages were more dependent on agriculture and manufacturing while those in non-project areas were more dependent on livestock production. Project villages also had higher per-capita expenditure. The full estimation results are given in Appendix 3.

Table 5 summarises estimates of the primary equation (Equation (1)), showing that diarrhoea incidence and the severity of illness of all members and children five years and below not significantly different between project and non-project areas. These results do not lend support to the claim in the PCR of the PCWSS of a reduction in waterborne diseases (ADB 2003, para. 31),[25] but are consistent with the earlier findings reported by Fewtrell and Colford (2004) and Jalan and Ravallion (2003) showing no significant impact

Table 5. Impact of water supply and sanitation intervention on health.

Health impact	Impact estimate	Significance level
A. Waterborne disease		
Diarrhea incidence, All ages	0.002[a]	0.521
Diarrhea incidence, 5 and under	0.003[a]	0.812
Diarrhea sick days, All ages	0.853[b]	0.167
Diarrhea sick days, 5 and under	0.901[b]	0.727
B. Drudgery		
Pain from fetching water [c]	(0.051)[b]	0.000

[a] Pain from fetching water refers to muscle strain, backache, and blisters.
[b] Marginal effect.
[c] Incidence rate ratio.

on health of water supply interventions. The already low incidence of diarrhoea in the sample households may have made it difficult for the project to cause a further and significant impact.

In the case of drudgery, the impact was negative and statistically significant; the project lowered the proportion of households with members complaining of pain from fetching water. The estimated marginal effect[26] shows that the reduction in the proportion attributable to the project was about 5 per cent. Note that the regression estimates simply replicates the results of the comparison of means, indicating that there are no confounding impacts from other determinants. Even the estimate of the impact on drudgery was virtually identical. The full estimation results appear in Appendix 4.

Education impact

The projects were expected to improve education and human resource development in the project area, as stated in the project document that 'the girls, who share the responsibility of water collection, will now be enrolled in schools' (ADB 2002, para. 65). The impact on education was measured by school attendance, (ii) by the proportion of households with children refusing to go to school due to lack of clean drinking water, and by the proportion of households with children refusing to go to school due to lack or poor toilet facilities. A special attention is given to the attendance of girls.

Attendance rates were higher in the project than in non-project areas, but the differences were not significant, except for the 11–13 (middle school) and 14–17 (high school) age groups (Table 6). Overall, the attendance rates by age group ranged from 77 to 80 per cent for 6–10 years (primary), from 73 to 80 per cent for 11–13 (middle school), from 52 to 59 per cent for 14–17 (high school), and from 15–24 per cent for 18–24 (tertiary). By gender, the difference in attendance rates was only significant in the same age groups for females (that is, 79 per cent vs. 70 per cent in the 11–13 years age group, and 53 per cent vs. 45 per cent for the 14–17 years age group). For males, the difference was significant only in the 14–17 years age group (that is, 65 per cent vs. 58 per cent). The attendance rates of males were generally higher than those of females regardless of location. The survey estimates were on the high side compared with existing estimates for Punjab. For instance, the net primary attendance rate based on the Demographic and Health Survey 2006–2007 is 75 per cent for both sexes, 76.5 per cent for males, and 73.2 per cent for females. For the middle/secondary (aged 10–14 years) the estimated net enrolment rate for Punjab was 31.2 per cent for all and 31.9 per cent for males and 30.6 per cent females. Based on the Pakistan Social and Living Standards Measurement Survey 2006–2007, the total net primary enrolment rate in Punjab province was 66 per cent (67 per cent for male and 65 per cent for female). For middle school (aged 10–14 years), the net enrolment rate was estimated at 34 per cent for all, 36 per cent for males and 32 per cent for females.

The proportion of households with children not going to school due to lack of clean drinking water was significantly lower in project (2 per cent) compared with non-project (4 per cent) areas. On the other hand, there was no significant difference in the proportion of households with children not going to school due to lack of toilet facilities between project and non-project areas, which ranges from 4 per cent to 5 per cent. These differences could not be used to establish causality because of the likely differences in household and community characteristics. To control for these differences, regression models controlling for these differences were estimated. From human capital models and education production functions, education outcomes were determined by personal, household and community

Table 6. Education indicators in project and non-project areas (proportion).

Variables		Project		Non-project		Difference	T	Sig. level
		Mean	Frequency	Mean	Frequency			
Proportion attending:								
All	6–24 years	0.507	1,111	0.496	1,136	0.011	0.61	0.541
	6–10 years	0.804	535	0.774	553	0.030	1.30	0.194
	11–13 years	0.800	437	0.733	450	0.067	2.40	0.016
	14–17 years	0.589	528	0.520	552	0.070	2.45	0.014
	18–24 years	0.193	669	0.185	664	0.008	0.41	0.681
Female	6–24 years	0.468	891	0.450	897	0.018	0.82	0.414
	6–10 years	0.774	316	0.762	315	0.012	0.36	0.718
	11–13 years	0.785	214	0.701	242	0.084	2.07	0.039
	14–17 years	0.531	292	0.449	319	0.082	2.07	0.039
	18–24 years	0.145	452	0.150	446	(0.005)	(0.24)	0.812
Male	6–24 years	0.578	884	0.546	922	0.032	1.52	0.128
	6–10 years	0.825	360	0.782	393	0.043	1.55	0.122
	11–13 years	0.802	262	0.781	254	0.020	0.56	0.575
	14–17 years	0.646	356	0.582	359	0.064	1.81	0.071
	18–24 years	0.239	428	0.211	419	0.027	1.00	0.317
Not going to school due to lack of water (prop.)		0.020	1295	0.038	1301	(0.018)	(2.68)	0.007
Not going to school due to lack of toilet (prop.)		0.040	1295	0.047	1301	(0.007)	(0.84)	0.401

Note: ( ) = negative, Sig. = significance, T = student's t-statistics.
Source: Socio-economic survey, 2008.

characteristics. The determining household characteristics and community characteristics were identical to those used in the health models mentioned above.

School attendance can be modelled as independent individual decisions or as a joint household decision (for example, using the proportion of school-age children attending school). The use of proportion, estimated as a fractional logit model (Papke and Wooldridge 1996), is preferred when the school attendance of school-age children is jointly decided by parents.[27] Otherwise, a probit model is used. The households with children not going to school because of lack of water or toilet facilities were binary and, thus, were estimated using a probit model. The results show that the projects had a significant positive impact on school attendance, particularly, at the high school levels (14–17 years); that is, the project increases the school attendance of high school-age children. It also reduced the proportion of children refusing to go to school due to lack of clean water (Table 7). It is noteworthy that there was an increase in enrolment found for girls in high school, but no such impact among the boys. The marginal effect estimates showed that the project increased the proportion of children attending high school by 5 per cent, and for girls the increase was even higher at 8 per cent. This result supports the claim in the PCR of PCWSSP for an increase in enrolment for girls (ADB 2003, para. 31).[28] This result, however, contradicts the *no significant impact* of drinking water on school attendance reported by Khandker (1996), particularly in the case of girls. The proportion of households with children not going to school due to lack of clean water also declined by 2 per cent because of the project ($p < 0.05$).

A comparison of the differences in means/proportion in Table 6 and the marginal effects in Table 7 indicates some confounding effects of other determining variables. Some

Table 7.   Impact of water supply and sanitation intervention on education.

Impact on school enrolment		Marginal effects	Significance level
Proportion enrolled by age group			
All	6–24 years	(0.008)	0.676
	6–10 years	0.028	0.282
	11–13 years	0.046	0.135
	14–17 years	0.053	0.092
	18–24 years	(0.016)	0.468
Female	6–24 years	0.002	0.929
	6–10 years	0.019	0.610
	11–13 years	0.068	0.136
	14–17 years	0.084	0.061
	18–24 years	(0.036)	0.164
Male	6–24 years	0.038	0.163
	6–10 years	0.038	0.437
	11–13 years	(0.072)	0.475
	14–17 years	0.110	0.113
	18–24 years	0.008	0.843
Household reporting children not going to school due to lack of water (proportion)		(0.018)	0.006
Household reporting children not going to school due to lack of toilet (proportion)		(0.011)	0.205

Note: ( ) = negative.

of the significant differences in the comparison of means are no longer significant in the multivariate regression results; that is, the total and disaggregated proportion of attendance for 11–13 age groups. There are also differences in the magnitude of the impact derived from the differences in proportions and those from the multivariate models. For instance, while the impact from differences in proportion for children aged 14–17 years is 7 per cent, the multivariate estimate is only 5 per cent. For girls in high school, the estimated impact from the differences in proportion is 8.2 per cent, while the computed impact from the multivariate model is 8.4 per cent. The full estimation results are provided in Appendix 5 for school attendance and Appendix 6 for the proportion of households with children not going to school due to lack of water or toilet facilities.

Impact on labour supply

The study examined impact of WSS on labour supply in terms of increase in labour force participation and increased hours of work, based on the assumption that time saved from fetching water and reduced sick days would be used for income-generating activities. Based on difference in the means, the estimates show that the project has had no significant impact on labour force participation and hours worked, except for the 11–17 age group where the differences are 2 per cent lower and 5 hours longer in the project areas, respectively. These imply that even though there was a decline in proportion of working children aged 11–17 years because of the project, working children in the project areas worked longer than their counterparts in non-project areas. The estimated labour force participation rate in the project and non-project areas were between 30 and 31 per cent for those 10 years and above; 4 and 6 per cent for 11–17 years old; and 24 and 26 per cent for 18–24 years old (Table 8). These estimates are relatively lower than the most recent estimates from the Labour Force

Table 8. Labour force participation and hours worked in project and-non project areas.

Variables		Project		Non-project		Difference	T	Sig. level
		Mean	Frequency	Mean	Frequency			
With job (proportion),	10 years and above	0.301	6,118	0.308	6,112	(0.008)	(0.940)	0.347
	11–17 years [a]	0.043	1,344	0.059	1,398	(0.016)	(1.844)	0.065
	18–24 years	0.235	1,223	0.260	1,216	(0.025)	(1.442)	0.149
Hours worked per week,	10 years and above	58.457	1,810	58.135	1,850	0.322	0.649	0.516
	11–17 years [a]	57.552	58	52.263	76	5.289	1.830	0.070
	18–24 years	57.117	281	56.632	310	0.485	0.381	0.703

Note: ( ) = negative, Sig. = significance, T = student's t-statistics.
[a] Age groups 11–13 and 14–17 merged to increase cell sample size.
Source: Socio-economic survey, 2008.

Survey of the Pakistan Federal Bureau of Statistics (FBS) for 2006–2007,[29] showing the labour force participation rate at 48.6 per cent for all of Punjab, and 52.1 per cent and 41.6 per cent for rural and urban areas, respectively. The age-group specific labour force participation rate for 10–14, 15–19, and 20–24 age groups were 13.3 per cent, 37.4 per cent, and 53 per cent, respectively. In the case of average hours worked in the past week, Table 8 shows that household members aged 10 years and above worked for about 58 hours per week, working children 11–17 years old worked for about 52–58 hours per week, while older children aged 18–24 worked for about 57 hours. The reported average hours work per week is clearly way above the 35-hour week the Pakistan FBS considers a full-time equivalent.

Time allocation models point to the seminal paper of Becker (1965) and the subsequent modification by Gronau (1977) as the guiding framework. These papers provide the basic framework for identifying individual, household, and community characteristics in time allocation decisions that motivate labour supply models. Ilahi and Grimand (2000) also provide a more recent rendition of the framework for water supply and time allocation problems. To account for the likely difference in household and community characteristics, a regression model was estimated for each of these indicators using individual, household and community controls.

Labour force participation, being a binary variable, was estimated using a probit model, while hours worked, being a continuous variable, was estimated using ordinary least squares. The estimation results show that the projects had no significant impact on any of the labour market indicators (Table 9). The simple comparison of means, however, showed significant impacts on both the labour force participation and the average hours worked by household members 11–17 years old. This contradiction indicates the impact of the confounding variables. Given that the computed labour force participation rate was low on average compared with the official estimates from Pakistan FBS, the no significant impact result is somewhat surprising. This result also does not support the earlier findings of Ilahi and Grimard (2000) showing a significant impact on labour market time of better access to water supply, at least for women. Considering the prevailing high number of average hours worked, however, it would be more difficult for the project to generate a significant effect. Hence, no significant result is plausibly less surprising. Appendix 7 shows the full estimation results.

Table 9.   Impact on labour force participation and work hours.

Labor supply impact	Impact estimate	Significance level
Labor force participation rate (respondents proportion with job)		
10 years and above	(0.006)[a]	0.489
11–17 years	(0.014)[a]	0.136
18–24 years	(0.018)[a]	0.354
Hours worked per week		
10 years and above	0.613[b]	0.719
11–17 years	59.013[b]	0.899
18–24 years	(98.986)[b]	0.388

Note: ( ) = negative.
[a]Marginal effects.
[b]Coefficients.

Impact on broad socio-economic groups

The impact of a project on different socio-economic groups is seldom uniform. It is therefore important to know how the impact varies across socio-economic groups. To measure the impact of the projects on different socio-economic groups, the treatment variable was interacted with the socio-economic group dummy variables[30] such as the education attainment of the household head.[31] To represent different socio-economic status levels, education of the household head was divided into three subgroups: up to Grade Five or primary; Grade Six to Grade 10 or middle and high school; and Grade 11 and above or post-high school.

The estimation results show an interesting finding. For instance, in the case of health, while the average impact on diarrhoea incidence for all ages was insignificant, the disaggregated estimates shows it was significantly positive for the lowest socio-economic group, and became negative and significant for the middle group and insignificant for the highest socio-economic groups (Table 10). The contrasting impact across socio-economic groups led to the insignificant pooled estimate. This means that the benefits from the projects in terms of reducing diarrhoea incidence was only realised by higher socio-economic groups, particularly the middle class, but not for the lower socio-economic group. This result differs from Gross et al. (1989), who found no differential impact of water supply on diarrhoea between lower and upper income groups. The disaggregated estimates also show no significant impact on diarrhoea incidence for children younger than five years of age, and on the duration of diarrhoea for all the socio-economic groups. The insignificant average impact on these variables therefore implies insignificance for all socio-economic groups. Drudgery, on the other hand, however, was found to be highly significant for the lowest socio-economic group, but not significant for the middle and weakly significant for the top most socio-economic group. The full estimation results are given in Appendix 8.

A positive impact on school attendance was observed for the upper socio-economic groups. For the lower socio-economic groups, the impact was either significant negative or insignificant (Table 11). In the case of households with children refusing to go to school because of lack of clean water, however, the significant negative effect was only valid among the lowest socio-economic groups. For the upper socio-economic groups, the impact was insignificant. The insignificance of the impact on children refusing to go to

Table 10.   Impact on health by socio-economic group.

Health impact	Marginal effects on socio-economic group		
	Lowest	Middle	Highest
A. Waterborne disease			
Diarrhea incidence, All	0.005	(0.01)[a]	(0.00)
Diarrhea incidence, 5 and under	0.009	(0.02)	0.01
Diarrhea sick days, All	0.813	1.133	1.092
Diarrhea sick days, 5 and under	0.943	0.821	0.983
B. Drudgery			
Pain from fetching water	(0.039)[b]	(0.011)	(0.037)

Note: ( ) = negative.
[a] Signifcance at 5 per cent level.
[b] Significance at 1 per cent level.

Table 11.   Impact on education by socio-economic group, marginal effects.

Impact on school enrolment	Marginal effects on socio-economic group		
	Lowest	Middle	Highest
All (by age group)			
6–24 years	(0.054)	0.106[a]	0.043
6–10 years	(0.004)	0.098[a]	(0.029)
11–13 years	0.006	0.118[a]	(0.023)
14–17 years	(0.010)	0.148[a]	0.044
18–24 years	(0.082)[a]	0.144[a]	0.108[b]
Female			
6–24 years	(0.032)	0.079[b]	0.031
6–10 years	(0.030)	0.133[a]	0.006
11–13 years	0.074	0.037	(0.157)
14–17 years	(0.003)	0.200[a]	0.090
18–24 years	(0.067)[b]	0.053	0.090
Male			
6–24 years	(0.009)	0.120[a]	0.015
6–10 years	0.002	0.122	(0.023)
11–13 years	(0.117)	0.187[b]	0.020
14–17 years	(0.011)	0.313[a]	0.153
18–24 years	(0.068)	0.156[b]	0.136
Household reporting children not going to school due to lack of water (proportion)	(0.021)[b]	0.009	(0.003)
Household reporting children not going to school due to lack of toilet (proportion)	(0.013)	0.005	(0.002)

Note: ( ) = negative.
[a] Significance at 1 per cent level.
[b] Significance at 5 per cent level.

school due to lack of toilet facility was true for all socio-economic groups. Appendix 9 provides full estimation results.

Finally, in terms of the impact on the labour supply, the overall insignificant impact masks the significant negative impact on both having a job and average hours worked for children aged 11–17 and 18–24 for the middle socio-economic group (Table 12). For this socio-economic group, the projects reduced the probability of having a job for the

Table 12.   Impact on labour supply by socio-economic group.

Labor supply impact	Marginal effects on socio-economic group		
	Lowest	Middle	Highest
Labor force participation rate (Respondents proportion with job)			
10 years and above	0.001	(0.020)	0.003
11–17 years	0.002	(0.038)[a]	(0.013)
18–24 years	0.022	(0.098)[a]	(0.021)
Hours worked per week			
10 years and above	0.793	0.348	(2.265)
11–17 years	25.790	(14.168)[b]	(30.982)
18–24 years	(95.982)	(0.405)	(0.833)

Note: ( ) = negative.
[a]Significance at 1 per cent level.
[b]Significance at 5 per cent level.

11–17 years age group by 3.8 per cent and reduced average work hours per week by 14 hours. The projects also reduced the employed proportion of 18–24 age group for the same socio-economic group by 9.8 per cent. However, for both the lowest and highest socio-economic groups there are no significant impacts. Full estimation results are presented in Appendix 10.

Summary and conclusions

This study aimed to provide estimates on the impact of rural WSS projects in Punjab, Pakistan. In doing so, it reviewed the relevant literature, presented an evaluation framework for estimation methodology and designs and implemented household and community surveys based on an ex-post treatment–comparison group design. The survey covered 230 villages (115 each for treatment and comparison groups), and 2602 households (1301 each) in seven out of 30 districts of Punjab included in the project. The treatment and comparison villages were matched based on four pre-intervention village indicators, namely: population size; absence of potable water source; geographic area of the village; and literacy rate. The impact estimation methodology included a comparison of means or proportions and treatment effect estimation using a control function approach following Wooldridge (2002).

The main findings suggest that the project had clear and large impacts on the intermediate outcomes – such as access to water supply, but a more limited and tentative impact on final outcomes, such as on health, education, and labour supply. The project had drastically changed the sources of water in project areas; increasing the proportion of households with piped water; and reducing their reliance on hand pump, tube well, or borehole. As a result, the time spent and the distances travelled to fetch the water reduced significantly. The impact on sanitation indicators, however, was negligible, which somehow reflects the very minimal allocation to the hygiene and other project components relative to the allocation for civil works, equipment, and materials that absorbed almost 90 per cent of project resources.

The positive impact of the project on health was consistently revealed in the drudgery or pain from fetching water. The project reduced the proportion of household members complaining of pains from fetching water. The impact on diarrhoea incidence and severity turned out to be statistically insignificant although there were specific cases where a significant reduction was found for diarrhoea incidence among the middle socio-economic class. There was also a clear impact on school attendance for girls of high school age but not for boys. On the labour force participation and work hours, the projects on average had no significant impact, although, at the disaggregate level, a significant impact was found in the middle socio-economic group. Thus, the higher attendance rates did not appear to have come from the withdrawal of working children from the labour force. The reduction of time spent in fetching water rather than the reduction in labour force participation appeared to be one of the explanations for the significant improvement in the attendance rate for high school-age children in project villages. The lack of impact on labour force participation and work hours indicated that the time saved from fetching water documented in the study had not been translated either into increased labour force participation or in increased hours worked.

The analysis also revealed that impact on the different socio-economic groups had some regressive effects on diarrhoea and school attendance but a progressive effect on drudgery and on the refusal to attend school due to lack of water facilities. For instance, overall, the impact of the projects on diarrhoea incidence and duration was insignificant but was found to have a negative impact in the higher income group but a significantly positive effect in the bottom socio-economic group. Only the impact on drudgery was found to favour the lower socio-economic group, with projects resulting in significant reduction in the proportion of households with members complaining of pain from fetching water among the poorest income group. A similar regressive effect was also found in school attendance. The impact on the poorest group was either negative or statistically insignificant. The positive impact was only clear among the better-off households. Again, the pro-poor impact was observed in the proportion of households with children refusing to go to school because of lack of clean water. Like in the case of drudgery, a significant reduction was only found among the poorest households. Finally, the impact on the reduction of work participation of children 11–17 age groups (middle and high school) was found to be only true for the richer households and insignificant for the poorer households.

The absence of baseline data guided the study to use the with-and-without project (single-difference method) rather than the difference-in-difference method to measure the impact. Given this method, the comparison households were, in a sense, 'synthetic' control rather than 'real' control households. While differences of the treatment and comparison households were minimised by controlling for relevant individual, household, and community characteristics, the unobserved differences could not be controlled for. With baseline data, the impact of time-invariant unobservable characteristics can be removed.[32] This constituted the primary limitation of the study. If rigorous evaluation has to be undertaken, the generation of valid baseline data for the treatment and comparison groups should be included in the project design.

Policy implications

The study findings suggest that there is a need for a two-pronged approach to the provision of WSS in the rural areas. Not all households can afford to front up the minimum amount required to access piped water connection to their dwellings and hence would benefit from the provision of public good such as community taps and sanitation facilities. Similarly, in order to bring about tangible sanitation impact, there is a need for concerted effort with due emphasis on investment in sanitation and associated education to local residents so that they can benefit from positive health impacts. Furthermore, economic benefit from time-saving varies from one country and cultural context to another. In a country such as Pakistan, such benefits are less likely as women and girls in particular are stretched in working longer hours in various household activities and any freed up time from fetching water from distant places is used for rest and/or social networking. Positive benefits in terms of education for the high-school-age girls suggest that there is a need for effectively linking access to the learning facilities in the rural areas. Moreover, the provision of rural water supply and sanitation project designs need to be flexible to suit various socio-economic and demographic groups to ensure tangible economic, social and environmental impacts.

Acknowledgements

The views expressed in this paper are those of the authors and do not necessarily reflect views or policies of the Asian Development Bank.

Notes

1. WSS interventions are critical to the achievement of Millennium Development Goal No 7: ensure environmental sustainability with its two indicators of access to improved water source and access to improved sanitation. The latest estimate for the Asia-Pacific region revealed that 18 out of the 38 countries are off-track in providing the rural population with access to safe water, and 17 out of the 32 are off-track in providing rural areas with access to basic sanitation (United Nations 2008).
2. The linear fit is better compared with a quadratic form for the distance variable.
3. More than 70 per cent of project resources are for civil works, and around 10–13 per cent are for equipment and materials. The more intensive institutional strengthening in the PCWSSP, as described in the project document, is not reflected in the actual disbursements. In fact, the allocated resources for this are relatively lower in the PCWSSP than that in the PRWSSP (that is, 1.1 per cent vs. 9.7 per cent).
4. These community organisations were called water user committees in the PRWSS and community-based organisations in the PCWSS.
5. There are more WSS than only water supply subprojects (58 per cent vs. 42 per cent), and about 80 per cent of the subprojects were new construction, while the remaining 20 per cent are rehabilitation, which were all funded in the PCWSSP. The rehabilitation projects were completed later than the new projects; that is, they have been in the community for 33 and 63 months, respectively. Most projects have been with the community for less than three years. The PRWSSPs handed over about 87 months ago, while the average for PCWSSPs is 34 months. The water supply subprojects were completed later (48 months), compared with the WSS (67 months).
6. The gold standard is of course a randomised experiment, where treatment and control groups are randomly assigned. Unfortunately, this approach could not be implemented since the study was conducted ex post. Another desirable counterfactual could have been baseline data for both treatment and comparison areas, so that one can use a double-difference method to control for the impact of not only the differences in observable characteristics but also the time-invariant unobservable differences.
7. Had more village-level data been available, propensity scores based on project participation using the variables could have been computed and used to match villages. Given the limited available indicators at the village level, matching draws also from knowledge of the local survey firm were employed to conduct the survey.
8. The superiority of pre-implementation village-level data over post-implementation data as matching variables was discussed in this paper. The obvious reason is that post-intervention data may have already been affected by the project.
9. Jalan and Ravallion (2001) and Rubin (1973) also show the superiority of estimation using differences in matched samples over that of using un-matched samples.

10. The propensity score matching at the household level could not be implemented due to lack of a large scale survey data in the study area that could have been used to provide statistically matching households.

11. It has been pointed out that the validity of this method is dependent on the similarity of the project and comparison households except for the presence of the project as in the case of a randomised experiment. When project and comparison households are not identical then the difference in outcomes includes also the effect of other characteristics. To generate an unbiased estimate, control for these other characteristics needed to be done, specifically in a multiple regression framework.

12. Rubin (1973) shows the superiority of estimation using differences in matched samples.

13. Demeaning a variable means that instead of using the original values of the variable, the difference between the actual and mean values of the variable is used. The term was adopted from Woodridge (2002). For any variable x, the demeaned value is $(x - \bar{x})$ where $\bar{x}$ is the mean of x.

14. It gives the likelihood of having the treatment given the values of independent variables. In estimating the propensity score, first one estimates a probit (or logit) model using the treatment dummy as a dependent variable and a set of explanatory variables. The predicted values of the probability of treatment using the estimated model are the estimated propensity scores.

15. This is known as the propensity score approach. Wooldridge (2002) argues that for continuous variables neither the linear nor the propensity score method dominates the other. Therefore, one can use both methods for continuous dependent variables. However, to arrive at the estimation form for linear models (Equation (4)), the linearity of $E(y|\mathbf{X})$ is assumed. This is non-tenable for non-linear models, hence the propensity score method is recommended (Woodridge 2002, p. 637). In estimating propensity score, first one estimates a probit (or logit) model using the treatment dummy as a dependent variable and a set of explanatory variables. The predicted values of the probability of treatment using the estimated model are the estimated propensity scores.

16. Under specific assumptions, the estimate of the average treatment effect can be derived from the generic expression: $E(y|\mathbf{X}, t = 1) - E(y|\mathbf{X}, t = 0)$. Note that no functional assumption is made here so that this is valid for any consistent estimate of y, be it linear or non-linear (Wooldridge 2002).

17. One can use the households with piped water as the treatment to generate the treatment on the treated effect. However, this is clearly an endogenous treatment variable. Estimation for endogenous treatment would require instrumental variable estimation for linear models; instrumental variables probit for discrete outcomes (Wooldridge 2002); and instrumental variables/generalised method of moments (GMM) approach for count models (Cameron and Trivedi 2005). The presence of the project in the village is a good instrument. It satisfies the conditions for instruments, namely: directly related to the treatment, and not related to the error term of the primary equation.

18. Since there were only very few sanitation only schemes, these were not considered separately in the sampling. The other project's feature such as hygiene education, capacity-building and livelihood activities were not applied because of their limited size and scope. The actual disbursement data revealed that hygiene education received less than 1 per cent; capacity-building accounted for about 10 per cent in PRWSS and only 1 per cent in PCWSS; and SUPER introduced only in the second phase received less than 1 per cent of project resources.

19. The results support claims made in the completion report for the PCWSSP that the project was highly effective in producing outputs (ADB 2008, para. 28), notwithstanding the *less efficient* rating of the PRWSSP.

20. The literature usually focuses on the diarrhoea incidence among children under five years of age; see, for instance, IEG (2008).

21. Available from: http://www.statpak.gov.pk/depts/fbs/statistics/pslm2006_07 and http://www.statpak.gov.pk/depts/fbs/statistics/pslm2006_07/pslm2006_07.html

22. The estimate of the Demographic and Health Survey 2006–2007 of diarrhoea incidence for children below six years of age with the last two weeks as the reference period is 22 per cent for all of Pakistan and 21 per cent for Punjab province.

23. See Mosley and Chen (1984) for a general framework discussing how personal, households and community characteristics determine the child morbidity and mortality outcomes.

24. In the first step, propensity scores for having a project with personal, household and community characteristics mentioned earlier as determinants are estimated, which are used as a

control function in the estimation of the primary equation. The propensity score estimate, aside from generating the control function, describes the characteristics of households in project vis-à-vis those in non-project villages ex post or at the time of the survey. While the comparison of means/proportions shown earlier are bivariate in nature, here it will be multivariate; that is, regression estimates are partial effects that already include the effects of all the other determinants.

25. There is no similar claim in the PCR of the PRWSSP.
26. This is a probit regression and the impact of the project is given the marginal effect.
27. Using the proportion of school-age children attending school as the dependent variable is closer to the spirit of the Becker and Lewis (1973) framework. Treating school attendance as individual decisions, by implication, adds the assumption of independence of the decision for each child in the same household.
28. There is no similar claim in the PCR for the PRWSSP.
29. Available from: http://www.statpak.gov.pk/depts/fbs/publications/lfs2006_07/lfs2006_07.html
30. Another way of estimating the impact by socio-economic group is to estimate separate equations by group. Orr (1997) argues that jointly estimating the impact using group dummies is superior because it provides more power because it uses the full sample to estimate the coefficients, and because it allows one to test whether there are statistically significant differences in impact among the subgroups taken as a set (rather than between pairs or subgroups).
31. Admittedly, income or expenditure is the more popular indicator of socio-economic status. Using it, however, will be problematic because it is endogenous. Education of the household head, on the other hand, is highly correlated with household income but can be considered exogenous because it is most likely to be earned before the project intervention.
32. Had there been a baseline, differencing could have removed the impact of unobserved characteristics; at least those that are deemed time invariant.

References

ADB, 1994. *Report and recommendation of the President to the board of directors: proposed loan to the Islamic Republic of Pakistan for the Punjab Rural Water Supply and Sanitation Project.* Manila: Asian Development Bank.

ADB, 2002. *Report and recommendation of the President to the board of directors: proposed loan to the Islamic Republic of Pakistan for the Punjab Community Water Supply and Sanitation Sector Project.* Manila: Asian Development Bank.

ADB, 2003. *Completion report: Punjab Rural Water Supply and Sanitation (Sector) Project in the Islamic Republic of Pakistan.* Manila: Asian Development Bank.

ADB, 2008. *Completion report: Punjab Community Water Supply and Sanitation Sector Project in the Islamic Republic of Pakistan.* Manila: Asian Development Bank.

Banerjee, A. and Duflo, E., 2007. The economic lives of the poor. *Journal of economic perspectives,* 21 (1), 141–167.

Becker, G., 1965. A theory of the allocation of time. *Economic journal,* 75, 493–517.

Becker, G. and Lewis, H.G., 1973. On the interaction between the quantity and quality of children. *Journal of political economy,* 81 (2), S279–S288.

Blackden, C. and Wodon, Q., eds, 2006. *Gender, time use, and poverty in sub-Saharan Africa.* Washington, DC: World Bank, Working Paper 73.

Burrows, G., Acton, J. and Maunder, T., 2004. *Water and sanitation: the education drain.* London: WaterAid. Available from: www.wateraid.org/documents/education20report.pdf

Cairncross, S. and Valdamanis, V., 2006. Water supply, sanitation and hygiene promotion. *In*: D. Jamison, J. Breman and A. Measham, eds. *Disease control priorities in developing countries.* 2nd ed. New York: Oxford University Press, 771–792.

Cameron, A. and Trivedi, P., 2005. *Microeconometrics: methods and applications.* Cambridge: Cambridge University Press.

Carvalho, S. and White, H., 2004. Theory-based evaluation: the case of social funds. *American journal of evaluation,* 25 (2), 141–160.

Dutta, S., 2005. *Energy as a key variable in eradicating extreme poverty and hunger: a gender and energy perspective on empirical evidence on MDG #1.* DFID/ENERGIA Project on Gender as a Key Variable in Energy Interventions. Draft version, September.

Fewtrell, L. and Colford, J., 2004. *Water, sanitation and hygiene: interventions and diarrhoea: a systematic review and meta analysis*. Washington, DC: World Bank, Health Nutrition and Population DP No. 34960.

Gronau, R., 1977. Leisure, home production, and work: theory of the allocation of time revisited. *Journal of political economy*, 85, 1099–1123.

Gross, R., Schell, B., Molina, M.C., Leao, M.A. and Strack, U., 1989. The impact of improvement of water supply and sanitation facilities on diarrhoea and intestinal parasites: a Brazilian experience with children in two low-income urban communities. *Revista de saude publica*, 23 (3), 214–220.

Hutton, G., Haller, L. and Bartram, J., 2006. *Economic and health effects of increasing coverage of low-cost water and sanitation interventions*. New York: United Nations Development Programme, Human Development Report Office Occasional Paper 2006/33.

IEG, 2008. *What works in water supply and sanitation? Lessons from impact evaluation*. Independent Evaluation Group. Washington, DC: World Bank.

Ilahi, N. and Grimard, F., 2000. Public infrastructure and private costs: water supply and time allocation of women in rural Pakistan. *Economic development and cultural change*, 48 (4), 45–75.

Jalan, J. and Ravallion, M., 2001. *Does piped water reduce diarrhoea for children in rural India?* Washington, DC: World Bank, Working Paper Series 2664.

Jalan, J. and Ravallion, M., 2003. Does piped water reduce diarrhoea for children in rural India? *Journal of econometrics*, 112, 153–173.

Khandker, S., 1996. *Education achievements and school efficiency in rural Bangladesh*. Washington, DC: World Bank, Discussion Paper 319.

Kremer, M., Leino, J., Miguel, E. and Zwane, A., 2007. Spring cleaning: a randomized evaluation of source water quality improvement. Paper presented at the Eleventh BREAD Conference on development economics, 5–6 October, London School of Economics.

Kumar M. and Snel, M., 2000. School sanitation and hygiene education in Mysore district. *Waterlines*, 19 (2), 16–18.

Mosley, H. and Chen, L., 1984. An analytical framework for the study of child survival in developing countries. *Population and development review*, 10, 25–45.

Orr, L., 1997. Social *experimentation: evaluating public programs with experimental methods*. Washington, DC: Department of Human Services.

Papke, L. and Wooldridge, J., 1996. Econometric methods for fractional response variables with an application to 401(k) plan participation rates. *Journal of applied econometrics*, 11, 619–632.

Pattanayak, S., Poulos, C., Wendland, K.M., Patil, S.R., Yang, Jui-Chen, Kwok, R.K. and Gorey, C.G., 2007. *Informing the water and sanitation sector policy: case study of an impact evaluation study of water supply, sanitation and hygiene interventions in rural Maharastra, India*. RTI Working Paper 06–04. Research Triangle, NC: Research Triangle Park.

Rubin, D., 1973. The use of matched sampling and regression adjustment to remove bias in observational studies. *Biometrics*, 29, 159–183.

Semenza, J., Roberts, L., Henderson, A., Bogan, J. and Rubin, C. 1998. Water distribution and diarrheal disease transmission: a case study in Uzbekistan. *American journal of tropical medicine and hygiene*, 59 (6), 941–946.

United Nations, 2008. *A future within reach. Regional Partnerships for the Millennium Development Goals in Asia and the Pacific*. New York: United Nations Economic and Social Commission for Asia and the Pacific/Asian Development Bank/United Nations Development Programme.

Wang, Z., Shepard, D.S., Zhu, Y.C., Cash, R.A., Zhao, R.J., Zhu, Z.X. and Shen, F., 1989. Reduction of enteric infectious disease in rural China by providing deep-well tap water. *Bulletin of the World Health Organization*, 67 (2), 171–180.

White, H. and Masset, E., 2007. Assessing interventions to improve child nutrition: a theory-based impact evaluation of the Bangladesh integrated nutrition project. *Journal of international development*, 19 (5), 627–652.

Wooldridge, J., 2002. *Econometric analysis of cross section and panel data*. Cambridge, MA: MIT Press.

Zwane, A. and Kremer, M., 2007. What works in fighting diarrhoea diseases in developing countries? A critical review. *World Bank research observer*, 22 (1), 1–24.

Appendix 1. Personal and household characteristics of treatment and comparison groups

Variables	Project		Non-project		Diff.	T	Sig. level
	Mean	Freq.	Mean	Freq.			
A. Personal characteristics							
Age, All	25.376	7682	25.295	7520	0.081	0.277	0.782
Male, All (proportion)	0.526	7682	0.525	7520	0.001	0.113	0.910
Education (in years), 5 years and above	5.066	6919	4.791	6863	0.275	3.757	0.000
B. Household characteristics							
Characteristics of household head							
Age	46.324	1293	45.958	1296	0.366	0.681	0.496
Male (proportion)	0.952	1293	0.943	1296	0.009	1.043	0.297
Education (in years)	5.719	1287	5.529	1290	0.189	1.032	0.302
Household size	5.893	1293	5.760	1296	0.133	1.425	0.154
Expenditures (rupees)							
Health exp., per capita[a]	47.011	885	46.805	932	0.207	0.029	0.977
Education exp., per attending child[a]	327.880	605	311.817	628	16.063	0.822	0.411
Total expenditure, per capita	1,560.025	1293	1,542.904	1296	17.121	0.492	0.623
Occupation of household head (proportion)							
Professional	0.048	1301	0.049	1301	−0.001	−0.091	0.928
Service	0.288	1301	0.301	1301	−0.012	−0.688	0.492
Agricuture	0.449	1301	0.437	1301	0.012	0.592	0.554
Crafts, mach operators, assemblers	0.045	1301	0.040	1301	0.005	0.584	0.559
Unskilled	0.170	1301	0.173	1301	−0.003	−0.208	0.835
Sector household head working (proportion)							
Agriculture	0.447	1301	0.441	1301	0.005	0.276	0.782
Industry	0.167	1301	0.179	1301	−0.012	−0.829	0.407
Services	0.186	1301	0.169	1301	0.017	1.128	0.259
Not specified	0.058	1301	0.065	1301	−0.007	−0.736	0.462
Housing							
No of rooms in house	3.274	1301	3.047	1301	0.228	4.188	0.000
No of rooms for sleeping	2.303	1301	2.168	1301	0.135	3.458	0.001
With finished floor (proportion)	0.572	1301	0.510	1301	0.061	3.152	0.002
structured roof	0.906	1301	0.912	1301	−0.005	−0.477	0.634
structured wall	0.906	1301	0.912	1301	−0.005	−0.477	0.634
Own house (proportion)	0.984	1301	0.978	1301	0.006	1.142	0.253
Use elec, gas & kerosene for cooking (prop.)	0.077	1301	0.062	1301	0.015	1.464	0.143
Has electricity (proportion)	0.965	1301	0.972	1301	−0.006	−0.898	0.370

[a]Substantial number of households did not provide breakdown on expenditure.
Source: Socio-economic survey, 2008.

Appendix 2. Community characteristics of treatment and comparison groups

Variables	Project		Non-project		Diff.	T	Sig. level
	Mean	Freq.	Mean	Freq.			
A. School							
With (proportion):							
Primary school	0.974	115	0.870	115	0.104	2.990	0.003
Middle school	0.461	115	0.426	115	0.035	0.529	0.597
High school	0.235	115	0.200	115	0.035	0.637	0.525
Vocational school	0.009	115	0.017	115	−0.009	−0.579	0.563
College/university	0.000	115	0.009	115	−0.009	−1.000	0.318
Distance to (in kms.):							
Primary school	0.078	115	0.443	115	−0.365	−2.881	0.004
Middle school	2.043	115	3.061	115	−1.017	−2.229	0.027
Secondary school	5.043	115	5.365	115	−0.322	−0.494	0.622
Vocational school	19.183	115	19.456	114	−0.274	−0.148	0.883
College/university	22.843	115	23.809	115	−0.965	−0.382	0.703
B. Health facilities							
With (proportion):							
Maternal and child health centers	0.211	114	0.149	114	0.061	1.206	0.229
Basic health unit	0.191	115	0.184	114	0.007	0.137	0.891
Rural health center	0.044	114	0.035	115	0.009	0.352	0.725
Dispensary	0.148	115	0.113	115	0.035	0.781	0.436
Hospital	0.000	114	0.017	115	−0.017	−1.414	0.159
Distance to (in kms.):							
MCH centers	5.500	114	6.460	113	−0.960	−1.127	0.261
BHU	5.217	115	6.430	114	−1.212	−1.559	0.120
RHC	9.982	114	11.009	115	−1.026	−0.974	0.331
Dispensary	6.878	115	7.239	113	−0.361	−0.395	0.694
Hospital	19.219	114	18.667	114	0.553	0.321	0.749
C. Water system							
With water system (proportion)	0.922	115	0.078	115	0.843	23.710	0.000
Percentage served by:[a]							
Water system	72.500	115	5.765	115	66.735	19.900	0.000
Deep well	3.835	115	5.730	115	−1.896	−0.871	0.385
Hand pumps	24.391	115	54.087	115	−29.696	−7.202	0.000
Tubewell	40.000	115	24.522	115	15.478	3.461	0.001
Shallow well	0.348	115	0.174	115	0.174	0.447	0.655
D. Other indicators							
With (proportion):							
Garbage disposal facility	0.009	115	0.009	115	0.000	0.000	1.000
Bus service	0.696	115	0.609	115	0.087	1.384	0.168
Taxi service	0.304	115	0.243	115	0.061	1.033	0.303
Motorbikes	0.530	115	0.539	115	−0.009	−0.132	0.895
Rikshaw	0.443	115	0.409	115	0.035	0.531	0.596
Electricity	0.983	115	0.983	115	0.000	0.000	1.000

(Continued)

Appendix 2. (*Continued*)

Variables	Project		Non-project		Diff.	T	Sig. level
	Mean	Freq.	Mean	Freq.			
Population							
Male	1893	115	2304	115	−411	−1.630	0.104
Female	1994	115	2332	115	−338	−1.393	0.165
Total	3887	115	4636	115	−749	−1.532	0.127
Number of households	392	114	441	113	−49	−1.001	0.318
Major sources of livelihood[b] (%)							
Crop production	61.009	115	60.870	115	0.139	0.059	0.953
Livestock	11.930	115	12.304	115	−0.374	−0.211	0.833
Manufacturing goods	3.191	115	2.583	115	0.609	0.429	0.669
Trading	16.722	115	14.391	115	2.330	0.843	0.400
Laborer	8.809	115	10.209	115	−1.400	−0.977	0.329

[a]No community served by artesian well or commercial refill station.
[b]No community dependent on fisheries.
Source: Socio-economic survey, 2008.

Appendix 3. First-stage probit estimates: probability of having project for health impact

Variables	First stage, indiv.		First stage, HH	
	Coeff.	Sig. level	Coeff.	Sig. level
Personal characteristics				
Age	(0.004)	0.070		
Age squared	0.000	0.039		
Male	0.000	0.997		
Education (in years)	(0.002)	0.422		
Household characteristics				
Male, household head (HH)	0.001	0.992	0.008	0.954
Age, HH	(0.003)	0.571	(0.007)	0.514
Age square, HH	0.000	0.347	0.000	0.399
Education (in years), HH	0.002	0.000	0.002	0.067
Household size	0.013	0.006	0.004	0.738
Professional, HH	(0.173)	0.031	(0.237)	0.212
Services, HH	(0.010)	0.875	(0.094)	0.555
Agriculture, HH	0.141	0.000	0.083	0.391
Crafts, mach operators, assemblers, HH	(0.083)	0.331	(0.074)	0.709
Industry, HH	0.156	0.025	0.205	0.229
Services sector, HH	0.331	0.000	0.347	0.040
Not specified sector, HH	0.096	0.226	0.154	0.438
No of rooms in house	0.073	0.000	0.056	0.007
With finished floor	0.230	0.000	0.220	0.000
With structured roof	(0.172)	0.000	(0.203)	0.052
Own house	0.023	0.776	0.150	0.440
Mother tongue Punjabi	(0.075)	0.053	(0.068)	0.472

(*Continued*)

Appendix 3. (*Continued*)

Variables	First stage, indiv.		First stage, HH	
	Coeff.	Sig. level	Coeff.	Sig. level
Community characteristics				
With primary school	(0.057)	0.550	0.059	0.847
middle school	(0.297)	0.000	(0.213)	0.011
high school	0.350	0.000	0.312	0.002
Distance to primary school (kms)	(0.419)	0.000	(0.408)	0.000
middle school (kms)	(0.088)	0.000	(0.071)	0.000
high school (kms)	0.029	0.000	0.029	0.000
With Maternal and Child Health	0.580	0.000	0.543	0.000
(MCH) centers				
basic health unit	(0.432)	0.000	(0.401)	0.000
rural health center	0.439	0.000	0.435	0.003
dispensary	0.624	0.000	0.638	0.000
Distance to MCH centers (kms)	(0.006)	0.095	(0.012)	0.168
basic health unit (kms)	(0.047)	0.000	(0.038)	0.000
rural health center (kms)	0.009	0.000	0.007	0.165
dispensary (kms)	0.027	0.000	0.024	0.000
With bus service	0.153	0.000	0.205	0.002
motor cycle service	(0.018)	0.506	0.002	0.971
rikshaw service	(0.113)	0.000	(0.150)	0.018
Total population	0.004	0.322	0.011	0.311
Prop of hh on crop production	0.000	0.989	0.000	0.841
on livestock production	(0.006)	0.000	(0.007)	0.004
in manuf. of goods	0.021	0.000	0.023	0.000
who are laborers	(0.006)	0.000	(0.006)	0.092
Village ave. per capita income	0.162	0.000	0.136	0.045
Bhawalpur	1.148	0.000	1.194	0.000
Chakwal	0.792	0.000	0.945	0.000
DGKhan	1.174	0.000	1.193	0.000
Faisalabad	0.842	0.000	0.839	0.000
RYKhan	1.051	0.000	1.127	0.000
Sargodha	1.073	0.000	1.132	0.000
Constance	(1.269)	0.000	(1.374)	0.006
Sample	14,597		2,511	
Pseudo $R2$	0.124		0.116	

Source: Analysis of survey data.

Appendix 4. Impact on health indicators: diarrhoea and drudgery

Variables	Diarrhea, all			Diarrhea, 5 and under			Diarrhea sick days, all			Diarrhea sick days, 5 and under			With family member suffering pain from fetching water		
	Coeff.	Sig. level	Mar. eff.	Coeff.	Sig. level	Mar. eff.	Coeff.	Sig. level	IRR	Coeff.	Sig. level	IRR	Coeff.	Sig. level	Mar. eff.
Treatment (Have project=1)	0.034	0.521	0.002	0.026	0.812	0.003	(0.159)	0.167	0.853	(0.104)	0.727	0.901	(0.485)	0.000	(0.051)
Propensity score (PS)	0.193	0.312	0.008	(0.052)	0.882	(0.006)	0.074	0.823	1.077	(0.445)	0.508	0.641			
Treatment* (demeaned[a] PS)	(0.684)	0.014	(0.030)	(0.552)	0.311	(0.065)	0.738	0.172	2.091	1.546	0.246	4.694			
Propensity score (PS)													1.115	0.000	0.114
Treatment* (demeaned[a] PS)													(2.500)	0.000	(0.255)
Constant	(2.196)	0.000		(1.523)	0.000		1.185	0.000		1.075	0.004		(1.881)	0.000	
Sample	14,597			1,588			260			95			2,511		
Pseudo R2	0.003			0.003			0.007			0.009			0.054		
Estimation	Probit			Probit			Poisson			Poisson			Probit		

[a]Variable-mean (variable).
Source: Analysis of survey data.

Appendix 5. Education: attendance by age group and by sex (estimation: GLM)

	6–24			6–10			11–13			14–17			18–24		
	Coeff.	Sig. level	Mar. eff.	Coeff.	Sig. level	Mar. eff.	Coeff.	Sig. level	Mar. eff.	Coeff.	Sig. level	Mar. eff.	Coeff.	Sig. level	Mar. eff.
Both sexes															
Treatment (Have project=1)	(0.033)	0.676	(0.008)	0.165	0.282	0.028	0.256	0.135	0.046	0.214	0.092	0.053	(0.102)	0.468	(0.016)
Propensity score (PS)	0.527	0.043	0.132	0.375	0.399	0.063	0.798	0.101	0.143	0.488	0.242	0.121	1.410	0.002	0.215
Treatment*(demeaned[a] PS)	(0.069)	0.869	(0.017)	(0.258)	0.742	(0.043)	0.497	0.575	0.089	(0.129)	0.847	(0.032)	(0.667)	0.369	(0.102)
Constant	(0.244)	0.049		1.045	0.000		0.627	0.007		(0.123)	0.532		(2.111)	0.000	
Sample	2184.000			1058.000			869.000			1053.000			1293.000		
Chi-square	6.457			2.762			12.280			7.532			10.944		
Significance level	0.091			0.430			0.006			0.057			0.012		
Female															
Treatment (Have project=1)	0.009	0.929	0.002	0.103	0.610	0.019	0.355	0.136	0.068	0.336	0.061	0.084	(0.288)	0.164	(0.036)
Propensity score (PS)	0.228	0.471	0.057	0.404	0.513	0.073	0.615	0.350	0.119	(0.375)	0.523	(0.094)	1.439	0.022	0.178
Treatment*(demeaned[a] PS)	0.413	0.412	0.103	(0.831)	0.412	(0.150)	0.280	0.810	0.054	0.936	0.316	0.234	0.256	0.815	0.032
Constant	(0.307)	0.042		0.950	0.001		0.540	0.090		(0.056)	0.837		(2.380)	0.000	
Sample	1737.000			611.000			447.000			592.000			872.000		
Chi-square	3.998			1.001			6.640			5.594			8.832		
Significance level	0.262			0.801			0.084			0.133			0.032		
Male															
Treatment (Have project=1)	0.152	0.163	0.038	0.238	0.437	0.038	(0.511)	0.475	(0.072)	0.466	0.113	0.110	0.052	0.843	0.008
Propensity score (PS)	0.574	0.103	0.142	0.591	0.520	0.095	(1.064)	0.627	(0.147)	1.214	0.207	0.288	1.936	0.068	0.296
Treatment*(demeaned[a] PS)	(0.343)	0.546	(0.084)	0.319	0.832	0.052	(2.095)	0.533	(0.290)	(0.623)	0.676	(0.148)	(0.963)	0.510	(0.147)
Constant	(0.117)	0.491		0.942	0.029		2.462	0.011		(0.347)	0.423		(2.474)	0.000	
Sample	1,310			284			83			240			398		
Chi-square	7.407			2.369			4.295			7.286			4.517		
Significance level	0.060			0.500			0.231			0.063			0.211		

[a]Variable-mean (variable).
GLM: Fractional Logit (Papke and Wooldridge 1996).

Appendix 6. Children refusing to go to school due to lack of water and toilet facilities (probit estimates)

	Refused to go to school due to lack of water			Refused to go to school due to poor toilet		
	Coeff.	Sig. level	Mar. eff.	Coeff.	Sig. level	Mar. eff.
Treatment (Have project=1)	(0.291)	0.006	(0.018)	(0.121)	0.205	(0.011)
Propensity score (PS)	0.955	0.008	0.059	0.698	0.041	0.064
Treatment*(demeaned[a] PS)	(2.007)	0.004	(0.124)	(0.643)	0.252	(0.059)
Constant	(2.197)	0.000		(1.983)	0.000	
Sample	2511			2511		
Psuedo $R2$	0.031			0.006		

[a] Variable-mean (variable).

Appendix 7.   Economic impact: labour force participation rates and hours worked

Variables[a]	Have a job, all			Have a job, 11–17 yrs			Have a job, 18–24 yrs			Hours worked, all		Hours worked, 11–17		Hours worked
	Coeff.	Sig. level	Mar. eff.	Coeff.	Sig. level	Mar. eff.	Coeff.	Sig. level	Mar. eff.	Coeff.	Sig. level	Coeff.	Sig. level	Coeff.
Treatment (Have project=1)	(0.018)	0.489	(0.006)	(0.132)	0.136	(0.014)	(0.057)	0.354	(0.018)	0.613	0.719	59.013	0.899	(94.774)
Propensity score (PS)	0.071	0.413	0.025	0.013	0.963	0.001	0.032	0.873	0.010					
Treatment* (de-meaned[b] PS)	(0.275)	0.042	(0.096)	(0.466)	0.339	(0.048)	(0.616)	0.052	(0.195)					
Age										0.401	0.001	(14.377)	0.586	0.707
Age square										(0.004)	0.006	0.469	0.601	(0.009)
Male										9.571	0.000	48.079	0.017	15.232
Education (in years)										(0.095)	0.223	(1.795)	0.053	(0.046)
Male, Household head (HH)										1.632	0.373	1.694	0.897	(1.139)
Age, HH										(0.255)	0.059	0.653	0.460	(0.275)
Age square, HH										0.002	0.141	(0.004)	0.535	0.002
Education (in years), HH										(0.043)	0.000	(0.016)	0.883	(0.021)
Household size										0.360	0.020	0.525	0.723	0.899
Professional, HH										(7.365)	0.002			(1.559)
Services, HH										(4.740)	0.011			(3.763)
Professional and services, HH												8.852	0.478	
Agriculture, HH										(1.974)	0.152	(1.367)	0.862	(2.522)
Crafts, mach operators, assemblers, HH										(2.450)	0.289			10.333
Industry sector, HH										4.361	0.036			1.823
Services sector, HH										4.115	0.051			(3.934)
Not specified sector, HH										5.028	0.021			3.294
No of rooms in house										0.083	0.766	1.023	0.690	0.066
With finished floor										(1.549)	0.026	9.835	0.217	(6.022)
With structured roof										0.935	0.479	(4.109)	0.854	0.729
Own house										4.058	0.017			12.010
Mother tongue Punjabi										2.542	0.020	21.290	0.007	3.954
With primary school										6.447	0.009			5.782
middle school										(3.583)	0.001	9.102	0.517	(0.752)

(Continued)

Appendix 7. (*Continued*)

Variables[a]	Have a job, all			Have a job, 11–17 yrs			Have a job, 18–24 yrs			Hours worked, all		Hours worked, 11–17		Hours worked
	Coeff.	Sig. level	Mar. eff.	Coeff.	Sig. level	Mar. eff.	Coeff.	Sig. level	Mar. eff.	Coeff.	Sig. level	Coeff.	Sig. level	Coeff.
high school										(3.528)	0.022	15.754	0.174	(11.326)
Distance to primary school middle school										1.878	0.005	(1.105)	0.771	0.023
high school										(0.378)	0.003	1.199	0.448	0.461
With MCH centers basic health unit										0.004	0.968	(0.151)	0.823	(0.535)
rural health center										2.622	0.086	2.822	0.875	2.930
dispensary										1.451	0.375	(28.438)	0.154	8.478
Distance to MCH centers basic health unit										(2.390)	0.271	(14.262)	0.683	(1.768)
rural health center										5.381	0.000	7.591	0.636	11.488
dispensary										0.352	0.011	(0.768)	0.409	0.864
With bus service										(0.044)	0.757	(0.423)	0.756	(0.327)
mot or c ycle service										(0.265)	0.000	0.921	0.283	(0.176)
rikshaw service										(0.020)	0.843	0.251	0.815	(0.342)
Total population										3.101	0.000	19.776	0.115	4.873
Prop of hh on crop production										(2.260)	0.005	(8.100)	0.233	(3.176)
on livestock production										(1.144)	0.129	3.443	0.696	(2.261)
on manuf of goods										0.063	0.699	1.025	0.289	(0.554)
who are laborers										0.035	0.246	(0.003)	0.992	0.132
Village ave. per capita income										(0.251)	0.000	0.027	0.955	(0.470)
Bhawalpur										0.097	0.128	(0.688)	0.703	0.867
Chakwal										0.082	0.036	(0.122)	0.791	0.080
DGKhan										(0.702)	0.343	7.411	0.388	2.813
Faisalabad										17.301	0.000			21.157
RYKhan										0.140	0.947			1.226
Sargodha										5.830	0.035			10.283
Northern Districts										7.791	0.003			1.307
Treatment* demeaned[b] Age										4.635	0.066			8.235
Age square										10.017	0.000			10.972
Male												(8.767)	0.508	
Education (in years)										(0.086)	0.598	(3.388)	0.913	12.624
Male, Household head (HH)										0.001	0.597	0.109	0.919	(0.296)
										(1.377)	0.666	(42.811)	0.040	(7.963)
										0.092	0.400	2.574	0.018	(0.527)
										(1.711)	0.523	151.610	0.014	(0.665)

Age, HH	0.226	0.230	3.082	0.073	(0.231)
Age square, HH	(0.002)	0.220	(0.029)	0.073	0.002
Education (in years), HH	0.047	0.004	(0.227)	0.166	0.038
Household size	(0.339)	0.120	(1.250)	0.521	(0.368)
Professional, HH	6.361	0.111			(9.302)
Services, HH	6.495	0.049			(3.096)
Professional and services, HH			(3.027)	0.830	
Agriculture, HH	(1.363)	0.464	10.528	0.350	(1.379)
Crafts, mach operators, assemblers, HH	2.644	0.513			(23.078)
Industry sector, HH	(6.410)	0.083			4.623
Services sector, HH	(7.439)	0.038			6.661
Not specified sector, HH	(8.450)	0.022	(1.401)	0.670	(2.151)
No of rooms in house	0.036	0.920	(11.345)	0.221	(0.396)
With finished floor	2.739	0.006	51.690	0.054	9.142
With structured roof	3.915	0.028			3.800
Own house	(2.893)	0.224	(6.234)	0.514	(11.261)
Mother tongue Punjabi	0.479	0.749			3.183
With primary school	12.080	0.032			21.002

[a] Some determining variables are either removed or collapsed because of perfect prediction or collinearity.
[b] Variable-mean (variable).

Appendix 8. Impact on health by socio-economic group: diarrhoea and drudgery

	Diarrhea, all			Diarrhea, 5u			Diarrhea sick days, all			Diarrhea sick days, 5u			With family member suffering pain from fetching water		
	Coeff.	Sig. level	Mar. eff.	Coeff.	Sig. level	Mar. eff.	Coeff.	Sig. level	IRR	Coeff.	Sig. level	IRR	Coeff.	Sig. level	Mar. eff.
Treatment (Have project=1)	0.104	0.092	0.005	0.077	0.550	0.009	(0.208)	0.098	0.813	(0.058)	0.856	0.943	(0.388)	0.000	(0.039)
Treatment (Have project=1)*Class 6–10	(0.174)	0.027	(0.007)	(0.191)	0.220	(0.021)	0.125	0.499	1.133	(0.197)	0.649	0.821	(0.114)	0.447	(0.011)
Treatment (Have project=1)*At least Class 11	(0.086)	0.392	(0.004)	0.050	0.782	0.006	0.088	0.719	1.092	(0.018)	0.964	0.983	(0.538)	0.056	(0.037)
Propensity score (PS)	0.193	0.312	0.008	(0.052)	0.882	(0.006)	0.074	0.823	1.077	(0.445)	0.508	0.641			
Treatment* (demeaned[a] PS)	(0.622)	0.028	(0.027)	(0.502)	0.358	(0.059)	0.681	0.196	1.976	1.714	0.222	5.551			
Propensity score (PS)													1.115	0.000	0.111
Treatment* (demeaned[a] PS)													(2.362)	0.000	(0.235)
Constant	(2.196)	0.000		(1.523)	0.000		1.185	0.000		1.075	0.004		(1.881)	0.000	
Sample	14597			1588			260			95			2511		
Pseudo R2	0.005			0.006			0.008			0.010			0.058		
Estimation	Probit			Probit			Poisson			Poisson			Probit		

[a]Variable-mean (variable).

Appendix 9. Impact on school attendance by socio-economic group

Appendix A9.1. Education: attendance by age and socio-economic group.

Variables	6–24 Coeff.	6–24 Sig. level	6–24 Mar. eff.	6–10 Coeff.	6–10 Sig. level	6–10 Mar. eff.	11–13 Coeff.	11–13 Sig. level	11–13 Mar. eff.	14–17 Coeff.	14–17 Sig. level	14–17 Mar. eff.	18–24 Coeff.	18–24 Sig. level	18–24 Mar. eff.
Both sexes															
Treatment (Have project=1)	(0.217)	0.022	(0.054)	(0.025)	0.890	(0.004)	0.032	0.872	0.006	(0.039)	0.797	(0.010)	(0.540)	0.003	(0.082)
Treatment (Have project=1)*Class 6–10	0.426	0.000	0.106	0.665	0.005	0.098	0.759	0.006	0.118	0.622	0.001	0.148	0.828	0.000	0.144
Treatment (Have project=1)*At least Class 11	0.173	0.246	0.043	(0.168)	0.546	(0.029)	(0.127)	0.701	(0.023)	0.182	0.451	0.044	0.617	0.024	0.108
Propensity score (PS)	0.527	0.043	0.132	0.375	0.399	0.062	0.798	0.101	0.142	0.488	0.242	0.121	1.410	0.002	0.212
Treatment*(demeaned[a] PS)	(0.223)	0.596	(0.056)	(0.408)	0.606	(0.067)	0.395	0.660	0.070	(0.275)	0.685	(0.068)	(1.082)	0.154	(0.163)
Constant	(0.244)	0.049		1.045	0.000		0.627	0.007		(0.123)	0.532		(2.111)	0.000	
Sample	2,184			1,058			869			1,053			1,293		
Chi2	20.670			12.616			19.024			18.182			28.458		
Significance level	0.001			0.027			0.002			0.003			0.000		
Female															
Treatment (Have project=1)	(0.129)	0.264	(0.032)	(0.171)	0.461	(0.030)	0.390	0.191	0.074	(0.012)	0.955	(0.003)	(0.539)	0.038	(0.067)
Treatment (Have project=1)*Class 6–10	0.316	0.019	0.079	0.867	0.006	0.133	0.201	0.594	0.037	0.820	0.002	0.200	0.401	0.150	0.053
Treatment (Have project=1)*At least Class 11	0.124	0.491	0.031	0.031	0.932	0.006	(0.721)	0.108	(0.157)	0.363	0.278	0.090	0.613	0.101	0.090

(Continued)

Appendix A9.1. (*Continued*)

Variables	6–24 Coeff.	Sig. level	Mar. eff.	6–10 Coeff.	Sig. level	Mar. eff.	11–13 Coeff.	Sig. level	Mar. eff.	14–17 Coeff.	Sig. level	Mar. eff.	18–24 Coeff.	Sig. level	Mar. eff.
Propensity score (PS)	0.228	0.471	0.057	0.404	0.513	0.072	0.615	0.350	0.118	(0.375)	0.523	(0.094)	1.439	0.022	0.177
Treatment* (demeaned[a] PS)	0.306	0.548	0.076	(1.057)	0.301	(0.188)	0.427	0.723	0.082	0.741	0.444	0.185	(0.011)	0.992	(0.001)
Constant	(0.307)	0.042		0.950	0.001		0.540	0.090		(0.056)	0.837		(2.380)	0.000	
Sample	1,737			611			447			592			872		
Chi2	9.271			9.401			9.471			14.725			11.937		
Significance level	0.099			0.094			0.092			0.012			0.036		
Male															
Treatment (Have project=1)	(0.036)	0.785	(0.009)	0.011	0.974	0.002	(0.893)	0.251	(0.117)	(0.046)	0.889	(0.011)	(0.447)	0.212	(0.068)
Treatment (Have project=1)*Class 6–10	0.501	0.002	0.120	0.934	0.090	0.122	2.206	0.043	0.187	1.688	0.002	0.313	0.894	0.030	0.156
Treatment (Have project=1)* At least Class 11	0.062	0.762	0.015	(0.140)	0.808	(0.023)	0.168	0.895	0.020	0.725	0.217	0.153	0.759	0.122	0.136
Propensity score (PS)	0.574	0.103	0.141	0.591	0.520	0.094	(1.064)	0.627	(0.135)	1.214	0.207	0.284	1.936	0.068	0.291
Treatment* (demeaned[a] PS)	(0.504)	0.383	(0.124)	0.364	0.810	0.058	(5.462)	0.204	(0.694)	(1.169)	0.460	(0.274)	(1.581)	0.301	(0.238)
Constant	(0.117)	0.491		0.942	0.029		2.462	0.011		(0.347)	0.423		(2.474)	0.000	
Sample	1,310			284			83			240			398		
Chi2	17.458			4.503			8.011			15.709			9.992		
Significance level	0.004			0.479			0.156			0.008			0.075		

[a]Variable-mean (variable).

Appendix A9.2. Impact on refusal to go to school due to lack of water or toilet facilities (by socio-economic group).

Variables	Refused to go to school because of lack of water facility			Refused to go to school because of lack of toilet facility		
	Coeff.	Z	Mar. eff.	Coeff.	Z	Mar. eff.
Treatment (Have project=1)	(0.338)	0.016	(0.021)	(0.138)	0.241	(0.013)
Treatment (Have project=1)*Class 6–10	0.131	0.458	0.009	0.052	0.707	0.005
Treatment (Have project=1)*At least Class 11	(0.046)	0.857	(0.003)	(0.022)	0.908	(0.002)
Propensity score (PS)	0.955	0.008	0.059	0.698	0.041	0.064
Treatment*(demeaned\a PS)	(2.019)	0.004	(0.124)	(0.651)	0.250	(0.060)
Constant	(2.197)	0.000		(1.983)	0.000	
Sample	2,511			2,511		
Pseudo R2	0.032			0.007		

Appendix 10. Impact on labour force participation rates and hours worked by socio-economic group

Variables[a]	Have a job, all			Have a job, 11–17 yrs			Have a job, 18–24 yrs			Hours worked, all		Hours worked, 11–17		Hours worked, 18–24	
	Coeff	Sig. level	Mar. eff.	Coeff	Sig. level	Mar. eff.	Coeff	Sig. level	Mar. eff.	Coeff	Sig. level	Coeff	Sig. level	Coeff	Sig. level
Treatment (Have project=1)	0.002	0.956	0.001	0.020	0.840	0.002	0.069	0.340	0.022	0.793	0.653	25.790	0.956	(95.982)	0.401
Treatment (Have project=1)*Class 6–10	(0.058)	0.122	(0.020)	(0.490)	0.001	(0.038)	(0.335)	0.000	(0.098)	0.348	0.724	(14.168)	0.040	(0.405)	0.868
Treatment (Have project=1)*At least Class 11	0.007	0.880	0.003	(0.139)	0.424	(0.013)	(0.067)	0.566	(0.021)	(2.265)	0.177	(30.982)	0.157	(0.833)	0.837
Propensity score (PS)	0.071	0.413	0.025	0.013	0.963	0.001	0.032	0.873	0.010						
Treatment*(de-meaned[b] PS)	(0.262)	0.055	(0.092)	(0.312)	0.530	(0.031)	(0.443)	0.167	(0.140)						
Age										0.401	0.001	(14.377)	0.594	0.707	0.944
Age square										(0.004)	0.006	0.469	0.608	(0.009)	0.969
Male										9.571	0.000	48.079	0.020	15.232	0.000
Education (in years)										(0.095)	0.223	(1.795)	0.058	(0.046)	0.831
Male, Household head (HH)										(1.632)	0.373	1.694	0.899	(1.139)	0.773
Age, HH										(0.255)	0.059	0.653	0.469	(0.275)	0.447
Age square, HH										0.002	0.142	(0.004)	0.543	0.002	0.684
Education (in years), HH										(0.043)	0.000	(0.016)	0.885	(0.021)	0.374
Household size										0.360	0.020	0.525	0.729	0.899	0.044
Professional, HH										(7.365)	0.002			(1.559)	0.834
Services, HH										(4.740)	0.011			(3.763)	0.476
Professional and services, HH												8.852	0.487		
Agriculture, HH										(1.974)	0.152	(1.367)	0.864	(2.522)	0.481
Crafts, mach operators, assemblers, HH										(2.450)	0.289			10.333	0.106
Industry sector, HH										4.361	0.036			1.823	0.760
Services sector, HH										4.115	0.051			(3.934)	0.506

Not specified sector, HH	5.028	0.021	1.023	0.696	3.294	0.580
No of rooms in house	0.083	0.766	9.835	0.227	0.066	0.937
With finished floor	(1.549)	0.026	(4.109)	0.857	(6.022)	0.002
With structured roof	0.935	0.480			0.729	0.848
Own house	4.058	0.017			12.010	0.092
Mother tongue Punjabi	2.542	0.020	21.290	0.008	3.954	0.179
With primary school	6.447	0.009			5.782	0.435
middle school	(3.583)	0.001	9.102	0.526	(0.752)	0.803
high school	(3.528)	0.022	15.754	0.182	(11.326)	0.015
Distance to primary school	1.878	0.005	(1.105)	0.775	0.023	0.991
middle school	(0.378)	0.003	1.199	0.457	0.461	0.218
high school	0.004	0.968	(0.151)	0.827	(0.535)	0.057
With MCH centers	2.622	0.086	2.822	0.877	2.930	0.438
basic health unit	1.451	0.375	(28.438)	0.162	8.478	0.128
rural health center	(2.390)	0.271	(14.262)	0.688	(1.768)	0.702
dispensary	5.381	0.000	7.591	0.643	11.488	0.007
Distance to MCH centers	0.352	0.011	(0.768)	0.418	0.864	0.011
basic health unit	(0.044)	0.757	(0.423)	0.761	(0.327)	0.413
rural health center	(0.265)	0.000	0.921	0.292	(0.176)	0.343
dispensary	(0.020)	0.843	0.251	0.818	(0.342)	0.269
With bus service	3.101	0.000	19.776	0.122	4.873	0.046
motor cycle service	(2.260)	0.005	(8.100)	0.242	(3.176)	0.114
rikshaw service	(1.144)	0.129	3.443	0.701	(2.261)	0.298
Total population	0.063	0.699	1.025	0.298	(0.554)	0.244
Prop of hh on crop production	0.035	0.246	(0.003)	0.992	0.132	0.123
on livestock production	(0.251)	0.000	0.027	0.956	(0.470)	0.018
on manuf of goods	0.097	0.128	(0.688)	0.709	0.867	0.000
who are laborers	0.082	0.036	(0.122)	0.795	0.080	0.417
Village ave. per capita income	(0.702)	0.343	7.411	0.398	2.813	0.254

(Continued)

Appendix 10. (*Continued*)

Variables[a]	Have a job, all			Have a job, 11–17 yrs			Have a job, 18–24 yrs			Hours worked, all		Hours worked, 11–17		Hours worked, 18–24	
	Coeff	Sig. level	Mar. eff.	Coeff.	Sig. level	Mar. eff.	Coeff.	Sig. level	Mar. eff.	Coeff.	Sig. level	Coeff.	Sig. level	Coeff.	Sig. level
Bhawalpur										17.301	0.000			21.157	0.009
Chakwal										0.140	0.947			1.226	0.856
DGKhan										5.830	0.035			10.283	0.238
Faisalabad										7.791	0.003			1.307	0.861
RYKhan										4.635	0.066			8.235	0.320
Sargodha										10.017	0.000			10.972	0.180
Northern Districts												(8.767)	0.517		
Treatment*demeaned[b] Age										(0.084)	0.607	(1.562)	0.960	12.787	0.372
Age square										0.001	0.597	0.032	0.976	(0.300)	0.378
Male										(1.466)	0.647	(42.640)	0.048	0.032	0.275
Education (in years)										0.120	0.358	2.826	0.013	(7.865)	0.188
Male, Household head (HH)										(1.802)	0.503	260.445	0.024	(0.508)	0.932
Age, HH										0.226	0.231	4.785	0.043	(0.542)	0.646
Age square, HH										(0.002)	0.216	(0.044)	0.045	(0.228)	0.647
Education (in years), HH										0.072	0.003	0.048	0.871	0.002	0.647
Household size										(0.350)	0.108	(1.186)	0.518	0.045	0.389
Professional, HH										6.659	0.096			(0.384)	0.565
Services, HH										6.738	0.041			(9.156)	0.483
Professional and services, HH												(1.225)	0.930	(2.914)	0.790
Agriculture, HH										(1.382)	0.458	9.055	0.425	(1.354)	0.763
Crafts, mach operators, assemblers, HH										2.752	0.495			(22.968)	0.068
Industry sector, HH										(6.513)	0.078			4.524	0.700
Services sector, HH										(7.652)	0.033			6.606	0.567
Not specified sector, HH										(8.521)	0.021			(2.252)	0.851
No. rooms in house										0.064	0.858	0.299	0.925	(0.356)	0.744
With finished floor										2.642	0.009	(17.070)	0.083	9.149	0.001
With structured roof										3.812	0.033	70.498	0.038	3.812	0.418
Own house										(2.951)	0.214			(11.224)	0.185

[a]Some determining variables are either removed or collapsed because of perfect prediction or collinearity.
[b]Variable-mean (variable).

Impact evaluation of infrastructure investments: the experience of the Millennium Challenge Corporation

Ariel BenYishay and Rebecca Tunstall

School of Economics, University of New South Wales, Sydney, NSW 2052, Australia

In many developing countries, aging or inadequate infrastructure is a binding constraint to economic growth. The Millennium Challenge Corporation (MCC), a US government agency providing development assistance, has committed more than $4 billion to upgrade or rehabilitate roads, ports, electricity, water, sanitation and major irrigation systems in 16 countries between 2004 and 2010. In at least eight of these countries, the MCC has developed evaluations that will assess the causal impacts of these investments on a variety of outcomes, including household incomes and consumption. These evaluations primarily rely on difference-in-differences estimation, complemented by random assignment, propensity score matching, geographic information systems (GIS) models, and regression discontinuity designs. The relatively large number of evaluations (13 in all) and the diversity in their approaches offer a unique opportunity to compare these evaluations in terms of the techniques used, their ability to control for selection bias, and their flexibility under changing implementation plans. This paper studies the conditions that led to the design of each evaluation, including differing mechanisms for selecting infrastructure to be upgraded. It compares the propensity score matching approaches used in many of these evaluations, noting key observable characteristics used to match treatment and control communities. It also studies the GIS modelling approaches used in four of the roads evaluations. Finally, it reviews the flexibility of each evaluation design in response to changes in the project implementation plans that arise when there are cost over-runs and/or poor policy performance, there are delays in construction, or there are changes to the roll-out strategy. Several of these evaluations will provide the first rigorous evidence on the impacts of highway or secondary road improvement in developing country contexts. Similarly, a number of evaluations will offer important evidence on the extent to which water and sanitation improvements can raise the income level of households. By incorporating multiple methods, a number of these evaluations will also illustrate whether these methods produce different impact estimates, another notable contribution to the literature.

1. Introduction

In many developing countries, aging or inadequate infrastructure is a binding constraint to economic growth. Weaknesses in transport networks, for example, limit connections between farmers, urban markets and producers, and international markets. Where they exist in good condition, rural roads connect villages and small towns, allowing farmers to deliver produce to local markets and obtain agricultural inputs. These roads also feed into larger secondary roads, on which these goods travel to and from larger urban markets. Access to these broader markets spurs non-agricultural production in rural areas. National highways link these urban centres and markets in neighbouring countries, as well as ports and airports used to export products.

Many developing countries' governments, however, have been unable to devote the considerable capital expenditures required to rehabilitate, maintain, or upgrade road networks and other infrastructure to their optimal condition. As a result, many rural roads are impassable for large parts of the year, and the time and vehicle damage incurred in travelling along them make transport prohibitively costly for the areas' farmers. Conditions along secondary and primary roads also force users to travel more slowly than they would otherwise and incur higher costs in operating their vehicles. Other types of infrastructure – including electricity and water systems and major irrigation canals – are also frequently inadequate, limiting the extent of output that an economy can generate. To ease these constraints, the Millennium Challenge Corporation (MCC), a US government agency providing development assistance, has partnered with 16 developing countries to support infrastructure improvements these countries have identified as crucial for economic growth. Since its creation in 2004, the MCC has committed more than $4 billion to improve infrastructure systems in these countries, including $2.3 billion to upgrade or rehabilitate primary, secondary and rural roads in 14 countries. Along with these capital investments, the MCC has also recommended – and in some cases required – that recipient country governments enact new arrangements for funding ongoing maintenance of their infrastructure.

Until recently, many of the claims about the impacts of infrastructure improvement on economic growth were not substantiated with empirical evidence. Advances in programme evaluation in the past 15 years, however, have allowed investigators to study these impacts with some confidence in their attribution. This development has been due in part to the broadening use of difference-in-difference (DD) estimation and propensity score matching (PSM) to control for selection bias in non-experimental data (sparked by Rosenbaum and Rubin 1983, Heckman *et al.* 1997, 1998a, 1998b, Dehejia and Wahba 1999). These methods rely on controlling for pre-intervention differences between treatment and comparison groups, and so have been bolstered by the growing availability of pre-intervention data.

Despite these advances and the resulting spate of work on the impacts of infrastructure in developing countries, major gaps in our understanding of these impacts and their mechanisms remain. While the impacts of rural roads on households' material well-being have been studied in a variety of settings, almost no causal evidence exists on the impacts of national highways and major secondary roads on the surrounding populations. Similarly, while the effects of improved water and sanitation access on child mortality has been well studied, impacts of these improvements on households' near-term income generation and consumption patterns are yet to be documented. More broadly, the behavioural response of households to improved access to electricity, water, sanitation, and irrigation in terms of off-farm employment activities and on-farm crop diversification remains an area of much-needed study.

Against this evidentiary background, the MCC has launched evaluations that will assess the causal impacts of its infrastructure investments in eight countries. Evaluations of road investments will estimate effects on transport costs, local prices, and/or household and business incomes, while water, sanitation, and electricity evaluations will track household health, education, and time use, as well as productive uses of this infrastructure. Similarly, an evaluation of irrigation investments in Armenia will estimate shifts in crop compositions and the associated gains in agricultural productivity and total household income as a result of these investments.

The MCC's road evaluations study the impacts of improvements along roads of varying type, length, pre-project condition, and geographic region (Fideg 2008, NORC 2007, 2009a, Torero 2009a, Struyk et al. 2010). The evaluations themselves include both some notable similarities and differences. All of them rely on difference-in-differences estimation, often complemented by PSM. As such, they include a comparison group for the communities that are treated with improved roads, while controlling for both observed differences between the treatment and comparison groups and time invariant unobservable differences. In addition, several of the evaluations include continuous treatment estimators that consider the degree of improvement in travel time and costs as the treatment that communities experience, and relate the intensity of this treatment to gains in household well-being. Geographic information systems (GIS) data will also play a key role in a number of these evaluations, integrating into the matching of treatment and comparison groups, the measurement of continuous treatment effects, and the estimation of the network effects of improving individual segment. Finally, several evaluations are attempting to use thresholds in the selection of segments or the timing of their improvements to identify their impacts.

In a similar vein, evaluations of MCC investments in electricity distribution, water and sanitation systems, and major irrigation canals in five countries are rigorously estimating counterfactual scenarios to capture the impact of these investments on household well-being (Chaplin et al. 2009, Komives et al. 2009, NORC 2009b, 2009c, Torero 2009b). These evaluations similarly rely on DD estimations, often coupled with matching of communities in treatment and comparison areas. In several cases – rural water in Lesotho and electrification in El Salvador and Tanzania – the evaluation involves random assignment of communities and/or households into the treatment group. Looking at macro effects of infrastructure improvement, the evaluation of Georgia's Regional Infrastructure Development activity complements household and firm-level analysis with a computable general equilibrium (CGE) model estimating effects on national output, prices, employment and expenditures.

The relatively large number of MCC infrastructure evaluations and the calibre of and diversity in their approaches offers a unique opportunity to compare these evaluations in terms of the techniques used, their ability to control for selection bias, and their flexibility under changing implementation plans. This paper studies the conditions that led to the design of these evaluations, noting how the MCC's pre-investment analysis process sometimes precludes randomised evaluations but can facilitate credible evaluation designs. We assess the PSM and GIS approaches used in the evaluations, highlighting how the combination of these approaches will enable the evaluations to identify the impacts of highway and secondary road improvements in developing countries. These results will provide important information for developing country governments, donor agencies, and individual stakeholders as they consider alternative investments of scarce resources.

We also compare the outcomes studied in each evaluation, noting that some evaluations will identify effects on the prices of agricultural goods, inputs, and consumption goods, while most will also capture effects on agricultural and non-farm production and labour income. Taken together, the evaluations will illustrate the conditions under which different effects of infrastructure improvements are likely to emerge.

Finally, our paper reviews the flexibility of each evaluation design in response to changes in the implementation plan of each project that arise when there are cost overruns and/or poor policy performance, there are delays in construction, or there are changes to the roll-out strategy.

While we largely focus on evaluations of MCC road improvement investments, which make up a substantial portion of the overall infrastructure evaluation portfolio, we note how these differ from MCC evaluations of other types of infrastructure.

The paper is organised as follows. In Section 2, we discuss the existing literature studying the effects of infrastructure improvement on material well-being in developing countries. In Section 3, we discuss the MCC's infrastructure investments and its impact evaluations of these investments. In Section 4, we describe the designs of the MCC's evaluations, delving into the PSM and GIS methods used in a number of these evaluations in Sections 5 and 6. In Section 7, we compare the outcomes studied in the road evaluations, while Section 8 investigates the flexibility of these evaluations in response to project implementation changes. Finally, we offer recommendations for future evaluations in Section 9.

2. Existing literature

As previously noted, advances in programme evaluation in the past 15 years have added substantially to the body of knowledge on infrastructure improvement impacts. Evidence on improvements in road systems has been particularly strengthened. Estache (2010) provides a useful review of these studies, which have primarily focused on rural roads. Repeated surveys of the population around these roads allowed evaluators to compare the changes in costs and production levels around both improved and non-improved roads, controlling for any time-invariant differences between these roads (Van de Walle 2008). Matching improved roads to statistically comparable non-improved roads further allowed evaluators to control for differential time trends that were correlated with observable characteristics of these roads. Van de Walle and Cratty (2002) provide an important early example of how PSM could be combined with DD estimators to assess the impact of rural roads in Vietnam. Escobal and Ponce (2004) and Lokshin and Yemtsov (2005) study related issues in Peru and Georgia. Dercon *et al.* (2006) and Khandker *et al.* (2006) instead rely on household-level panel data to control for differences both across and within communities in the likely impact of the road improvements in Ethiopia and Bangladesh. All of these studies find significant effects on household material well-being, with several of the studies pointing to gains in agricultural prices and production, lower input costs, and higher wages as the channels for income or consumption gains.

The mounting evidence in support of the impacts of rural road improvement contrast sharply with the lack of empirical evidence on the effects of highway or secondary road improvements, particularly in developing countries. Evaluators of non-rural roads have struggled to identify a counterfactual that was actually observed in the form of a comparison group. Instead, as Estache (2010) notes, most evaluators have turned to computable general equilibrium models to simulate these outcomes. One notable exception is Garcia-Mila and Montalvo (2007), who use data from GIS to separate 20 km segments of Spain's national highway system and find no statistically significant effects on business creation as certain segments are improved and others not. To date, there is little written about the effects of improvements in highways or secondary roads in developing country contexts.

Evidence on the effects of other types of infrastructure improvements in developing countries has similarly been strengthened significantly in recent years. Access to piped water, for example, has been demonstrated to improve child survival and health outcomes in a number of developing countries (Lee *et al.* 1997, Jalan and Ravallion 2003). Rauniyar *et al.* (2010) find that Pakistani households in areas that gained access to water and sanitation saw their high-school-aged daughters attend school more frequently. The latter authors do not find evidence that households use time savings to increase labour force participation or hours worked. As such, this stream of evidence suggests that water and sanitation improvements can increase the income an economy generates primarily over a longer time horizon, when children's survival and human capital eventually translates into gains in output in their adult years.

Similarly, gains in household access to electricity can lead to additional investments in child welfare, but the degree to which they affect a household's near-term earning potential remains unclear. Chowdhury and Torero (2009) provide some evidence that access to electricity raised Bangladeshi women's labour income, but this additional income was not necessarily compensated with less time spent on unpaid work at home. Thus, while gains in off-farm microenterprise and employment opportunities and on-farm productivity from access to electricity are often posited, these channels are not well documented in the literature.

Finally, irrigation infrastructure improvements might be expected to more directly influence rural incomes by increasing agricultural productivity and enabling transitions toward higher value crops that require significant water inputs. White (2008) presents evidence that improvements in several large irrigation canals in India did raise yields, but not by the expected amount. Moreover, the expected diversification into higher value crops did not take place following these irrigation improvements. As this diversification often determines whether income growth among farmers will be sufficient to justify the large costs associated with irrigation investments, it remains to be seen whether such investments in other countries can yield cost-effective poverty reduction.

3. MCC infrastructure investments and evaluations

The MCC was created in January 2004 by the US Congress. The MCC provides low-income and lower-middle-income countries with five-year large-scale grants, called compacts, to fund investments aimed at reducing poverty through sustainable economic growth. Eligible countries are invited to identify their constraints to achieving sustainable economic growth and poverty reduction and then develop proposals to address these constraints in broad public consultations. In Armenia, for example, the compact proposal was developed through a consultative process in which more than 1200 individuals participated and some 230 written proposals were received on particular investment projects. Improved physical infrastructure was highlighted as a priority area, so the Government of Armenia selected improvements in irrigation infrastructure and roads as the main areas for MCC support.

In El Salvador, in contrast, the proposal to the MCC was based on an existing national plan that had resulted from a process led by the National Commission for Development with broad participation from local governments, private enterprises and civil society. The Northern Zone portion of the plan was selected for MCC investment and it included, among other investments in community infrastructure, education and business development, the Northern Transnational Highway that had been promised to the people of the Northern Zone for over 50 years.

To increase aid effectiveness, the MCC has created an analytical framework that systematically includes a strong focus on results, including significant ex ante analysis. Benefit–cost analysis in the form of economic rate of return (ERR) models and distributional analysis are conducted to assess the economic justification of the proposed investments and the distribution of the expected benefits. Current MCC policy is that ex ante ERRs are calculated on a large share of project activities, and road sections that fall below the minimum hurdle for an ERR are not usually included in compact programmes.[1] For roads, the most commonly used ERR model is the Highway Development and

Management system (HDM-IV), which captures the expected changes in road quality (roughness), speed and traffic and calculates the expected savings in vehicle operating costs and travel time.[2] In some cases, increases in agriculture production, land values along the road, and income related to improved access to health and education facilities are also modelled as benefits.

ERR models for other types of infrastructure are not as standardised as the HDM-IV used for road modelling. These models must take into account the intermediate results of productivity and behavioural changes that occur from improving the infrastructure. For a water and sanitation project, for example, the ERR may include the value of time savings from no longer having to travel long distances and wait in line for water or the benefits of less disease in the form of more days at work and lower medical costs. The benefits for an electricity project may include cost savings from no longer having to buy alternative sources of energy, new business development within a newly electrified household or increased study time for children in the evenings.[3]

Once a compact proposal is agreed upon and implementation begins, the MCC requires strict monitoring and reporting, complemented with rigorous, independent impact evaluations. Evaluations have been commissioned when there are lessons that could be applied to future funding decisions or project design, when there is a need for evidence about a particular intervention, and when they are feasible.[4]

To date, the MCC has signed 20 compacts with partner countries committing $7.2 billion in assistance. Thirty-three percent, or $2.3 billion, has been allocated for transportation activities, the largest sector in which the MCC is investing. These road investments comprise 14 projects, and impact evaluation strategies have been developed for half of them (Table 1). These seven projects – each in a distinct country – represent $1.14 billion and 2189 km of road improvements. They include all types of road improvements from new

Table 1. MCC road projects with impact evaluations.

Country	Project	Budget allocation	Distance to be improved	Evaluation designer
Armenia	Rural road rehabilitation	$67 million	24 km[a]	Mathematica Policy Research
El Salvador	Secondary road openings and upgrades	$233 million	290 km	Social impact with the International Food Policy Research Institute
Georgia	Main road rehabilitation	$204 million	120 km	National Opinion Research Center
Ghana	Feeder road rehabilitation	$70 million	357 km	National Opinion Research Center
Honduras	Secondary and tertiary roads	$21 million	750 km	National Opinion Research Center
	Highway	$119 million	109 km	
Nicaragua	Main and secondary roads	$58 million	74 km	Millennium Challenge Corporation
Tanzania	Trunk roads and rural roads	$369 million	465 km	Economic Development Initiatives Ltd

[a]The Armenia budget allocation was originally committed to rehabilitate up to 943 km; however, the activity is currently on hold. Twenty-four kilometres is the revised target for number of kilometres to be completed even though the budget allocation has not officially changed.

Table 2.   Other MCC infrastructure projects with impact evaluations.

Country	Project	Budget allocation	Expected beneficiary count	Evaluation designer
Armenia	Irrigated Agriculture Project[a]	$146 million	420,000	Mathematica Policy Research
El Salvador	Rural Electrification Activity	$33 million	235,000	Social impact with the International Food Policy Research Institute
El Salvador	Water and Sanitation Activity	$24 million	90,000	Social impact with RTI International
Georgia	Regional Infrastructure Development Activity	$57.7 million		Tbilisi Business Service Center and ACT Consulting
Lesotho	Water Sector Project	$164 million	644,000	National Opinion Research Center
Tanzania	Electricity: Distribution Rehabilitation & Extension	$206.47 million	1,080,000	Mathematica Policy Research

[a]This project includes activities in various sectors. The evaluation discussed in this paper is covering only a portion of the infrastructure activities – the tertiary canal rehabilitation.

roads, to upgrading rural roads and rehabilitating highways. Similarly, the MCC's evaluations of non-road infrastructure projects also cover an array of activities in a number of different countries (Table 2).

To date, none of the MCC infrastructure projects considered in this study has been completed as originally planned; however, the Honduras road project, which was one of the first compacts to be signed, will finish this year. Table 3 displays the state of implementation of the projects in these eight countries.

One can reasonably ask how these projects were selected for evaluation from the MCC's broader portfolio of infrastructure investments. The investments being studied in these impact evaluations total more than $1.5 billion, or slightly more than one-third of the MCC's overall infrastructure investments. In determining how rigorous an evaluation of a given project should aim to be, the MCC considers several factors. Technical feasibility is always a prerequisite, but learning potential, need for evidence justifying the programme, and cost also play an important role in evaluation selection.

The share of infrastructure investments with existing impact evaluations may be slightly misleading because a number of these investments are still quite early in their implementation and may yet have impact evaluations, as may be the case with road improvement projects in Burkina Faso, Moldova, and Senegal, for example. Once the evaluations of these recently launched projects are designed, we expect that the share of MCC infrastructure funding covered by impact evaluations may rise above 50 per cent.[5]

4.   Evaluation designs

The MCC compacts in the eight countries considered in this paper are funding improvements of infrastructure of varying type, scope, and pre-project condition. In all of these compacts, the selection of projects for investment was the result of a process that explicitly

Table 3. State of implementation as of March 2010.

Country	Compact begin date	Compact end date	Road completion Percentage complete[a]	Road completion Distance complete	Construction progress on other infrastructure activities
Armenia	September 2006	September 2011	100%	24 km	7%
El Salvador	September 2007	September 2012	32%	0 km	0% water, 8% electricity
Georgia	April 2006	April 2011	48%	0 km	20%
Ghana	February 2007	February 2012	12%	0 km	n/a
Honduras	September 2005	September 2010	43%	310 km	n/a
Lesotho	September 2008	September 2013	n/a	n/a	0%[b]
Nicaragua	May 2006	May 2011	99%	74 km	n/a
Tanzania	September 2008	September 2013	0%	0 km	0%[3]

[a]Percentage complete is measured as the amount disbursed divided by the total amount contracted for construction works.
[b]Urban water: design work for distribution systems continues this quarter. Rural water: the procurement process has begun for 25% of the rural water systems and latrines.
[c]In Tanzania, design, environmental and social preparatory work associated with the upgrade of transmission systems and distribution line extensions in six underserved regions of the country continues.

considered the likely economic impacts of rehabilitating or upgrading each piece of infrastructure, as well as other features of the infrastructure that are likely to be correlated with outcomes. As described in Section 3, the project selection process involved public consultations in the country, prioritisation by the government, and benefit–cost and distributional analysis of proposed investments. We discuss these in greater detail below and note how evaluation designs must take each of these selection features into account.

It is worth noting that the impact evaluations of these investments can be designed to answer two questions. The first is 'what is the impact of MCC investment in infrastructure improvements?' An evaluation designed to answer this question will model the counterfactual and estimate the impact of the MCC's funding. If road improvements, for example, are made on any of the comparison roads, then that would reduce the measured impact and imply that those roads may have been improved even without MCC funding. In some instances, the fungibility of public finances means that MCC funding may actually enable some of the improvements along comparison roads, which raises concerns about contamination of the comparison group. The second question that the evaluation can be designed to analyse is 'what is the impact of infrastructure improvements, regardless of the funding source?' An evaluation designed to answer this question would include all improved infrastructure in the treatment group even if it had been improved by another funding source such as another donor or the host country government. The impact evaluations discussed herein contain a mix of these two approaches, offering an important contribution to the existing literature.

Because road investments are a broad treatment and the MCC's consultative and analytical process frequently leads to selection of individual road segments, random assignment of individual, communities, or road segments to treatment and comparison groups is frequently not possible. To nonetheless generate a comparable group and attribute impacts to the MCC's road investments, all of the organisation's roads evaluations utilise PSM and DD. In addition, several evaluations are using continuous treatment methods that measure the actual changes in transportation access for different communities and compare

Table 4.   Evaluation methods.

Country	Project	DD	Randomised assignment	PSM	Continuous treatment	RD	CGE
Armenia	Irrigation	Y					
Armenia	Roads	Y					
El Salvador	Electricity	Y	Y	Y			
El Salvador	Roads	Y		Y	Y	Y	
El Salvador	Water and sanitation	Y		Y			
Georgia	Regional Infrastructure	Y					Y
Georgia	Roads	Y			Y		
Ghana	Roads	Y		Y	Y		
Honduras	Roads	Y		Y	Y		
Lesotho	Rural water	Y	Y				
Lesotho	Urban water	Y				Y	
Nicaragua	Roads	Y	Y				
Tanzania	Roads	Y		Y			
Tanzania	Electricity	Y	Y	Y		Y	

communities for whom these changes are greater with those where changes are smaller. Finally, several evaluations have attempted to use regression discontinuity methods based on a number of thresholds in the selection and roll-out of road segments, with varying success.

Investments in extending the electricity and water and sanitation distribution systems can be more targeted, as they require connection by households or businesses to these systems. In several cases, MCC evaluations involve random assignment of communities, clusters, or households to treatment groups receiving earlier access to improved water systems and coupons to facilitate connections to the electric grid. In other cases, regression discontinuity methods using threshold levels of costs/pricing are being attempted, meeting varying degrees of success (much as in the roads evaluations).

Table 4 details the methods being used in the MCC's infrastructure impact evaluation. For road investments, the consultative and analytical basis for funding some individual road segments and not others precludes the use of randomisation for most of the MCC's road improvement project evaluations. In other types of projects, the selection process may determine interventions that are feasible – say, training on intercropping for maize farmers in Malawi – but may not determine the optimal allocation of these interventions across observably homogeneous communities or individuals. That is, the pool of people who are eligible to receive the treatment and for whom the impact of the treatment is indistinguishable ex ante is sufficiently large that the treatment can be randomly allocated among them with no effect on the ex ante estimates of its returns. For example, a farmer training programme may be designed to inform maize farmers about the benefits of intercropping, but whether these effects will be larger for farmers in certain communities may not be well known. The programme may therefore be randomly assigned within the pool of otherwise homogeneous communities.

Road improvement, on the other hand, is a rather broad treatment – an intervention that is not targeted to individuals or communities, but to stretches of road. One cannot randomly assign treatment and control communities along the same segment selected for improvement. If one conducts ex ante ERR analysis on individual road segments as the basis for selection, all communities along these segments would be intended for treatment. The level of analysis and the level of treatment coincide entirely, meaning allocation of the programme based on the ex ante analysis precludes random allocation of the programme among lower level units. Given the MCC's focus on ex ante analysis at the lowest unit for which confident estimates are possible, it is not surprising that few road improvement evaluations involve randomisation. In fact, in only one case – Honduras' rural roads programme – was randomisation a realistic option. In this case, there were not sufficient data available to estimate the segment-by-segment returns accurately, making randomisation among the potential segments a possibility. Although a randomisation was initially considered, implementation plans eventually ruled out his possibility.

If a country's initial proposal includes a set of rural road segments, the ERR from investment in each segment is estimated, and a subset of segments for which this rate exceeds a pre-determined hurdle rate may be recommended for funding. The variation in the flow and composition of existing traffic and the population base along the road segments is the primary determinant of the expected rates of return for improving each segment. This selection process thus links the existing conditions, traffic, and population base of each road segment to its probability of being selected for investment. Of course, the appraisal process produces estimates that have a good deal of uncertainty of the true gains from improving each road segment. Nonetheless, if the noise in these estimates is not too great, the set of road segments recommended for improvement will exhibit significant positive selection.

When a large pool of road segments is considered for potential improvements, the ERR-based selection process provides a natural discontinuity that can be exploited to evaluate the effects of these improvements. Segments with ERRs that are just above the hurdle rate may not differ significantly from those just below the rate, except in their probability of investment. The most rigorous regression discontinuity (RD) approach would limit the sample to those roads near the hurdle rate, and make the aforementioned comparison between those just above and just below the hurdle rate. Unfortunately, in none of the MCC's impact evaluations was the pool of potential road segments so large that this approach would yield a large enough sample to precisely detect the project's impacts. The evaluation of Armenia's Rural Road Rehabilitation Project (RRRP) offers a useful example of an alternative approach. The evaluation was designed to include the full range of road segments considered for rehabilitation in the sample, while controlling for a smooth function of the pre-investment ERR (Fortson and Rangarajan 2008). If the relationship between the ERR and the outcome variables studied in the evaluation exhibit a stable relationship that is accurately modelled in the estimation, the sharp discontinuity in the ERR at the hurdle rate will identify the programme's impacts.

In the case of Armenia's RRRP, road segments were initially divided into three packages of potential road segments that would be rehabilitated. The intention prior to the launch of construction was to select roads from each package using the ERR hurdle rate criteria. All of the road segments in the first package cleared the ERR hurdle rate, making the RD design dependent on the second and third packages to generate a control group of segments. However, the subsequent appreciation of the Armenian Dram caused the costs of rehabilitation to rise substantially. At the new costs, only the road segments in the first package could be funded. Rather than raise the hurdle rate and fund a smaller share of roads from each package, the most efficient project re-design involved funding only the first package of roads. As we discuss in Section 8, modifications to the RD approach and alternative designs were also considered in response. More generally, the validity of the RD design relies on the consistent use of an explicit analytical framework for road segment selection – a practice that has been challenging to follow even among donors who mandate it as part of their 'best practices'.

When road segment selection does not follow such an explicit analytical framework, or when the pool of potential segments is relatively small, other methods must be used to estimate the counterfactual. This is particularly true of improvements to national highways or other major roads, for which the number of potential segments for improvement may be limited. For these situations, DD estimators could control for differences in initial conditions across road segments. DD estimation compares the *changes* in outcome variables along treated roads to those along comparison roads. Since most of the parameters used in the HDM-IV and Roads Economic Decision models vary across road segments only in terms of their initial characteristics, if these models were the sole basis for selection from a known pool of potential segments, DD estimators would effectively control for selection bias. However, these conditions are frequently not met. For example, a country eligible for an MCC compact may propose only a small set of segments for funding, with all or most of these segments appraised as having ERRs above the hurdle rate. For this and other reasons, one cannot confidently say that the ERR model parameters were the sole basis for the selection. Without explicit comparison with alternative segments that were not selected, the possibility of selection bias remains a key issue.

To overcome this bias, evaluations are increasingly turning to PSM. As previously noted, Van de Walle and Cratty (2002) provide a seminal example of how PSM, in combination with DD, can be used to control for differences between treatment and comparison road segments based on their observable characteristics. Taken together, PSM and DD limit the effect of selection bias to the effect of unobserved characteristics on differential trends across segments. This approach is used in all seven MCC evaluations considered herein (although it was originally conceived as a 'back-up' alternative in several of these evaluations). The core elements of this approach require panel data married with observing a broad range of initial characteristics on which to match units. In the next section, we discuss the varying data and matching process used across the seven MCC evaluations.

Four of these evaluations (El Salvador, Georgia, Ghana, and Honduras) utilise GIS to generate data on physical and agricultural conditions along road segments and incorporate this information into the PSM. For example, in Honduras, GIS data allow roads to be matched in terms of their elevation and the surrounding areas' soil type, soil fertility, and rainfall (in addition to other observables). Where it is regularly updated, GIS information can also capture improvements in comparison roads that are funded by other non-MCC projects (including domestic roads rehabilitation programmes). Importantly, GIS information can be used to model network spillovers that are likely to occur from improvements along specific segments. This integration of GIS into these evaluations is relatively unique and represents a real contribution to the literature. In Section 6, we highlight how this practice has varied across these four evaluations and what we are likely to learn about this practice based on results of these studies.

In addition to the traditional delineation of communities into treatment and comparison categories, a number of the evaluations also consider treatment as a continuous variable based on the changes in accessibility that occur when a nearby road is improved. The recently developed methods analysing continuous treatment (Imbens 2000, Behrman *et al.* 2004, Hirano and Imbens 2004) can be likened to a 'dose–response' framework in the medical field. Evaluations of MCC-funded improvements in El Salvador, Georgia, Ghana and Honduras will assess the impact of incremental reductions in travel costs (both time and direct costs) to the nearest market, major towns, or a weighted composite of destinations.[6] In this framework, it is the intensity of treatment that varies, and there is no formal control

group (no group receives zero treatment). The average dose–response function charac-
terises the mean impact estimate per unit reduction in travel costs, which can be multiplied
by the mean reduction experienced in the sample to obtain the mean total impact. This
offers a cross-validation of the PSM-DD results that will be obtained in these evaluations.

Estimating travel costs in this framework is most carefully accomplished by considering costs reported by households or communities, estimates derived from GIS pathway
models, and additional cost data from transport operators. Several of the evaluations utilise
primarily GIS-based data, in which the characteristics of each road are considered in terms
of the operating costs for vehicle owners (say, the 'wear and tear' and fuel costs of driving along a hilly, circuitous, unimproved road). The El Salvador evaluation calibrates these
costs using data from domestic transport companies. Other road evaluations calculate an
'accessibility index' that converts the minimum-cost path to predetermined destinations
onto a normalised scale. Generally, such continuous measures therefore provide robust
estimates that can be used to estimate continuous treatment effects.

Finally, one road evaluation has also attempted to utilise the variation in timing of construction along different segments to identify the impacts of these improvements. In El
Salvador, the construction of five road segments has followed a timeline that includes distinct dates of completion for each segment (see Figure 1). The evaluation will thus use
an RD design, where the thresholds for treatment are the dates of completion of segment.
Controlling for a smooth function of time trends, this approach compares earlier implemented segments with later completed segments, with the assumption that the timing of
construction was not selected based on the differences in the likely impacts of the construction (that is, upgrading roads with higher existing traffic first, and so forth). To the
extent that the timing of construction is driven by engineering requirements or contracting
variation that are different from historical features of the areas around each road segment,
this approach can provide valid estimates of impact.

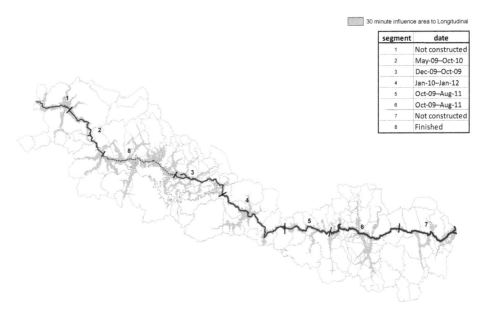

segment	date
1	Not constructed
2	May-09–Oct-10
3	Dec-09–Oct-09
4	Jan-10–Jan-12
5	Oct-09–Aug-11
6	Oct-09–Aug-11
7	Not constructed
8	Finished

30 minute influence area to Longitudinal

Figure 1.   El Salvador road improvement timeline.
Source: Reproduced from Torero (2009, p. 9).

While treatment of a population with improvement in roads can be fairly broad or continuous, treatment with access to other types of infrastructure is often more discrete. Households access water, sanitation, electricity, and irrigation services via discrete connections, and these connections can vary within communities. These types of infrastructure offer additional opportunities for evaluation designs that are not feasible for roads improvements. The MCC's evaluation of extensions of the electricity grids in El Salvador and Tanzania involve random assignment of coupons to facilitate household connections to the extended grids. The MCC's rural water supply project in Lesotho involves a random assignment of the timing of construction of 100 small rural water systems (bore holes, gravity systems, and other technologies). Meanwhile, an evaluation of improvements in access to water and sanitation in urban Lesotho is using discontinuities in the pricing of connections to the main lines based on thresholds in the distance between a residence and the main lines.

At the same time, evaluation designs for rural roads and other types of infrastructure do not differ substantially in every case. Evaluations of water and sanitation improvements in rural El Salvador, investments in major irrigation canals in Armenia, and regional infrastructure development in Georgia are being carried out using matching and DD techniques similar to those used in evaluating many roads projects. The latter evaluation in Georgia will complement the household and firm-level analysis with a CGE model estimating the effects of the improved infrastructure on national-level output, prices, employment, and expenditures.

The randomised assignment approaches used in Lesotho, El Salvador, and Tanzania are particularly noteworthy because they will offer some of the most rigorous evidence on the effects of rural water and electricity supply in very poor countries. In Lesotho, the Department of Rural Water Supply identified 250 small community water systems (each serving 100–180 people) that would be fully designed and, if feasible, implemented under the MCC compact. One hundred of these systems were designed by August 2008, and these were randomly assigned into early and late construction groups. These 100 systems were dispersed across 10 districts, with each district having exactly 10 systems. In August 2008, a public randomisation was held in which five of the 10 eligible systems in each district were selected for implementation in the first year of the project, with the remaining systems slated for implementation in the second year. The evaluation will thus identify the effects of the improved water systems by the differential timing of changes in outcomes among treatment ('early') and comparison ('late') groups.

In El Salvador and Tanzania, random assignment of coupons to facilitate connection to the electric grid among subsamples will supplement PSM-based estimates across the full evaluation samples. Both projects will involve extending new distribution lines to communities, with households in these communities facing costs to connect to the new lines. The coupons can therefore be considered a randomised encouragement design, in which some households would have connected to the new lines even in the absence of the coupons and some won't connect even if offered the coupons. The effects of electrification will thus be identified by the share of households that connect to the grid only because of the coupons.

This random assignment is a crucial cross-validation of the PSM approaches taken in the broader sample, about which significant concerns remain. One challenge is that a major characteristic determining propensity of connection to the newly extended grid may be the distance of a household from the new lines. In comparison communities, however, the location of those lines is unknown as of yet, and thus identifying households that would be close to the hypothetical lines and offer good comparisons is challenging. This is problematic if the location of the lines is correlated with other unobserved geographic features, which may or may not be major sources of bias.

Finally, thresholds in costs or prices associated with extending the electric grid and offering water and sanitation connections can also serve as useful RD-based identification strategies. In Lesotho, the Urban Water and Sewerage Authority uses a 'distance from the main' standard to determine the connection fee for a particular residence or business, with a step scale fee structure. A particularly crucial cutoff takes place at the distance of 100 metres from the main, with households just a metre closer to the main paying 3000 *maloti* and those just a metre farther paying 4000 *maloti*. The distribution of households around the 100-metre mark provides a reasonably large, balanced sample over which to estimate the programme effects.

In Tanzania's energy evaluation, however, attempts by evaluators to retrofit an RD design based on an imputed threshold rule for subproject funding were not successful. Evaluators explored the degree to which subproject funding decisions were based on a threshold level of projected revenue/capital expenditure ratios for subproject locations, finding that only 13 out of 240 subprojects were both below the threshold level and not funded. Evaluators therefore turned to PSM and randomised assignment of coupons to identify the programme's effects.

One additional feature of several of the evaluations considered herein is their use of multiple methodologies to identify the programme impacts. These evaluations are particularly informative because they can be used to compare and cross-validate the methodologies. Taken together, this set of evaluations can provide a sense of what the probable results may have been of using alternative approaches in some of these evaluations. For example, if (hypothetically) Georgia's continuous treatment estimates show effects that are 20 per cent lower than those based on PSM-DD estimates, this might suggest that Nicaragua's PSM-DD estimates may overstate the programme's effects.

5. Propensity score matching

In combination with a DD approach, the use of PSM is intended to control for differences in trends between communities. That is, some communities may experience faster growth in agricultural productivity, gains in land values, and diversification of products available in local markets. These changes may be closely related to the reasons that infrastructure in or near these communities is selected for rehabilitation or upgrading. For example, some communities may be politically represented by parliamentarians who are very successful at obtaining funding for their districts for both road improvements and other key investments in, say, land tenure systems or agricultural extension services. If such correlated investments are made over similar timeframes, the selection of treatment communities will be spuriously correlated with trends in outcomes of interest. Controlling for such cross-sectional differences thus remains crucial even when DD estimators are used.

In many studies conducted using existing samples, these cross-sectional differences must simply be controlled for using observed characteristics. However, in studies designed with such considerations explicitly in mind, investigators can directly consider these differences when drawing their samples. The primary benefit of doing so is that one can select these treatment and comparison community samples to be as similar as possible in their observable characteristics. PSM provides a statistic that summarises the comparability of these two samples and thus allows one to draw samples that maximise this comparability.

Of course, this approach depends not only on what characteristics are observable but on which characteristics are actually observed. Observing these characteristics generally means using secondary data from existing government or other sources and adding to that primary information gathered through pre-intervention surveys. There is a core tension, however, between observing as much information as possible prior to conducting a PSM exercise and maintaining a large analytical sample. If matching is done *after* a baseline survey, many communities covered by the survey may subsequently be deemed to be poor comparisons and dropped from the analytical sample. Thus, most of the MCC evaluations attempted to gather as much information as possible from existing sources.

The Tanzania road evaluation is using a modified approach. Using existing Government of Tanzania data, comparison roads were first selected to ensure that they would be in the same district and agro-climatic zone and would be of a similar initial quality as the treatment roads to which they are to be compared. In most cases, a comparison road is also within the same ward and electoral constituency as the treatment road. Once this sample of roads was complete, villages along each road were randomly sampled, and sub-village neighbourhoods (known locally as *vitogoji*) were stratified as being near or far from each road, based on whether the travel time by foot to the road is <30 minutes ('near') or ≥30 minutes ('far'). The full community and household pre-intervention surveys were then administered in these *vitongoji*. These *vitongoji* were then matched using PSM on the basis of this data (see Table 5). Because the intervention roads run through five districts with varying features, the matching was first conducted district by district. Comparing the propensity score distributions of treatment and comparison *vitongoji* highlights the challenge in finding a common support (ensuring that only *vitongoji* with propensity scores that are similar to those of the other (treatment/comparison) group are included in the estimation). As Imbens and Wooldridge (2008) highlight, neglecting this common support can be a source of substantial bias in PSM estimates. In the case of Tanzania's district-by-district estimates, a substantial number of comparison *vitongoji* were dropped from the sample because their propensity scores were lower than any of those exhibited by treatment *vitongoji*. To preserve a larger sample, the matching was conducted for the whole sample jointly, with district fixed effects controlling for district-level unobserved differences in mean outcomes. Figure 2 shows the distributions for these alternative specifications. The full-sample matching weakens the ability of the evaluation to claim that all district-level effects have been controlled for through the matching, as district-level heterogeneity may still be present in the responsiveness of outcomes to the literacy rates or other covariates in a *vitongoji*. Nonetheless, this multi-stage approach allowed for better matching using a larger set of observables than would have been the case had the matching been done prior to the baseline surveys and had only secondary data from the Government of Tanzania been used. At the same time, the possibility that a greater share of the sample may be dropped because of the lack of common support remains an important consideration for future evaluations.

One other feature of matching roads or communities within relatively narrow boundaries (like wards) may be that spillovers from treatment roads/communities may affect comparison groups. For example, a road improvement in one part of the ward may reduce the effective price of agricultural produce from that part of the ward at the market located at this ward. One result may be that a comparison community located in this ward struggles to compete with these lower prices and sells less of its produce at this market. If the evaluation compares changes in agricultural production in these two parts of the ward, it would suffer from comparison group contamination. One thus needs to carefully balance the higher quality of matching based on geographical closeness and the possibility of spillovers threatening the validity of the evaluation.

Table 5. Propensity score matching for full Tanzania sample.

	PS1	PS2
Distance to road	−0.005 (0.003)	−0.005 (0.003)
Crop income	0.548 (0.805)	0.303 (0.840)
Literacy rate	−0.705 (0.763)	−0.668 (0.771)
Poverty headcount	−0.059 (0.368)	−0.127 (0.373)
Moved up LoL (%)	−0.321 (0.393)	−0.341 (0.400)
Female-headed households (%)		−3.663 (3.005)
TLU		−0.116 (0.090)
District dummies	Yes	Yes
Pseudo R^2	0.03	0.04

Note: Standard errors in parentheses. LoL is the 'Ladder of Life' survey instrument used to capture individuals' general well-being. TLU is Tropical Livestock Units, a count of the livestock each household owns, normalised by FAO weights.
Source: Reproduced from Economic Development Initiatives Ltd (2009, p. 85).

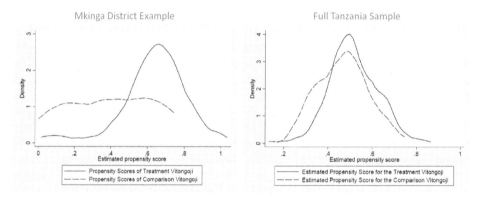

Figure 2. Propensity score distributions: Mkinga district and full Tanzania sample.
Source: Reproduced from Economic Development Initiatives Ltd (2009).

6. Geographic information systems

As previously discussed, evaluations of road improvements can be particularly strength-ened by integrating GIS data into their designs. GIS information can be useful in improving the matching process, in estimating changes in road quality due to other programmes, and in estimating the network effects of improvements in individual segments. GIS informa-tion on roads is generally derived from maps and databases maintained by national roads authorities, satellite imagery, and census/surveys information. This information can also be merged with other national data on natural resources and other infrastructure to create a multi-layered database that allows one to better characterise each community's relation-ship to these features. Naturally, the ability to use GIS data in evaluations depends on the amount of such data that exists within each country, particularly data on the national road network maintained by the national roads authority. Also important is the regular updating of this database to reflect changes in conditions over the course of the project, both along roads targeted for improvement and those outside the project's scope.

GIS can be used to strengthen the matching process by more precisely measuring the geo-physical and road conditions each community experiences. One important set of these features are agricultural factors, including soil quality, average rainfall, and elevation, which are likely to be correlated with the impact of transport improvements on agricultural production in the area. Information on each road segment is also particularly important, including the quality of the road, the volume of existing traffic, and the amount of congestion regularly experienced on it. In addition, GIS information can be used to calculate the transport costs to types of destinations. In El Salvador, for example, the targeted destination was the nearest town/city with 25,000 or more inhabitants. The minimum-cost route taking into account travel time and road type was identified for each community, and communities can be matched using this factor as one of the variables in the propensity score estimation.

Because GIS data are generally national in scope, they can be used to calculate transport costs for all communities in the country. Thus, these data can allow one to estimate the network effects of road improvements. That is, one can estimate the changes in outcomes for out-of-sample communities for which the minimum-cost pathways run through segments improved by a given project. This is most crucial when the improvements affect major national highways, which are likely to affect many communities in the country. In the Honduras evaluation, for example, the GIS model implemented by National Opinion Research Center found that the improvement of the CA-5 highway will probably benefit every village in the country, if all major potential destinations are considered (including cities and ports). By using the continuous treatment methodology to estimate the outcomes per unit reduction in travel costs, one can then impute the likely outcomes that would occur in out-of-sample communities based on their calculated reductions in travel costs. These estimates can provide a more complete sense of improvements in national infrastructure, particularly when they are based on updated data on road quality and usage throughout the network. In Georgia, for example, origin-destination studies are expected to provide context for estimates of these national-level spillovers by detailing the volume and paths of traffic flows after the improvement of the Samtskhe–Javakheti road. More generally, validating the changes in travel costs along the entire network with survey responses or global positioning system data and merging these with outcomes estimated in the evaluation sample can provide estimates of national-level impacts from major road improvements. In essence, this approach helps to determine the total scale of the effects of these improvements by considering the total number of communities for which travel costs change as a result of the project.

7. Outcomes studied

The MCC's investments in infrastructure improvements are aimed at generating higher economic activity and incomes. Projections of the impacts of road improvements are based on the aforementioned recent evidence from the evaluation literature identifying significant effects on household material well-being, with several of the studies pointing to gains in agricultural prices and production, lower input costs, and higher wages as the channels for income or consumption gains. The MCC's impact evaluations will contribute to this growing body of evidence by analysing a variety of outcomes from infrastructure improvements.

The outcomes studied in each of the impact evaluations discussed herein are related to the original economic analysis and to the purpose of the evaluation. As a standard across all countries, enough information is collected during and after implementation to calculate an ex post ERR using traditional methods, as discussed in Section 2.

For roads investments, the MCC collects the following common indicators across all countries:

- Average annual daily traffic.
- International roughness index.
- Number of kilometres completed.

These indicators allow for the calculation of changes in travel time and cost that result from the road improvements.

Beyond these measures of travel time and costs, the road impact evaluations considered in this study assess the effects of these travel-specific changes on the broader economy. Because the MCC's mission focuses on poverty reduction, many of these evaluations directly measure the change in economic well-being of individuals affected by the road improvements. As the MCC's Chief Economist writes, the:

> MCC's mandate starts with the recognition that income-based poverty measures are broadly accepted and used around the world; if an agency has as its mission the reduction of measured poverty, it needs to be able to demonstrate that it is raising incomes.[7]

Because of this mandate, MCC's road impact evaluations are designed to estimate the change in household income resulting from a new or improved road.

Most of the household surveys implemented for this type of analysis are similar to the World Bank's Living Standards Measurement Study,[8] and they include detailed modules collecting information on household consumption. Consumption is used more frequently than income since survey respondents are more likely to remember and feel comfortable sharing information on their consumption of goods rather than income. In addition, in rural areas, households have so many different sources of income that it is difficult to capture them all. Finally, consumption is preferred over income because it is smoother over time whereas income is more prone to change based on short-term factors. Analysis of intra-household allocation of resources is not conducted in a quantitative manner, but, when practical, qualitative information is collected along with the impact evaluation survey data to understand how road improvements affect men and women differently.

Collecting data on household income or consumption can be challenging, time consuming and expensive, so in some countries the analysis is limited to changes in prices and availability of goods at local markets. The theory behind this is that improved roads will open up markets to more competition and the prices of goods will fall, which will automatically result in savings of income for households in that area. Often this strategy is used in countries that do not have an ongoing annual national household survey that would provide an easy basis from which to over sample for the evaluation. This approach also makes sense when the project includes improvements in rural roads for communities that before the project had very limited access to major markets. Another advantage to this approach is that changes in prices are expected to take place in the short term whereas changes in income may take longer to develop.

Certain evaluations are designed to answer not only the question of how household income/consumption has changed, but why. This is portrayed as the shaded boxes in the logic diagram (Figure 3). For example, in El Salvador, the compact programme includes upgrading and opening sections of the main road in the Northern Zone of the country, in a primarily agricultural area. The evaluation survey was designed to capture information

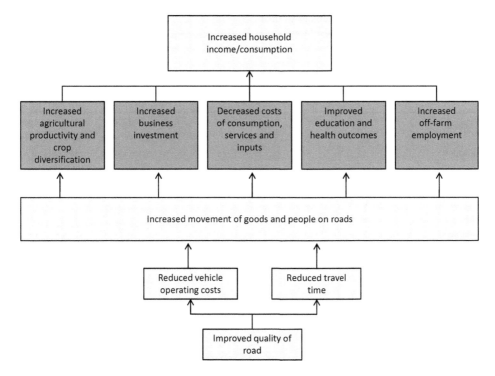

Figure 3. Road program logic.

not only on agricultural productivity and crop diversification, but also on employment and time use. The hypothesis is that as farmers gain greater access to nearby towns and cities, rural–urban trade increases, and markets become more integrated, opportunities for rural non-farm income generation should expand. It is expected that there will be changes in labour allocation between farm and non-farm activities.

Many countries project increases in business income from road improvements when they submit their project proposal justifications to MCC. Business income is not included in ex ante ERR estimates because of the lack of evidence and concern about double-counting; however, recognising that it is an important area for more research, analysis of business development has been included in the road impact evaluations in Georgia and Honduras in addition to household income. Enterprise surveys are being conducted in addition to household surveys to capture business investment, employment, and income changes. Likewise, the Tanzania and El Salvador evaluations include analysis of how the improved roads affect access to public services and their impacts on health and education outcomes. Table 6 summarises the key outcomes included in each of the seven road impact evaluations.

An array of data collection instruments are being used to capture information on these outcomes, as illustrated in Table 7. All of the surveys involve panel data at either the community level or the household level, a crucial element for the DD analysis described in Section 3.

The road evaluations discussed herein will not only assess the average increase in income among broad populations from road improvements, but also will look at the heterogeneity in benefits throughout these populations. Understanding who receives these

Table 6. Road improvement outcomes studied.

Country	Household income/consumption	Local market prices of inputs/outputs	Business income/growth	Agricultural productivity	Transport access, time, costs	Access to health and education services	Land values	Additional outcomes
Armenia	Y			Y	Y			
El Salvador	Y			Y	Y	Y	Y	Labour allocation between farm and non-farm activities
Georgia	Y		Y		Y			
Ghana		Y			Y			
Honduras	Y	Y	Y		Y	Y	Y	
Nicaragua		Y			Y			Availability of goods
Tanzania	Y	Y			Y	Y		Availability of transport services Capital investment Employment Migration patterns

benefits is crucial for future policy decisions allocating scarce aid resources across potential projects. Traditional road analysis considers the users of the road to be the main beneficiaries, and this is reflected in the ex ante economic analysis of time and cost savings for road users. However, for standard reporting across countries, the MCC uses a common definition of road beneficiaries as the population that lives within 5 km of the improved road. The reality is probably a mix of these two – road users benefit, and people living near the road benefit as well. To understand who the main beneficiaries are of road improvements, the MCC is analysing the impact of the road on households with different levels of access to the road. For example, the evaluation sample in Tanzania was purposefully stratified based on distance from the road, so that results could be compared between households within 30 minutes of walking time of the road and those farther than 30 minutes from the road. In addition, MCC conducts beneficiary analysis both pre-construction and post-construction, which disaggregates the increases in income from the ERR into income groups to estimate the distributional benefits of road improvements.

The MCC's evaluations of investments in electricity, water and sanitation and irrigation will also involve analysis of income and consumption effects across the baseline distribution of beneficiaries. In monitoring the progress of these activities, the MCC uses the common indicators presented in Table 8 in all water and sanitation and irrigation projects when relevant (common indicators for electricity investments have not yet been developed).

As discussed, the MCC impact evaluations take the analysis a step further by analysing the changes observed in households or businesses as a result of having, for example, increased water consumption and lower disease rates, and comparing them with a group who has not received the improvements. The household surveys, business surveys and community surveys used for these impact evaluations do not vary substantially from those used in the MCC's road impact evaluations. In fact, in El Salvador, the same survey is

Table 7.   Road improvement evaluation surveys.

Country	Data sources	Data collector	Survey sample
Armenia	Integrated Living Conditions Survey	National Statistical Service of Armenia	Households selected by chance into main sample, plus an additional sample of 1700 households served by project and comparison roads (panel of road sections)
El Salvador	Connectivity Household Survey and Community Survey	El Salvador Office of Statistics and Census	Panel of 5388 households
Georgia	Integrated Household Survey and Village Infrastructure Census	Department of Statistics of Georgia	Over-sample of national household survey of 3382 households (panel of communities)
Ghana	Ghana Market Survey	National Opinion Research Center and Pentax (private firms)	Panel of 308 communities
Honduras	Household Survey, Business Survey and Price and Product Survey	National Institute of Statistics of Honduras	2000 households. Panel of 200 enterprises. Panel of 100 communities
Nicaragua	Price Survey	Fideg (private firm)	Panel of 435 observations in 33 communities
Tanzania	Household and community surveys	Economic Development Initiatives, Ltd (private firm)	3000 households and panel of 200 communities for trunk roads. 1200 households for rural roads on Zanzibar

being used to collect data for the road evaluation and the rural electrification evaluation because of the overlapping locations of the two projects. Thus, the income and consumption effects of road improvements can be compared with those generated from the electrification intervention. As noted previously, estimating the effects of water and sanitation

Table 8.   Common indicators.

Water and sanitation	Irrigation
Persons trained in hygiene and sanitary best practices	Hectares under improved or new irrigation
Number of water points constructed	Hectares under production
Number of sanitation systems constructed	
Volume of water produced	
Number of households with access to improved water supply	
Number of households with access to improved sanitation	
Domestic water consumption	
Commercial water consumption	
Incidence of water-borne diseases	

Table 9. Electricity, irrigation, and water and sanitation improvement outcomes studied.

Country and project	Household income/ consumption	Business income/ growth	Time/cost savings	Water/ electricity consumption	Additional outcomes
Armenia Irrigation	Y			Y	Agricultural productivity
El Salvador Electricity	Y		Y	Y	
El Salvador Water	Y		Y	Y	Health
Georgia	Y	Y	Y	Y	Health
Lesotho Water	Y	Y	Y	Y	Health
Tanzania Electricity	Y	Y		Y	Health, education

programmes on household income and consumption will be a major contribution of the MCC's evaluations.

One difference between the MCC's road and other infrastructure evaluations is that some of these other evaluations make use of administrative data such as utility company records. Information from the utilities on electricity used or water consumed and amount paid is collected to check household and business responses on surveys. Table 9 summarises the key outcomes included in each of the non-road infrastructure impact evaluations.

The MCC's evaluations of electricity, water, and sanitation investments will also address how time saved from daily household activities will be reallocated. There is generally consensus that providing an improved energy or water source will free up time for household members. However, whether this time will be allocated to leisure or to other productive activities remains less clear. Three of MCC's infrastructure evaluations discussed here have questionnaires that include time use modules to determine what effects time savings have on the household's productive activities.

Finally, even though a great deal of the existing literature on water and sanitation improvements in developing countries focuses on reductions in disease incidence, not all of the MCC's evaluations highlighted herein are designed specifically to address this particular outcome. In Lesotho, the evaluation of the rural water supply programme will indeed focus on gastrointestinal morbidity among children under five years of age. The evaluation of the urban water investments, however, will not, as urban water quality is already quite good and water-borne disease is not a significant problem. In El Salvador, the MCC encountered a trade-off in terms of what outcomes could be analysed with high precision. To capture the best data possible on coping costs (time costs associated with collecting water and the monetary cost of relying on alternative water sources such as vendors), surveys would have had to be done in the dry season when water shortages are more likely. To capture data on disease incidence, however, surveys would have had to be done during the wet season when disease rates are highest. Given budget limitations, the MCC could not commission dual surveys in both seasons and opted to give priority to the measurement of changes in household income and coping costs by conducting surveys in the dry season. This was due in large part to the fact that coping costs accounted for most of the expected benefits in the ERR and because diarrhoea rates had dropped substantially in recent years due to a variety of public health interventions.

8. Implementation

Even though none of the MCC's infrastructure impact evaluations have yet been completed, there are many lessons from the past six years about how implementation can affect impact evaluation design – ranging from creating opportunities for evaluation where there was none to preventing the opportunity for any rigorous evaluation at all. The impact evaluation concept is developed before a compact is even signed. Usually the final evaluation design is agreed upon during the first year of implementation once implementation strategies are better defined. The final agreed upon design is completed in the first year of the compact term so that baseline data can be collected before construction begins. Implementation plans change throughout all five years of the compact term. So far, three common issues have been encountered during implementation that complicate the impact evaluation effort. Those are: project scope changes because of cost over-runs and/or poor policy performance; delays in construction; and changes to the roll-out and/or contracting strategy. Each one is discussed in turn.

In many countries, compacts are signed before feasibility studies, detailed designs, environmental impact assessments, and resettlement plans are completed. Therefore, at compact signing when the impact evaluation design is initially agreed upon, the scope of infrastructure to be improved (the number of kilometres of roads, for example) is usually an upper bound. As studies are completed, the number of kilometres to be completed is refined. This takes place over a couple of years. Between collecting baseline data and finalising the detailed design of the roads, currencies fluctuate and input prices change. In the recent past, input prices have increased, so the reasonable pre-investment cost estimates have turned into underfunded budgets and fewer road sections have been improved. Given a different global financial situation, one could imagine that the opposite could take place – more road sections than originally planned could be constructed.

In addition to designs, currency fluctuations, and input price changes, projects can be changed because of poor policy performance by a country. As explained in Section 2, eligibility for MCC assistance is based on countries meeting certain requirements in terms of ruling justly, investing in people, and economic freedom. If countries backslide on policy performance during implementation, MCC funding can be put on hold, suspended, or terminated. This occurred in two of the countries considered in this paper – Armenia and Nicaragua.

The effect of project scope changes or 're-scoping' on the impact evaluation could be either positive or negative. As road projects get smaller in terms of the number of kilometres completed and the number of beneficiaries, the treatment group for the evaluation also gets smaller. If the baseline survey was completed and then a re-scoping takes place and the treatment survey sample is reduced, the power of the evaluation is reduced. As explained in Section 4, in Armenia an RD design was chosen because road sections had been packaged for construction in three packages based on ERRs. However, subsequent challenges in the country led MCC to put a hold on the road activities. Only 24 kilometres were built by MCC, which was too small of a treatment group to conduct the originally planned impact evaluation.

In at least one case thus far, re-scoping has led evaluators to consider including in the comparison group road segments that would no longer be improved. In Nicaragua, sections that were initially slated for improvement but were not launched when compact funding was terminated were relatively comparable with those roads on which construction had already begun. Nonetheless, in order to make use of such evaluation opportunities, evaluators must carefully investigate whether the differential timing of improvements along particular segments is correlated with factors related to outcomes along these roads.

Preparing for road construction requires a large effort, especially when done under the MCC model of country ownership. Countries are required to develop their own terms of reference for construction and construction supervision, as well as all of the environmental assessments and resettlement plans. The MCC then reviews and approves each of these. This process often takes months and has resulted in projects starting later than originally planned in some cases. Delays can also be caused by poor performance by design contractors, new information about environmental considerations, resettlement negotiations, or problems encountered during construction. All of the MCC's road projects must be completed by the end of the compact, which has a five-year term. It is very common for construction projects to be delayed such that the construction is completed in the last year of the compact.

Delays create a challenge for evaluating the impact of the road improvements. An evaluation at the end of the compact will only capture short-term effects, and if the project is in an agricultural area, at least a year will have to pass for any agricultural changes to take place before doing the final data collection. In addition, if an evaluation based on differential timing of construction was planned, construction delays could end up condensing construction into a short time period towards the end of the compact term, making this type of analysis impossible. There are also risks for matching evaluations. If a matching evaluation was planned and the treatment takes years to be completed, it is possible that other road projects funded by the government or other donors could be started and completed in the comparison group at the same time as the MCC treatment group.

A third complication is changes to the project roll-out and/or contracting strategy. An evaluation based on differential timing of construction requires that certain road segments are improved before others. Sometimes final designs including environmental issues and resettlement become more complicated on a certain section than originally thought. This could delay construction on a particular section and completely change the order of section completion. If the construction coincides with later sections, the analysis based on differential timing of construction can no longer be implemented. Changes to contracting strategies can also result in schedule changes if road sections were packaged differently than originally planned. Combining construction packages could complicate an evaluation based on the differential timing of construction, since it would reduce the statistical power. Conversely, separating construction packages into smaller units could create an opportunity for analysis based on differential timing of construction (although timing between them may not be sufficient).

The evaluation issues experienced in implementation of road improvement projects have been similar to those experienced by projects focused on other types of infrastructure. In El Salvador, both the water and sanitation and rural electrification evaluations were designed based on pre-feasibility studies; and as final designs were completed, scope changes occurred, which caused several complications for the evaluations. In water and sanitation, many of the treatment projects were determined to be unfeasible and dropped from the project, leaving the evaluation with a smaller treatment sample than expected. As a result, a second baseline including the final list of treatment projects may have to be undertaken, as the first baseline only included a sample of expected projects (luckily for the evaluation, implementation is behind so there is time for another baseline). In the case of El Salvador's rural electrification evaluation, some of the final designs for extending the electrical grid left out households included in the baseline survey as part of the treatment group based on the pre-feasibility designs. The evaluation team is working with the implementation team to identify these households and include them in future phases of electrical grid extensions when possible.

9. Recommendations

The 13 MCC evaluations studied herein offer useful lessons for evaluators and are likely to generate several key pieces of information that will guide policy-makers considering investing resources in potential infrastructure improvement projects. Most notably, the evaluations in El Salvador, Honduras, Nicaragua, Georgia, and Tanzania are likely to provide the first set of empirical evidence on the impacts of improvements in highways and major secondary roads in developing countries. Evaluations of rural road improvements will help quantify the effects of these improvements on the access to and use of public services, such as medical clinics, as well as on other channels through which households' material well-being may be affected. The MCC's evaluations of water and sanitation improvements will include some of the first experimental and quasi-experimental results on the effects on income generating opportunities for households in developing countries. Meanwhile, electrification evaluations will provide rigorous evidence on the extent to which access to electricity leads to changes in the level and composition of household income, including the wages earned by women and the amount of unpaid work they do at home.

The MCC portfolio of evaluations also offers several more immediate implications for infrastructure evaluation. First, one important question not tackled by these evaluations is what effect MCC's engagement with recipient countries on reforming institutional arrangements for maintaining the improved infrastructure has had on the affected population. For example, new road maintenance policies with fuel tax revenues devoted to newly created road maintenance funds are being implemented along with MCC's capital investments in a number of countries. Although such issues are frequently national in scope and variation in treatment is often difficult to identify, these reforms would differentially affect areas where existing roads had languished longest without adequate maintenance. Evaluators should attempt to study these heterogeneous effects to assess the likely value of such reforms.

The second implication is that comparison of non-experimental and experimental methods for evaluation of rural road improvements is crucial to confirming the validity of the former. The overlap of methods within a number of the MCC evaluations will allow for a comparison of these methods. In particular, the El Salvador roads evaluation's RD design could be compared with estimates obtained through PSM-DD, giving a sense of the effectiveness of PSM-DD in providing precise, unbiased estimates of programme impact. At the same time, it would be invaluable to compare these alternative approaches with experimental results. While random assignment is being used in several evaluations of water and electricity network expansion, governments and aid organisations should employ random assignment of rural road improvements to build an experimental benchmark against which other evaluation methods could be compared. Random assignment of rural road improvements may be most appropriate in cases where segment-by-segment cost–benefit analysis is not possible. In such a case, a comparison of the random assignment results to those obtained from PSM-DD and continuous treatment estimators would be extremely valuable to the roads evaluation literature.

The MCC's evaluation experience also suggests that evaluators must build multiple methods into their evaluation designs if they are to remain robust to project implementation changes. Evaluations that rely on selection processes or construction timing can offer rigorous results, but they are naturally sensitive to changes in these processes or timing. In particular, regression discontinuity designs appear to be particularly susceptible to these changes, especially when they rely on future funding decisions for a given portfolio of potential sub-projects. In these cases, changes in costs or project scope can dramatically alter the composition of projects around a given threshold. On the other hand, evaluations using statistical matching are much more robust to such changes, although the degree of rigour they offer depends on how much of the treatment-comparison differences one can directly observe. Combining these methods in evaluations is thus highly recommended.

When statistical matching is employed, careful thought should be given to the geographic proximity of matched units. On the one hand, nearby roads, for example, might be more comparable in terms of unobservables with treatment roads than would be roads located in other districts of a country. On the other hand, intra-district heterogeneity may be more pronounced in some respects than inter-district heterogeneity. This may be the case when a given district may only have a limited amount of resources to maintain all of its roads and devotes these resources to treatment roads but not to comparison roads. Such scenarios could result in ex ante differences between roads within a district – leading to problems in finding a common support if matching within district – as well as possible contamination of the comparison group. Evaluators should carefully consider the comparability of assignment units across geographic regions, weighing cross-region differences against within-region differences and contamination risk. Evaluators may find that, as in the case of Tanzania's roads evaluation, matching can be optimally done over the full sample, but with propensity scores controlling for differences across regions in the form of region fixed effects.

One core weakness in the existing literature is on the effects of improvements of primary roads or highways on traffic, household, and firm outcomes along other sections of the road network that are connected to the improved road. Several MCC evaluations are using GIS data to model these effects and to make out-of-sample predictions. GIS data are also useful in quantifying the degree of treatment that a given household or firm receives by enabling calculations of the travel time and costs to key destinations. We recommend that, whenever possible, evaluations of primary or even secondary roads include GIS analysis components.

We also find that continuous treatment designs are being successfully employed in several MCC road evaluations but in none of the evaluations of other types of infrastructure we examined. There is sufficient heterogeneity in the initial level of access to these other types of infrastructure to permit identification of differential improvements in access and relate them to changes in key outcomes. We highly recommend that evaluations of irrigation, water and sanitation and electricity improvements incorporate this design.

Finally, the MCC's evaluations are intended to enable comparisons of cost-effectiveness in terms of common outcomes within infrastructure types and, just as importantly, comparisons of cost-effectiveness in terms of household income gains across all interventions. The present value of income gains from roads improvements can be compared with the present value of investment costs and changes in maintenance costs to establish a benefit–cost ratio. An alternate version may include only income gains among households living on less than $2 per day in purchasing power parity (PPP) terms to assess the cost-effectiveness of these investments in terms of impacts on the poor. Calculating these measures requires not only some modelling of the future time path and sustainability of these gains, but also marrying this modelling with a detailed cost accounting for the activities. We recommend that infrastructure evaluations consistently include such cost-effectiveness calculations in order to inform policy-makers about the relative impacts of these infrastructure investments vis-à-vis investments in other sectors.

Acknowledgements

The authors are grateful to Jigar Bhatt, Ken Fortson, Celeste Lemrow, and Anne Pizer for the time and insights they shared with them. They also thank an anonymous referee and the editor for their suggestions. Thanks are also due to Andrew Carter and Algerlynn Gill for excellent research assistance. The views represented herein are the authors' own and do not represent those of the Millennium Challenge Corporation nor of any other organisation.

Notes

1. Hurdle rates for ERRs have historically fallen between 8 and 15 per cent, depending on the country and its recent growth experience. A standardised hurdle rate for new activities and changes to activities already under implementation is currently set at 10 per cent. All of MCC's economic rate of return models can be found on its website (http://www.mcc.gov/err).
2. In some cases, the World Bank's Roads Economic Decision model is used for low-volume roads, as it designed specifically for unpaved roads with high uncertainty of initial roughness and traffic measures.
3. Just as in the roads analysis, in some cases a portion of the expected benefits does not have a wealth of rigorous studies to pin down their magnitude. Therefore, the models are developed with the best available information at the time and key assumptions are highlighted for future analysis.
4. Descriptions of MCC's impact evaluations can be found on its website (www.mcc.gov) under 'Programs and Activities' and then 'Impact Evaluation'.
5. Even in cases where rigorous statements of causal impacts cannot be made, the MCC is devoting significant resources to evaluations of the outputs and outcomes of these activities. For example, for a number of activities, comparisons of conditions before and after the investments, although made without the observation of a comparison group, can yield helpful evidence on the bounds for the programme's potential effects.
6. The Tanzania evaluation will not consider treatment as a continuous variable, but communities have been categorised in terms of their travel time to a treatment/comparison road. The difference in outcomes for communities near an improved road (vis-à-vis communities near unimproved roads) can be compared with the difference in outcomes for communities farther from these improved roads (*vis-à-vis* outcomes for communities at a similar distance from unimproved roads). This difference-in-difference-in-difference approach can be likened to a more continuous treatment.
7. Franck Wiebe's MCC Working Paper 'Aid Effectiveness: Putting Results at the Forefront' (http://www.mcc.gov/mcc/bm.doc/mcc-112008-paper-results.pdf).
8. For more information, see www.worldbank.org/lsms

References

Behrman, J., Chen, Y. and Todd, P., 2004. Evaluating preschool programs when length of exposure to the program varies: a nonparametric approach. *Review of economics and statistics*, 86 (1), 108–132.

Chaplin, D., Chatterji, M. and Hankinson, D., 2009. *Final design report for the MCC impact evaluation design & implementation services – Tanzania Energy Sector Project*. Mimeo.

Chowdhury, S. and Torero, M., 2007. *Impact of infrastructure on income and work of rural households, women and the landless in the Northwestern region of Bangladesh*. Washington, DC: IFPRI.

Dehejia, R. and Wahba, S., 1999. Causal effects in nonexperimental studies: reevaluating the evaluation of training programs. *Journal of the American Statistical Association*, 94, 1053–1062.

Dercon, S., Gilligan, D., Hoddinott, J. and Woldehanna, T., 2006. *The impact of roads and agricultural extension on consumption growth and poverty in fifteen Ethiopian villages*. University of Oxford, CSAE WPS 2007-01. Mimeo.

Economic Development Initiatives Ltd, 2009. *Final report: consultancy services for the design and implementation of household survey and community profile for transport sector*. Mimeo.

Escobal, J., and Ponce, C., 2004. *The benefits of rural roads: enhancing income opportunities for the rural poor*. Lima, Peru, GRADE Working Paper 40. Mimeo.

Estache, A., 2010. *A survey of impact evaluations of infrastructure projects, programs and policies*. Université Libre de Bruxelles, ECARES Working Paper 2010-005. Mimeo.

Fideg, 2008. *Informe Final: Encuesta para medir el precio de la Canasta Básica en 30 Comunidades de León y Chinandega*. Mimeo.

Fortson, K., and Rangarajan, A., 2008. *Rural road rehabilitation project evaluation plan*. Mathematica Policy Research. Mimeo.

Garcia-Milà, T. and Montalvo, J. 2007. The impact of new highways on business location: new evidence from Spain. Universitat Pompeu Fabra. Mimeo.

Heckman, J., Ichimura, H. and Todd, P., 1997. Matching as an econometric evaluation estimator: evidence from evaluating a job training programme. *Review of economic studies*, 64 (4), 605–654.

Heckman, J., Ichimura, H. and Todd, P., 1998a. Matching as an econometric evaluation estimator. *Review of economic studies*, 65 (2), 261–294.

Heckman, J., Ichimura, H., Smith, J. and Todd, P., 1998b. Characterizing selection bias using experimental data. *Econometrica*, 66 (5), 1017–1098.

Hirano, K. and Imbens, G., 2004. The propensity score with continuous treatments. *In*: A. Gelman and X. Meng, eds. *Applied Bayesian modeling and causal inference from incomplete-data perspectives*. Oxford: Wiley, 73–84.

Imbens, G., 2000. The role of the propensity score in estimating dose-response functions. *Biometrika*, 87 (3), 706–710.

Imbens, G. and Wooldridge, J., 2008. *Recent developments in the econometrics of program evaluation*. National Bureau of Economic Research Working Paper 14251. Mimeo.

Jalan, S. and Ravallion, M., 2003. Does piped water reduce diarrhea for children in rural India? *Journal of econometrics*, 112 (1), 153–173.

Khandker, S., Bakht, Z. and Koolwal, G., 2006. *The poverty impact of rural roads: evidence from Bangladesh*. World Bank Policy Research Working Paper 3875. Mimeo.

Komives, K., Poulos, C. and Pattanayak, S., 2009. *Impact evaluation design for MCC water and sanitation interventions in El Salvador*. Social Impact, Inc. Mimeo.

Lee, L., Rosenzweig, M. and Pitt, M., 1997. The effects of improved nutrition, sanitation, and water quality on child health in high-mortality populations. *Journal of econometrics*, 77 (1), 209–235.

Lokshin, M. and Yemtsov, R., 2005. Has rural infrastructure rehabilitation in Georgia helped the poor? *The World Bank economic review*, 19 (2), 311–333.

National Opinion Research Center (NORC), 2007. *Design report: design and implementation of MCA Honduras program evaluation*. Mimeo.

National Opinion Research Center (NORC), 2009a. *Annual report: impact evaluation design & implementation services Georgia*. Mimeo.

National Opinion Research Center (NORC), 2009b. *Department of rural water supply evaluation mini-report*. Lesotho: Impact Evaluation Design & Implementation Services.

National Opinion Research Center (NORC), 2009c. *Water and sewerage authority evaluation mini-report*. Lesotho: Impact Evaluation Design & Implementation Services.

Rauniyar, G., Orbeta, A. and Sugiyarto, G., 2010. *Impact of water supply and sanitation assistance on human welfare in rural Pakistan*. Asian Development Bank. Mimeo.

Rosenbaum, P. and Rubin, D., 1983. The central role of the propensity score in observational studies for causal effects. *Biometrika*, 70 (1), 41–55.

Struyk, R., Caldwell, J., Felkner, J., Kysia, K. and Shova, K.C., 2010. *Impact evaluation of feeder roads: phase 1, baseline findings report*. National Opinion Research Center. Mimeo.

Torero, M., 2009a. *Impact evaluation design for MCC connectivity interventions in El Salvador*. Social Impact, Inc. Mimeo.

Torero, M., 2009b. *Impact evaluation design for MCC rural electrifications interventions in El Salvador*. Social Impact, Inc. Mimeo.

Van de Walle, D., 2008. *Impact evaluations of rural road projects*. World Bank Working Paper 47438. Mimeo.

Van de Walle, D. and Cratty, D., 2002. *Impact evaluation of a rural road rehabilitation project*. Washington, DC: World Bank.

White, H., ed., 2008. *An impact evaluation of India's second and third Andhra Pradesh irrigation projects: a case of poverty reduction with low economic returns*. Washington, DC: World Bank.

Achieving high-quality impact evaluation design through mixed methods: the case of infrastructure

Howard White

International Initiative for Impact Evaluation (3ie), New Delhi, India

A good-quality impact evaluation is based on an analysis of the theory of change for the intervention. Analysis of different parts of this causal chain, and the underlying assumptions, necessarily requires use of a variety of research methods. The method should fit the question, not the other way round. The challenge is to genuinely mix these methods rather than conduct parallel studies. The analysis needs to be rooted in a good understanding of context, which may come from anthropology or political science and political economy. Qualitative information sheds light on factors behind programme placement and self-selection. A key contribution from other disciplines is a proper understanding of the nature and distribution of benefits, enabling an impact evaluation design that captures the full range of benefits and socially-mediated impact heterogeneity.

1. Introduction

Impact evaluations address the attribution question, impact being defined as the difference in the indicators of interest with versus without the intervention.[1]

How attribution is best addressed depends on the nature of the intervention and the evaluation questions. For large *n* studies – that is, those in which there are a large number of units to which the intervention is assigned – statistical procedures using experimental or quasi-experimental approaches are the most appropriate means to quantify impact. Large *n* infrastructure interventions include water supply and sanitation, rural electrification, urban development such as slum upgrading, small infrastructure such as footbridges, and might also be applicable to regional or national programmes of rural road improvement or provision, as well as urban transport schemes. To capture macroeconomic impacts, which are particularly pertinent for large-scale infrastructure such as port development, trunk roads and establishment of a new grid, computable general equilibrium models (CGEs)[2] are more appropriate, such as used by Haddad (2011) in his contribution to this volume. When using CGEs, calibration of the transaction cost savings and associated behavioural responses may come from micro-econometric studies (Ravallion 2009).[3] Other forms of small *n* intervention, such as seeking change in the policy environment – for example, encouraging the adoption of a public private partnership model for infrastructure development, or indeed assessing the impact of impact evaluations on subsequent project design – require a qualitative approach based on stakeholder mapping and so on, although there is less consensus as to the appropriate qualitative toolkit for addressing the attribution question in the way there is for quantitative studies.

But measurement is not evaluation. An impact evaluation should not be solely concerned with producing a counterfactual measure of impact. Such an analysis should be embedded in a well-contextualised theory of change, which helps understand the causal pathways behind why an intervention works or does not work, not just if it does (see Pawson and Tilley 1997, Carvalho and White 2004, Rogers 2007, White 2009). Such an approach implies a combination of factual and counterfactual analysis drawing upon a range of data sources and methodological approaches. The method should be chosen to fit the evaluation questions, not the other way round. The purpose of this paper is to discuss this range of sources and approaches applicable to the evaluation of infrastructure interventions.

2. Establishing the base: theory-based evaluation design

The theory-based approach starts with a clear identification of the intervention, its objectives and outcomes (which may be intended and unintended), and the underlying theory of change. Impact evaluators from a range of perspectives all stress the importance of properly understanding the intervention, and its rationale, as a basis for evaluation design (Karlan 2009, Ravallion 2009, Rogers 2009).

The theory of change should be complemented by any counter-theories suggesting that the intervention may not work in the way its designers intended. For example, social funds were seen by their proponents as a means of constructing small-scale social sector infrastructure – schools and clinics – quickly and effectively. But the 'counter-theory' of critics of these projects was that such a decentralised approach undermined centrally-based resource allocation needed to ensure that facilities were constructed where they were most needed (Carvalho and White 2004). Unintended outcomes from infrastructure interventions may include adverse social and environmental consequences, loss of existing livelihoods, and undesirable aspects of contact with the outside world; for example, the transmission of HIV/AIDS along trunk roads.

A theory-based impact evaluation design (White 2009) stresses the complementarity of methods in different parts of the design. Development of the theory of change itself depends upon review of the project documents, interviews with project staff and other stakeholders, field visits including interaction with intended beneficiaries, and review of relevant academic literature on both the intervention and the context in which it is being implemented. The review should also encompass a review of other evaluation studies of similar interventions, though it is rare that an 'evaluation template' can be lifted from one context to another.

The theory of change may be laid out in the project documents, but often it is not. Rather, it is often taken for granted that implementing certain activities –which may be either 'business as usual' or the latest 'flavour of the month' – will lead to the expected outcomes. If there is a project or programme log frame, then this framework can be the starting point for the theory of change, since it does lay out the causal chain from inputs to outcomes; an example is provided in Broegaard et al. (2011). But the log frame is the framework for analysis, not the analysis itself, since the evaluation has to interrogate the assumptions underlying the causal chain implicit in the log frame.

Tables 1 and 2 lay out an evaluation framework for a programme of trunk road rehabilitation. Table 1 presents indicators corresponding to different levels of the causal chain, showing the 'indicator' and a more precisely defined measure of the data to be collected. Finally the assumptions are given. As is evident from the table, much of the data to be

Table 1.   Log frame and indicators for trunk road rehabilitation.

	Indicator	Measure	Assumptions
Inputs	Money, plans, institutional framework	Agreed work programme and responsibilities, disbursements	Plans technically sound, local buy in to plans and capacity to implement them, accurate costings
Activities/ processes	Award contracts for work, land acquisition, work undertaken	Contracts awarded through transparent tendering process; percentage of required land acquired	Reported work actually completed (and on time and budget); construction quality sufficient; legal framework exists for land acquisition
Outputs	Length of road rehabilitated	Kilometres of road rehabilitated	Suitable regulatory environment for public transport
	Increased traffic volumes	Public and private vehicular traffic	Availability of vehicles, spare parts and fuel
	Reduced vehicle operating costs	Vehicle operating costs	Road is maintained
Outcomes	*Positive*: increased market access resulting in higher income (and multiplier effects). Better access to services and/or better services in communities on road	Net household income	Profitable economic opportunities in catchment area, and capacity to respond to them
	Negative: traffic accidents, competition for local handicrafts, exposure to health hazards	Access health and education	
		Traffic fatalities Disease prevalence rates	

collected relate to process aspects of the project, such as land acquisition, which is a frequent source of delay in the implementation of infrastructure projects. Delays matter. Given large upfront costs, postponing the start of benefits will seriously affect the rate of return to the investment. Our study of the construction of a new irrigation scheme in Andhra Pradesh showed that delays, combined with cost overruns, pushed a potentially good investment, with large poverty reduction benefits, into negative returns (World Bank 2008).

Thinking about the causal chain also helps thinking about the timing of the impact study. People ask 'when is the right time to do an impact evaluation?' But there is no single answer to that question. It all depends on a realistic time frame for measurable changes in the outcome to be realistically expected. The current fashion for impact evaluation is creating pressure for premature impact evaluations. For the roads project, there is no point in conducting the evaluation until after the construction or rehabilitation is complete; in fact, preferably at least a year or so after that (Ravallion 2009). And a post-endline survey three or four years later is strongly advised to see whether benefits have accumulated and multiplied, or tailed off because of weak sustainability (see Woolcock 2009 on impact trajectories). At end line, sustainability should be assessed by evaluating whether systems are in place to ensure sustainability.

Table 2. Common questions for a theory-based impact evaluation of trunk road rehabilitation.

	Design	Implementation	Consequences
Relevance	What was the planning process? Who was involved? Was allocation consistent with national and local priorities (as reflected in political strategies rather than donor-backed documents)? Were resources allocated to priority areas with highest potential benefits?	Does project implementation follow the design?	Did the intervention satisfy a priority need of beneficiaries? What are their perspectives on positive and negative impacts?
Behaviour change	Are any necessary complementary inputs being provided?	Are complementary inputs being provided to the right people at the right time?	Are households increasing variety, size and scale of livelihood activities? Are travel patterns changing?
Impact: who benefits and by how much?	Are potential losers identified? What, if any, are the mechanisms to compensate losers?	Is compensation actually being paid, and is it to the right people?	Does the physical configuration of the infrastructure impede existing livelihoods? By how much have net incomes increased in beneficiary communities?
Sustainability	Is there a mechanism in place for maintenance?	Is the mechanism functioning correctly? Are institutional arrangements in place for it to continue to do so? Does technical capacity exist to undertake maintenance? Are adequate financial resources available?	Are income effects (including multiplier effects) sufficient to cover maintenance costs through taxation?

Process data may be available from the monitoring system, although the evaluation design should allow for independent verification of the monitoring data for a sample of activities. The data from inputs to outputs can be pieced together into a strong factual narrative on what actually happened, which is just as important as the counterfactual analysis as to what would have happened in the absence of the intervention. Too many evaluations pay insufficient detail to an account of what was actually done: what was the money used for?

For ex ante evaluation designs, process evaluations should take place whilst the intervention is being implemented. There are at least three advantages to such an approach: bringing timely findings to management for action to ensure a functioning feedback loop;

to be aware of changes in project design and implementation that may have implications for the design of the endline data collection for impact analysis; and it may be found that things are going so badly wrong at the lower reaches of the causal chain that there is no point in conducting the impact analysis. An unbuilt road will not improve lives in the communities that it was meant to serve.

Table 2 presents examples of the sorts of questions that may be addressed by the trunk road evaluation. It is not an exhaustive list. These questions can be classified according to subject (relevance, who benefits, and so forth), and whether they relate to the design or implementation of the intervention or its consequences. Again, many of these questions are process questions, requiring factual analysis of a variety of data sources.

Impact evaluations should consider the standard evaluation questions, including relevance and sustainability. Relevance needs to be assessed looking across the portfolio and considering other programmes going on. In rural Africa, most journeys are still made on local paths, so a footbridge may matter far more to most people than a trunk road. Both have their benefits, but external donors, who generally have a preference for large infrastructure, need to be sure that these local priorities are also being addressed.[4] It is easy for 'everything to be a priority' and so find a policy statement serving to demonstrate the relevance of any intervention. But a stronger case can be made for relevance if strong political commitment can be found for the intervention, as in the case of basic education in Ghana discussed below.

A commonly neglected area in intervention design is proper analysis of those who may be adversely affected by the project. The real world offers little scope for Pareto improvements. Most development interventions have winners and losers. Of course, there should be a positive net gain, so the losers can be compensated. From a road project, direct losers are those whose land is taken to construct the road. Indirect losers are local service providers who lose out from increased competition from 'imported' goods; for example, the displacement of local brews with bottled beer. Most project designs only provide compensation to the direct losers, leaving it to the market to provide opportunities for the indirect losers. How qualitative data can shed light on potential losers is discussed in Section 4.

A neglected area in impact evaluation design is the sustainability of the benefits. Impact evaluation quantifies the benefits at a specific point in time. Cost–benefit analysis requires projecting these benefits into the future, which assumes these benefits are sustainable. The 3ie review of water supply and sanitation studies showed that, although point of use treatment, is very cost effective, sustainability is weak, meaning that adoption rates fall off rapidly after the intervention (Waddington et al. 2009, Waddington and Snilstveit 2010). Sustainability is best addressed through a post-endline survey, a type of study that is conducted too infrequently.[5] Alternatively, a process evaluation can be made of mechanisms to ensure sustainability. Our study of social funds, for example, showed that water pumps were unlikely to be sustainable as no one in the village had the technical skills to perform maintenance and no revenue was being collected to pay for spare parts if needed (Carvalho et al. 2002, World Bank 2002).

The above discussion of a theory-based approach has mostly discussed aspects of the evaluation requiring a factual, rather than counterfactual, analysis of a range of data. Approaches to mixed-methods factual analysis are now discussed in more detail.

3. Approaches to combining mixed methods in rigorous impact evaluation

I have discussed elsewhere the use of mixed methods in poverty measurement and analysis (Carvalho and White 1997, White 2002), and specifically with respect to impact evaluation (White 2006, 2008). Here I will briefly summarise some main points from those discussions.

Mixed methods should be broadly conceived. It does not mean just commissioning some qualitative research alongside the main quantitative research, and certainly does not mean just doing a few focus groups, an increasingly overused and misused form of data collection. For both quantitative and qualitative data, the focus has to be on rigour. Both approaches are open to poorly designed or implemented research yielding biased and misleading results (White 2002).

In fact, everyone already practises mixed methods, as they at least read the project documentation for the intervention they are evaluating. Or, at least, it is to be hoped they do – although I have read evaluations for which one can wonder whether that was the case. Utilising the information in the project documents is qualitative research providing data on context. Context also comes from reading general studies on the political economy of the country, anthropological studies relevant to the setting and intervention, and sector reviews for the country; the latter may be grey material that is increasingly available online. Turning to the project, be sure to collect any evaluations that have been conducted as well as know what data are available in the monitoring system. If there are annual monitoring reports, get these. You should be fully familiar with all project documentation before you first meet programme staff so you do not waste their time, and your time, asking things you should already know about.

It will usually be necessary to commission some additional qualitative data collection in the field. The full range of participatory methods should be used, not just focus groups but mapping of various kinds, transects, oral life histories, and so forth (see Chambers 2009 for a list of suitable participatory methods for evaluating transport interventions). If possible some of the budget should be reserved for action research to address issues and questions that emerge as the work proceeds.

Whilst the qualitative work can be commissioned, it is impossible to overstate the importance of the lead researchers getting out into the field. As an extreme example, I saw with my own eyes a collapsed railway embankment 20 km outside Accra leaving a 200-metre gap in the rail, so treated with some scepticism the claim by an official two days later that the line was fully operational.

But mixed methods does not just mean using qualitative methods. It means also using the full range of appropriate quantitative methods. Of course, a credible counterfactual addressing selection bias is central to impact evaluation design for large n interventions. But other quantitative methods should also be used, such as cost–benefit analysis. A recent World Bank (2010) study showed that transport projects report an economic rate of return (ERR) more commonly than any other sector: but still 42 per cent of projects do not do so. And approximately two-thirds do not do so for water supply and urban development (63 and 68 per cent, respectively).

The greatest challenge in mixed-methods research is mixing the methods. The large majority of so-called interdisciplinary research is in fact merely multi-disciplinary, with quantitative and qualitative work proceeding in parallel with little or no integration of the two. Carvalho and White (1997) lay out various examples of how quantitative and quali- tative analysis can be combined. As a more recent example, 3ie has commissioned a set of studies on the impact of water supply and sanitation on child health outcomes using DHS data, but complemented by mixed-methods analysis. In Zambia we found a weak link between water and child health, which studies in the medical literature suggest is explained by the fact that piped water is in fact not safe to drink in much of the country, being itself a bearer of disease. In Egypt, qualitative fieldwork brought two issues to bear that can reduce the effectiveness of water supply. First, a very large proportion of the population lives in apartment buildings. Although they have piped water there are problems of poor water pressure, so people store water with all the attendant risks of contamination. Second, leaky septic tanks are very common, which contaminate local groundwater. More examples follow in the next section.

Successful mixed-methods research is of course a matter of team composition. The team needs the skills to conduct the planned research. But that does not ensure integration. Integration will be facilitated by joint meetings across the team early on to map out the causal chain and discuss the nature of evidence to be brought to bear on the different evaluation questions that emerge, and later on to discuss and interpret emerging findings. But experience suggests that such joint work alone is not enough. I believe it is essential that the core team leaders, the Principal Investigators in US terminology, have a very firm grasp of all the data collected, and are closely involved in the design and implementation of both quantitative and qualitative data. In the United Kingdom, professionals who have some background in development studies are usually better placed to play this role than those with single-discipline training. Unfortunately development studies is not so strongly established elsewhere, and is as good as absent in the United States.

I turn now to the issue of what insights qualitative work might bring to bear in the analysis of infrastructure investments.

4. Bringing qualitative insights to bear in the analysis of infrastructure investments

4.1. Preparing for the evaluation: understanding context

As already mentioned, understanding context is an important part of preparing for an evaluation. Political economy considerations can help understand programme placement for infrastructure investments, and also help explain why many governments have basically re-built a road every five to 10 years rather than maintain it. Facts pertinent to the latter are that traditionally aid money could be used for investment but not maintenance, although that has not been the case for some time, and there are more opportunities for rent-seeking in new construction than in maintenance. The latter fact also explains the proliferation of irrigation engineers on new projects compared with their shortage in operations and maintenance.

Sources for contextual reading vary. *Lonely Planet* guides, or Wikipedia, give good potted histories that provide the general context. These may sound rather like trivial sources, but it is better than turning up in a country without knowing the name of the ruling party, main opposition parties, major ethnic groups or even what languages are spoken. I recall from the early days of my career a consultant who was unable to correctly pronounce 'Lesotho' even at the end of his six months in the country, or learn that its residents are called Basotho not 'Lesothians', an ignorance that undermined the credibility of any advice he had to offer. For rural interventions, village studies are likely to be a rich source. Political economy can explain why projects are important and whether they really have government support or not.

An example of the latter comes from the context for an evaluation of World Bank support to basic education in Ghana (World Bank 2004). Rawlings came to power for the second time in a coup in 1981. He did not have a strong political base. He had alienated the urban middle class and political classes during his first stint in power with his strong anti-corruption stance and Robin Hood policies of seizing assets. He alienated his left-wing supporters once he began implementing liberalisation policies, turning to the International Monetary Fund and World Bank for support. Rawlings thus strove to build a rural power base, in large part through investments in roads, rural electrification and schools, all of which were supported by the World Bank. The evaluation question as to the relevance of these interventions in relation to national policy is clear from the political importance attached to them (Table 2).

As part of the attention to education, Rawlings pushed through an unpopular reform of the education system, reducing the length of pre-university education from 17 years to 12 years. To prevent obstruction from the education service, which opposed the reforms, all seven directors were sacked and replaced with party loyalists. New textbooks, printed with donor support, produced to support the new curriculum were distributed by the army; a failure to have distributed this material would have been a key weak link in the causal chain (Table 1). Meanwhile, the World Bank launched a nationwide construction programme. Hence in the late 1980s and through the 1990s, when the fashion in education aid was turning away from hardware toward software – that is, from the infrastructure of school buildings to paying attention to school management – the World Bank paid for the construction of new classroom blocks in 8000 schools across the country. Rawlings' commitment to education ensured students in the new classrooms had books, and other measures were taken to ensure teachers were in post. This strong political commitment was an important part of the success of this programme, ensuring that the other things needed to make the investment in buildings worthwhile were in place.

4.2.   Where are infrastructure investments made? Understanding programme placement

A crucial part of impact evaluation design is understanding how selection bias may result from programme placement and self-selection. Reading the project documents and talking to programme staff is a good place to start. But there may be other factors at play needing other data to bring them to light. You need to know what happens in practice.

Rural electrification usually has a very clear programme placement strategy. First, grid electricity must be present in the region (say a province), which, unless there is internal generation capacity, means that high voltage cables must be run into sub-stations from the national or regional grid. Extension of the gird is not random but a function of accessibility and economic and political importance. Medium-voltage cables are then run out to rural towns, such as district capitals, from whence they then go to rural communities. The lines are typically run along the line of road as the least cost solution, unlike high-voltage cables for which an 'as the crow flies' routing is usually the most cost-effective. Communities within a certain distance, say up to 10 km, from the line will be served provided there are sufficient households wealthy enough to connect.

But there will be complications in this story depending on the local context. I was analysing a dataset for Laos, expecting that distance from provincial capital, distance from road, and average village wealth would provide a good prediction of which communities in the sample had electricity. But the R^2 value was lower than expected, whereas an ethnic dummy remained significant in various model specifications. A visit to Laos soon explained things. I was taken to visit an off-gird (solar panel) project, which was being delivered to part of a village, the other part of which had electricity. Why did part of the village have electricity and the other part not? Because the part that did not was on an island in the Mekong river, and it is not economic to extend the grid to small islands. The data I was using did not have a variable as to whether the village was on an island. But that is where many of the Lao Loum ethnic group lives, explaining why there was a negative coefficient on the ethnic dummy for this group. Similarly, the Lao Soung live in the mountains in the east of the country, and it is not economic to run the grid over or around mountains, once again picked up in the ethnic dummy for that group. Had the data contained information of physical characteristics of the community – 'on an island' and 'in a mountainous region' (possibly proxied by altitude) – these variables would, I expect, have worked well and eliminated the significance of the ethnic dummies.

There are two stings in the tail of this tale. The first is that it is in fact not at all unlikely that the government is discriminating against the Lao Soung, as they supported in the United States in the secret war against Laos when the country suffered the heaviest aerial bombardment of any country in history. Government is urging resettlement into villages closer to the centre; whilst this is said to be on developmental grounds, such resettlement is a common means of political control. The second sting takes us back to the island the Mekong. The solar panel project was to serve the 32 households on the island. But 20 of them had moved to the mainland since the village got electricity. Households, even entire communities, move to be near better infrastructure. Impact studies may take geographical location as exogenous, an identifying variable. But this is not a valid identification strategy if households – especially if certain households – move to be near the infrastructure. Location of the household becomes endogenous with respect to the programme, with relocation being a function of wealth, education and other things that almost certainly matter to the outcome of interest. Such endogeneity of location was also a problem in the analysis of education in Ghana, where children frequently stay with relatives to access better schooling. Quasi-experimental approaches thus need to model participation in the programme using equations based on a model in which location is endogenous.

Ghana was a rather different story of programme placement, as I learned from a reading of the project files in preparation for a study of Dutch co-financing of the World Bank (Sowa and White 1997, White and Dijkstra 2003, ch. 5). As already mentioned, the Ghanaian President, Jerry Rawlings, was committed to bringing electricity to all 110 of the country's districts. A loan was being negotiated with the World Bank for this purpose. However, cost–benefit analysis showed that the rate of return from electrification in some districts was insufficient to warrant the investment, so the Bank proposed dropping these from the project. Rawlings was insistent that all must be included. As a compromise, the Bank offered to find another donor to co-finance the project in these districts.[6] As a result, all districts did indeed receive electrification, so the usual bias toward the more economically productive areas was not present.

4.3. Which benefits to look for: what are the benefits of infrastructure investments, and who gets them?

Drawing on a broader range of literature gives a deeper understanding of the costs and benefits of infrastructure, and the distribution of those benefits (as highlighted in Table 2). In the case of roads, traditional cost–benefit analysis has captured benefits such as reduced vehicle operating costs and increased agricultural value added (Bridger 1983). Most impact evaluations similarly focus on positive impacts of roads in terms of higher incomes and employment and lower poverty (for example, Escobal and Ponce 2003, Van de Walle 2009, Rand 2011). However, roads have a far broader range of impacts, both positive and negative.

Starting with economic effects, the road 'brings development' – encouraging outmigration of young men, the inward movement of foreign goods and modern health and education services, and opening up commercial agriculture (LeVine et al. 1996). Not everyone will view these developments positively, as they are a threat to the traditional way of life, and those, usually elders, holding power. Opposition to roads has resulted in active resistance, such as in Kandahar (Afghanistan) in the late 1950s, where tribal communities felt that modern roads would undermine their authority, but also their livelihood from caravan traffic (Emadi 2002, p. 19). There are other losers, such as artisans who lose their livelihood as modern goods become available, and there may be general adverse dietary consequences of the gradual switch from unprocessed to processed foods.

This unequal distribution of benefits is highlighted in Trankell's (1993) study of the impact of rural roads in Laos. She argues that men have benefitted more than women, as roads have opened up markets to goods produced by men and enabled mechanisation of men's tasks more than those of women. Moreover, the shift to production for the market has been accompanied by a concentration of land holdings, reflecting the unequal distribution of benefits as the better off are better placed to take advantage of improved market access. As these discussions make clear, analysis of distributional and poverty impacts should be rooted in an understanding of people's livelihood strategies, or, as we used to say, their relation to the means of production, rather than a meaningless classification of the population into quintiles (see Hanmer et al. 1999 for an elaboration of this point).

Impact studies often emphasise the positive consequences of improved access to facilities, especially health. This is undoubtedly true. Training of traditional birth attendants was widely abandoned in the 1990s on the grounds that there is no point training women to recognise when they should refer complicated deliveries when there is nowhere to refer them to. Bangladesh was given as an example where this was the case. But massive investments in rural roads in Bangladesh have seen access to clinics improve enormously, and a consequent increase in utilisation of Emergency Obstetric Care (World Bank 2006). But the story about health and roads is more complex, as the case of Bangladesh illustrates. The fact of good trunk roads, together with other infrastructure such as mobile phones and satellite televisions, means that well-qualified doctors are easier to attract and retain in provincial towns, and indeed there has been substantial growth in private clinics and hospitals outside Dhaka. Lower-level health workers, and teachers, will go and stay in communities that have a decent road, electricity and a safe water supply. Or, if they do stay in town, a road makes sure they can and do get to the village easily and quickly. That is, infrastructure reduces worker absenteeism, which has been an enormous problem in service delivery across the developing world (Chaudhury and Hammer 2003, World Bank 2004).

Access to education may also improve. I recall a visit to small rural town in the Volta region in Ghana in which the villagers took me to a fast-flowing although narrow river, saying they wanted a foot bridge as two children had drowned last month while crossing and now parents would not send their children to school.

But there are also negative health effects from traffic accidents and, for larger roads, pollution. In developed countries the fact that roads kill people has long been factored into cost–benefit analysis. 'Better' roads undoubtedly kill drivers, their passengers and those attempting to cross the road as traffic is moving more quickly. Indeed better roads can reduce access for this reason: Harriss et al.'s (2010) study of an Indian village reports a case of children not attending school as parents fear their crossing the road to get to it. These accident-related health costs are overlooked in impact studies. An exception is the Asian Development Bank (ADB) study of road rehabilitation in Kazakhstan, which did indeed find an increase in accidents and fatalities. To be fair, this apparent neglect is partly explained by the fact that the issue is perhaps less for rural roads than national ones. But only perhaps; evidence is needed.

Negative health impacts of 'better roads' also come from adverse environmental consequences, such as air and traffic pollution. Again, including these costs has been a routine aspect of assessing the impact of infrastructure in developed countries, although it is argued that economic costs consequent from noise and air pollution, such as lower house prices, need for double glazing and so on, do not outweigh the value of the economic benefits for those near the road. But there may be some – typically lower income households – for who the net benefit is negative, so there is an adverse distributional impact (Kirby 1982, pp. 130–132 after Wheeler 1976).

A final story on the distribution of benefits illustrates the wide range of qualitative data that may provide insights. Driving through Northern Province in Zambia, we passed near a village that had high-voltage cables running overhead on their way to the provincial capital Kasama. But this village, like nearly all others, did not have electricity. A rather post-modern protest was scrawled on a large rock by the side of the road: 'visit www.chiefndezulusvillage.com'. This piece of graffiti provided evidence of the disaffection felt at being so clearly passed by modernisation, and a reminder to us – as so many studies show – that utility is a function of comparison with peers, so the fact of making one person better off without providing anything to the other decreases the welfare of the other.[7]

Roads also open up the area to the state military and police apparatus, as discussed in Blaikie *et al.*'s (1976) analysis of rural roads in Nepal. Whether this is a positive or a negative – providing either security or repression – depends on your relation to the state. Herbst (2000, ch. 5) writes of importance of roads in political consolidation, which means of course repression of populations seen as subversive, such as the Ndbele in Zimbabwe in the 1980s. He notes also how roads facilitated the massacre of Tutsis in Rwanda.

The above examples come mostly from texts not primarily concerned with addressing impact. The richness of analysis that is possible when non-economists do turn their attention to these issues is shown in Tanja Winther's outstanding study of the impact of electrification in rural Zanzibar, from which I select just a couple of examples of how impact is mediated through local context.

One issue that you will not find addressed in conventional impact studies is that of billing in illiterate communities. In the communities studied by Winther (2008), the monthly visit of the revenue collector is a big event, relying on this person to read bills for illiterate household members. But not understanding the tariff structure can undermine the benefits to be had from household electrification. In most countries there is a flat tariff for low consumption levels, usually at 20 or 25 kilowatt hours (kWh) per month. Winther reports the case of an elderly man restricting his consumption to just half an hour of one light bulb a day in an effort to save money on his bill. He was consuming only 3 kWh a month, so he could have increased his consumption eight-fold without altering his bill. This example illustrates why the benefits are less than they should have been, and less than they would have been assumed to be at appraisal. This failure to realise benefits will affect the least educated, and so poorest, the most, and points to a policy conclusion of the benefits of proper information campaigns. Other issues discussed in the study include why electricity is not used for cooking, restrictions people face in buying electrical consumables for fear of the evil eye, and relationships around electricity theft; this electricity shows up as a system loss but is actually benefitting someone and so should be reflected as a transfer for cost–benefit analysis.

4.4. Mixed methods in confirming and understanding impact

Carvalho and White (1997) propose that when methods are mixed, one approach may serve to confirm, refute or enrich the other. Confirmation – often referred to as triangulation –

is very useful to improve the rigour of estimates, especially if the identification strategy is less than ideal. Broegaard *et al*. (2011) triangulate their findings across quantitative and qualitative approaches. The impact of irrigation on paddy yields in Andhra Pradesh was estimated by a variety of means, concluding rather robustly that post-irrigation yields are in the range of 4–5 tons per hectare, rather than the 7 tons per hectare assumed in the appraisal report for the project (World Bank 2008). In that same study, qualitative research from the state level to the field level yielded insights that explained continued low coverage at the tail end. In the field we witnessed evidence of farmers sabotaging control measures (for example, removing gates), and discussions at state level confirmed that tertiary-level water user associations were not an appropriate means to deal with system-wide water distribution issues.

5. Conclusion

Impact evaluations have become very important in recent years. If these studies are really to help improve development policies and programmes, and so improve lives, then the studies need to go beyond just reporting a counterfactual-based measure of the impact on selected outcomes. Impact analysis needs to be embedded in a well-contextualised analysis that unpacks the causal chain. Such analysis helps understand why an intervention works or not, or why it only works for certain people, or in certain places or at certain times.

A theory-based analysis of this sort is necessarily a mixed-methods evaluation. Mixed methods need to be broadly conceived as drawing on a wide range of disciplines and approaches. The methods have to be chosen to fit the questions not the other way round.

These points are increasingly widely recognised. The challenge is to truly integrate the approaches to get a mixed-methods study, not a set of parallel studies. Ensuring team-work helps, but the team leader, and other core team members, need to be fully engaged across all components of the study.

This paper has shown that mixed methods have plenty to offer in what may be thought of as the technically-oriented sector of infrastructure. There is undoubted scope for improving the use of mixed methods in other sectors, thus increasing the quality, relevance and poverty impact of studies, and thus making a larger contribution to improving lives across the developing world.

Acknowledgements

Thanks are due to Paul Shaffer and John Weiss for comments on an earlier version and to Yasmin Khalafallah for assistance in preparation of the paper. The usual disclaimer applies. The views expressed here are the author's own, and may not be taken to represent the views of 3ie or any of its members.

Notes

1. The term impact means something different to many evaluators. I have discussed this distinction in White (2010).
2. However, the assumption-driven nature of CGEs has generally limited their appeal to policy-makers and many researchers.
3. Large *n* approaches, including randomisation, should not be ruled out. Karlan (2009) lists some ways these approaches might be applied to large infrastructure projects.
4. An evaluation I conducted in Ghana in the 1990s included a review of a World Bank road project. There was considerable co-financing for trunk roads, driven partly by the commercial interest

in such projects. However, the task manager was unable to get co-financing for a feeder road construction programme to be implemented by poor rural women.

5. By one meaning of impact, studies conducted some time after the intervention are, by definition, impact evaluations. Most studies conducted by the World Bank Operations Evaluation Department (now the Independent Evaluation Group) that are classified as 'impact evaluation studies' are ex-post studies conducted five to 10 years after the project closed.

6. To complete the story, the Dutch realised they were being asked to fund what the Bank itself saw as bad investments. When this point was raised by the Netherlands government, bank staff essentially asked what rate of return the Dutch wanted and provided the necessary calculations. This story illustrates the need for rigorous impact evaluation to underpin quantification of the benefits stream for cost–benefit analysis to be credible.

7. The importance of equity or 'fairness' is routinely found in behavioural games that are increasingly being used by economists and political scientists in developing countries (Carpenter and Cardenas 2008). In one such game, person A is given a sum of money, of which they choose to give a certain amount to person B. Then person B can either accept or reject the offer; if they reject, person A also gets nothing. Conventional economics would suggest that person B would accept just one penny, since they are better off than if they did not have the penny. However, typically players do not accept offers that are less than around 20 per cent of the amount given to person A, their reason being 'fairness'.

References

Blaikie, P., Cameron, J. and Seddon, D., 1976. *The effects of roads in West Central Nepal.* Norwich: Overseas Development Group, University of East Anglia.

Bridger, G., 1983, *Planning development projects: a practical guide to the choice and appraisal of public sector investments.* London: Overseas Development Administration.

Broegaard, E., Freeman, T. and Schwensen, C., 2011. Experience from a phased mixed-methods approach to impact evaluation of Danida support to rural transport infrastructure in Nicaragua. *Journal of development effectiveness*, 3 (1), 9–27.

Carpenter, J. and Cardenas, J.-C., 2008. Behavioral development economics: lessons from field labs in the developing world. *Journal of development studies*, 44 (3), 337–364.

Carvalho, S. and White, H., 1997. *Combining the quantitative and qualitative approaches to poverty measurement and analysis. The practice and the potential.* Washington, DC: World Bank, World Bank Technical Paper 336.

Carvalho, S. and White, H., 2004. Theory-based evaluation: the case of social funds. *American journal of evaluation*, 25 (2), 141–160.

Carvalho, S., Perkins, G. and White, H., 2002. Social funds, sustainability and institutional development impacts: findings from an OED review. *Journal of international development*, 14 (5), 611–625

Chambers, R., 2009. So that the poor count more: using participatory methods for impact evaluation. *Journal of development effectiveness*, 1 (3), 243–246.

Chaudhury, N. and Hammer, J., 2003. *Ghost doctors: absenteeism in Bangladeshi health facilities.* Washington, DC: World Bank, World Bank Policy Research Working Paper No. 3065.

Emadi, H., 2002. *Repression, resistance, and women in Afghanistan.* Santa Barbara, CA: Praeger Publishers.

Escobal, J. and Ponce, C., 2003. *The benefits of rural roads. Enhancing income opportunities for the rural poor.* Lima, Peru: Grupo de Análisis para el Desarrollo (GRADE), Documentos de Trabajo 40.

Haddad, E., 2011. Assessing the ex ante economic impacts of transportation infrastructure policies in Brazil. *Journal of development effectiveness*, 3 (1), 44–61.

Hanmer, L., Pyatt, G. and White, H., 1999. What do the World Bank's poverty assessments teach us about poverty in sub-Saharan Africa? *Development and change*, 30 (4), 795–823.

Harriss, J., Jeyaranjan, J. and Nagaraj, K., 2010. Land, labour and caste politics in rural Tamil Nadu in the 20th century: Iruvelpattu (1916–2008). *Economic and political weekly*, 45 (31).

Herbst, J.I., 2000, *States and power in Africa: comparative lessons in authority and control.* Princeton, NJ. Princeton University Press.

Karlan, D., 2009. Thoughts on randomised trials for evaluation of development: presentation to the Cairo evaluation clinic. *Journal of development effectiveness*, 1 (3), 237–242.

Kirby, A., 1982. *The politics of location: an introduction*. London: Methuen.

LeVine, R.A., *et al.*, 1996. *Child care and culture: lessons from Africa*. Cambridge, MA: Cambridge University Press.

Pawson, R. and Tilley, N., 1997, *Realistic evaluation*. London: Sage Publications.

Rand, J., 2011. Evaluating the employment generating impact of rural roads in Nicaragua. *Journal of development effectiveness*, 3 (1), 28–43.

Ravallion, M., 2009. Evaluating three stylised interventions. *Journal of development effectiveness*, 1 (3), 227–236.

Rogers, P.J., 2007. Theory-based evaluation: reflection ten years on. In: *Enduring issues in evaluation: the 20th anniversary of the collaboration between NDE and AEA. New directions for evaluation*, 114, 63–67.

Rogers, P.J., 2009. Impact evaluation design: matching impact evaluation design to the nature of the intervention and the purpose of the evaluation. *Journal of development effectiveness*, 1 (3), 217–226.

Sowa, N.K. and White, H., 1997. *An evaluation of Netherlands cofinancing of World Bank activities in Ghana, 1983–1996*. The Hague, The Netherlands: Ministerie van Buitenlandse Zaken, Inspectie Ontwikkelingssamenwerking en Beleidsevaluatie.

Trankell, I.B., 1993. *On the road in Laos: an anthropological study of road construction and rural communities*. Uppsala, Sweden; Uppsala University Department of Cultural Anthropology, Uppsala Research Reports 12.

Van De Walle, D., 2009. Impact evaluation of rural road projects. *Journal of development effectiveness*, 1 (1), 15–36.

Waddington, H. and Snilstveit, B., 2009. Effectiveness and sustainability of water, sanitation, and hygiene interventions in combating diarrhoea. *Journal of development effectiveness*, 1 (3), 295–335.

Waddington, H., Fewtrell, L., Snilstveit, B. and White, H., 2009. *Water, sanitation and hygiene interventions to combat childhood diarrhea in developing countries*. New Delhi: International Initiative for Impact Evaluation.

Wheeler, J., 1976. Location dimensions of urban highway impact: an empirical analysis. *Geografiska annaler b*, 58 (2), 67–68.

White, H., 2002. Combining quantitative and qualitative approaches in poverty analysis. *World development*, 30 (3), 511–522.

White, H., 2006. Demographic and Health Survey.

White, H., 2008. Of probits and participation: the use of mixed methods in quantitative impact evaluation. *IDS bulletin*, 39, 98–109.

White, H., 2009. Theory-based impact evaluation: principles and practice. *Journal of development effectiveness*, 1 (3), 271–284.

White, H., 2010. A contribution to current debates in impact evaluation. *Evaluation*, 16, 153–164.

White, H. and Dijkstra, G., 2003. *Beyond conditionality: program aid and development*. London: Routledge.

Winther, T., 2008, *The impact of electricity: development, desires and dilemmas*. Oxford: Berghahn Books

Woolcock, M., 2009. Toward plurality of methods in project evaluation: a contextualized approach to understanding impact trajectories and efficacy. *Journal of development effectiveness*, 1 (1), 1–14.

World Bank, 2002. *Social funds: assessing effectiveness*. Washington, DC: OED, World Bank.

World Bank, 2004. *Books, buildings and learning outcomes: an impact evaluation of World Bank assistance to basic education in Ghana*. Washington, DC: OED, World Bank.

World Bank, 2006. *Project performance assessment report: Bangladesh Fourth Population and Health Project, and Health and Population Program Project*. Washington, DC: IEG, World Bank.

World Bank, 2008. *An impact evaluation of India's second and third Andhra Pradesh irrigation: a case of poverty reduction with low economic returns*. Washington, DC: IEG, World Bank.

World Bank, 2010. *Cost–benefit analysis in World Bank projects*. Washington, DC: IEG, World Bank.

Index

Page numbers in *Italics* represent tables.
Page numbers in **Bold** represent figures.

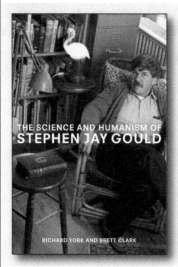

Critical Review of International Social and Political Philosophy

CO-EDITORS:

Richard Bellamy, *University College London, University of London, UK*
Preston King, *Emory University and Morehouse College, USA*

Critical Review of International Social and Political Philosophy focuses on individual thinkers, particular social and political concepts, such as power, equality, sovereignty and liberty, and various schools of thought, such as republicanism, liberalism and nationalism. In each case, particular regard is paid to the practical policy implications of the theories or ideas concerned. It also covers the theoretical assumptions and implications of such policy issues and socio-political-legal processes as democratization, multiculturalism, environmental protection, development aid, European Union, judicial legislation, globalization and social stratification.

Critical Review of International Social and Political Philosophy accepts articles from any branch of social and political philosophy that are accessibly written and concerned with the overlap between theory and practice. For details on how to submit a paper to **CRISPP**, please visit the journal homepage and click on the 'Instructions for Authors' link.

Highlights of **CRISPP** are now available FREE online, please visit:
www.tandf.co.uk/journals/fcri

View an online sample issue at:
www.tandf.co.uk/journals/fcri

Related titles from Routledge

ROUTLEDGE

Critical Perspectives in Rural Development Studies

Edited by Saturnino M. Borras Jr.

Agrarian transformations within and across countries have been significantly and dynamically altered during the past few decades compared to previous eras, provoking a variety of reactions from rural poor communities worldwide. The recent convergence of various crises – financial, food, energy and environmental – has put the nexus between 'rural development' and 'development in general' back onto the center stage of theoretical, policy and political agendas in the world today. Confronting these issues will require (re)engaging with critical theories, taking politics seriously, and utilizing rigorous and appropriate research methodologies. These are the common messages and implications of the various contributions to this collection in the context of a scholarship that is critical in two senses: questioning prescriptions from mainstream perspectives and interrogating popular conventions in radical thinking.

This book was previously published as a special issue of the *Journal of Peasant Studies*.

November 2009: 234 x 156: 258pp
Hb: 978-0-415-55244-8
£80 / $125

Available from all good bookshops

Improving Water Policy and Governance

Edited by Asit K. Biswas and Cecilia Tortajada

Old forms of governance in both public and private sectors are becoming increasingly irrelevant because of rapidly changing conditions. Improving water governance will require good and objective analyses of case studies from different parts of the world as to what has worked, why and the enabling environments under which good governance has been possible.

This book analyses case studies of good water governance from different parts of the world, and for different water use sectors. It concludes with an analysis of the critical issues that should be considered for water governance and a priority research agenda for improving water governance in the future.

This book was originally published as a special issue of the *International Journal of Water Resources Development*.

November 2010: 246 x 174: 208pp
Hb: 978-0-415-60628-8
£80 / $125

For Product Safety Concerns and Information please contact our EU representative GPSR@taylorandfrancis.com Taylor & Francis Verlag GmbH, Kaufingerstraße 24, 80331 München, Germany

Batch number: 08151665

Printed by Printforce, the Netherlands